TWAYNE'S WORLD AUTHORS SERIES

A Survey of the World's Literature

ITALY

Carlo Golino, University of Massachusetts

EDITOR

Dante Alighieri

TWAS 563

DANTE
CON L'ESPOSITIONE
DI CHRISTOFORO LANDINO
ET DI ALESSANDRO VELLVTELLO,

Sopra la sua Comedia dell'Inferno, del Purgatorio, & del Paradiso.

Con tauole, argomenti, & allegorie, & riformato, riueduto,
& ridotto alla sua uera lettura,

PER FRANCESCO SANSOVINO FIORENTINO.

In Venetia, Appresso Giou.ambattista, Marchiò Seßa, & fratelli. 1564.

Dante Alighieri

DANTE ALIGHIERI

By RICARDO J. QUINONES

Claremont Men's College

TWAYNE PUBLISHERS

A DIVISION OF G. K. HALL & CO., BOSTON

Published in 1979 by Twayne Publishers,
A Division of G. K. Hall & Co.
All Rights Reserved

Printed on permanent/ durable acid-free paper and bound
in the United States of America

First Printing

Library of Congress Cataloging in Publication Data

Quinones, Ricardo J
Dante Alighieri.

(Twayne's world authors series ; TWAS 563)
Bibliography: p. 204–206
Includes index.
1. Dante Alighieri, 1265–1325—Criticism and interpretation.
PQ4390.056   851'.1   79–9776
ISBN 0–8057–6405–4

For Andrew Bongiorno,
who cared for this volume with patient exactness.

Contents

About the Author

Preface

Acknowledgments

Chronology

1. Early Life and the *Vita Nuova*   13

2. *La Donna Gentile:* Dante's Philosophical Growth and the *Canzoni*   42

3. *Peregrino, quasi mendicando:* Exile, the *Convivio,* and *De Vulgari Eloquentia*   52

4. The Five-Year Drama of Henry VII: Dante's *De Monarchia* and the Political Epistles   89

5. *Commedia: Inferno*   100

6. *Commedia: Purgatorio*   131

7. *Commedia: Paradiso*   157

8. Conclusion   189

Notes and References   195

Selected Bibliography   204

Index   207

About the Author

Ricardo J. Quinones is Professor of English and Comparative Literature at Claremont Men's College and chairman of the Department of Literature. He received his Ph.D. in Comparative Literature from Harvard University, 1963, and is the author of *The Renaissance Discovery of Time* and numerous articles and reviews in such journals as *The Journal of the History of Ideas, The Renaissance Quarterly, Shakespeare Quarterly, Dante Studies* and others. His sequel to the Renaissance study, All We Have: Time and Development in Literary Modernism is being readied for press. Currently he is involved in a study of the Cain-Abel theme.

Preface

This study considers the *Commedia*, the work that elevates Dante to the status of a world classic, in the context of his changeful public career and as the product of his evolving thought and poetic practice. Introductory volumes normally adhere to the level of consensus, and this one is no exception; however, almost inevitably when dealing with poetry, personal readings will intrude. While my bias is historical my particular interest is in a Dante rewarding for today's reader.

This study abides by the TWAS policy of giving quotations in their English translations. Since of late the better renderings of Dante's poems have been in prose, most of my quotations from the poetry are consequently in English prose. This is an anomaly which I hope will not offend. Dante, after all, like a statue, is *meglio nudo che vestito*. In the nakedness of plain prose at least we are not being misled.

Conscious of limitations of space I have tried to keep the apparatus to a minimum. The bare bibliography and notes are in no way a complete record of my indebtedness to Dante scholars past and present.

Acknowledgments

Quotations from *The Divine Comedy of Dante Alighieri*, trans. John D. Sinclair (Oxford University Press, rev. 1958), used by permission of The Bodley Head, Covent Garden, London; quotations from *Dante's Lyric Poetry*, ed. and trans. by Kenelm Foster and Patrick Boyde (2 vols. 1967) used by permission of Oxford University Press.

Chronology

1215	Buondelmonte murder.
1250	Death of Frederick II.
1260	Battle of Arbia valley, where large Florentine force was routed.
1265	Dante born in Florence under Gemini.
1266	Guelph victory at Benevento over Manfred and Ghibellines.
1274	First meeting with Beatrice, believed to be Bice, daughter of Folco Portinari.
1277	Dante betrothed to Gemma di Manetto Donati; mother already dead, father remarries.
1283	By this date father also dead. Following this date and prior to 1295 Dante marries Gemma (three children, Jacopo, Pietro, and Antonia—perhaps four, Giovanni—from this union).
1290	Beatrice dies.
1292– 1293	*Vita Nuova* and start of philosophical studies.
1295	Enrolled in Guild; start of political life.
1300	Dante prior for bimester June 15–August 15.
1301	In July Dante opposes extending troop consignment to Boniface VIII; in October Dante one of three emissaries to Pope in Rome; in November, takeover by exiled Black Guelphs under Corso Donati.
1302	Dante ordered to appear to answer charges; failing to do so, March 10 sentenced to death. Years of exile begin.
1305	Clement new Pope; papacy in Avignon.
1308	Henry of Luxembourg elected and crowned emperor.
1310	Henry crosses Alps to Lombardy.
1312	After struggle, Henry crowned at St. John Lateran.
1313	In August, Henry, "the last Emperor," dies of fever near Siena.

1314   Dante's letter to Italian cardinals; *Inferno* completed.

1315   Possibility of pardon rejected by Dante; Dante settles in Verona with Can Grande della Scala.

1319   (?) Dante relocates in Ravenna with Guido Novello da Polenta. Correspondence with Giovanni del Virgilio. *Purgatorio* and part of *Paradiso* completed.

1321   September 13–14, Dante dies in Ravenna.

CHAPTER 1

Early Life and the Vita Nuova

I *The Emergence of Guelph Florence*

DANTE and the men of his time were witness to the break-up and defeat of two of the most powerful institutions of the medieval world, the Papacy and the Empire. Since at least the Carolingian epoch the difficult relationships between these two powers had dominated the affairs of Italy and of Europe. Dante's birth in 1265 preceded by one year the defeat of the Ghibelline forces and their attractive leader, Manfred, the illegitimate son of Frederick II, a defeat that prepared the way for the return of the exiled and now victorious Guelphs to Florence. That great reversal was brought about by the alliance of the Italian Guelph cities with the papacy and the French house of Anjou. Despite later conflicts, some of them important, and despite the emergence of other aspirants to the imperial crown, this defeat put an end to the Ghibelline cause in Italy. The house of Swabia—the line of Frederick Barbarossa, Henry VI, Frederick II—terminated, in effect, in this defeat. But on the other side, within a short period of time, that great succession of thirteenth-century Popes, including Innocent III and Innocent IV, met its humiliation in the violence done to Pope Boniface VIII by the forces of Philip of France, and soon thereafter the removal of the Papacy to Avignon, to be controlled by the French monarch.

Recognizing that the crucial events of his life were determined by the collapse of these two powers, Dante devoted his thought in his major prose works and in his great poem to understanding and explaining their proper relationships. And it is to Dante's credit that he perceived that, behind their real antagonism, they represented in actuality the twin ideals of the medieval world; they were, in the modern phrase, complementarities.[1] The claims of each transcended national boundaries, and were also coterminous. But, as with rival twin brothers, the very closeness of the relationship proved to be the cause of a serious ambiguity: it was almost impossible to define where the interests of the one left off and those of the other commenced. As the brilliant Belgian historian Henri Pirenne was to ask, "Charged as they were, the one with the government of men's souls, and the other with the government of their bodies, who was to indicate the exact limits of their competence?"[2] The nature of their ideal relationship Dante could only suggest by metaphor or by pointing to specific historical example. The Carolingian model seemed to him the one that came closest to his ideal: Pepin and his son were both guardians of the temporal order and protectors of the Church. They had at least some idea of the heavenly city, and their actions moved in step with those of the Church.

Such instances of perfect cooperation between the two powers were rare in human history (so rare, in fact, that their materialization Dante would come to see as the work of divine providence, high-water-marks left as a sign to the needy human race). Historically, except for such outstanding moments of cooperation, their relationship had been marked by exaggerated claims of each to superiority over the other. Following the needed Clunisian reforms of the eleventh century, the Papacy strengthened itself and sought to defend its own autonomy, leading to such reforms as having the College of Cardinals solely authorized to elect the Pope and to such strong figures as Pope Gregory VII, whose diplomatic and political victory over Henry IV in 1077 had come to symbolize papal resurgency. Support rallied behind Gregory because he was—on the surface, at least —merely asking for what should have been the Church's right to invest its own ecclesiastical offices. But the papal policy in its turn soon claimed the spiritual power to be the higher authority of the two. In the thirteenth century this aggressive papal policy encountered Frederick II, heir of the Swabian house that never shared the clear religious purposes of the Carolingians. As had happened before and was to occur again, the young Frederick was brought to the throne as a political maneuver on the part of Innocent III in order to defeat the far more threatening political rival Otto IV. Once secured in power, Frederick showed his true Ghibelline and imperial motives, and he, in turn, became an enemy of the papacy.

Dante's *Commedia* and his prose works will turn even sharper focus upon these conflicts (of necessity only sketched in here) at the time when the partisan divisions of Guelph and Ghibelline are fatally introduced into the life of Florence by the Buondelmonte murder of 1215. Following this assassination on Easter Sunday of the young man who jilted a young woman of the Amidei to whom he had been betrothed, the rival families reached for outside support to papal and imperial alliances, thus turning Florence into two bitterly divided camps. Referring back to that moment in 1215 from the heights of Paradise, Dante has Cacciaguida, that embodied voice of Florentine history, see the change of marriage plans as the origin of his city's troubles. "This is the house from which your wailing sprang," Cacciaguida tells Dante in *Paradiso* XVI. It would have been better for Florence had God consigned Buondelmonte's ancestors to the river Ema rather than allow them ever to settle in Florence. Dante's compressed description of Florence's tragic fate is powerful:

> Ma conveniesi a quella pietra scema
> che guarda il ponte, che Fiorenza fesse
> vittima nella sua pace postrema.
>
> But it was fitting that to the wasted stone
> which guards the bridge Florence should offer
> a victim in her last days of peace. (145–47) [3]

Instead of enjoying its just and glorious days of peace Florence was bound to make of itself the sacrifice to the broken statue of Mars, the god of war, that stood at the head of the Ponte Vecchio.

From 1248 to 1266 the political condition of Florence was one of intermittent civil war. Murder, pillage, the destruction of houses and towers, exile—these were the grave penalties both sides had alternatively to endure. The Hell that Dante describes was well known to his fellow citizens, and the unifying motif to several of its major encounters is the common experience of exile. In *Inferno* X, Farinata is proud that his Ghibelline forces chased the Guelphs out twice, but he is silenced by Dante's reply that they returned each time, something the Ghibellines never learned to do. And, in fact, following the battle of Benevento in 1266, the Ghibellines were scattered, and, while continuing to pose a threat in Tuscany, never did return to Florence.

This meant that Dante grew up in a great city that was flush
with victory, a frankly expansionist postwar society brimming
with civic pride. The apparently final settlement of the long
strife provided the conditions for a true economic, political, and
cultural upsurge. Prior to this time, in the words of Helene
Wieruszowski, "Florence was not yet ready for intellectual
leadership in Tuscany, let alone in Italy." [4] But with the return
of the exiles, all of this changed. New buildings were constructed
as an expression of justifiable civic pride. The Florentines compared themselves with Rome and the civilization of the ancient
city-states. On the walls of its public building, the Bargello,
were inscribed these words (I give the translation):

> Florence is full of all imaginable wealth;
> She defeats her enemies in war and in civil strife;
> She enjoys the favor of fortune and has a powerful population;
> Successfully she fortifies and conquers castles;
> She reigns over the sea and the land and the whole world;
> Under her leadership the whole of Tuscany enjoys happiness;
> Like Rome she is always triumphant. [5]

This burst of civic pride ushered in an era dominated by
devotion and dedication to the city. The city itself, its history and
its values, became the focus of attention and a powerful object
of identification. And it is this fact that accounts for the appeal
of Aristotle and of Cicero, the citizen-philosophers of the ancient
city-states. Even in the *Paradiso* Dante must still allow as being
beyond any possible dispute that it would be far worse for man
were he not a member of a city (VIII.117). Man was by his
very nature a social animal and his earthly well-being was
best realized in a city. Dante's own personal commitment to his
city can be perceived in the words of Cacciaguida, who, prophesying his banishment, speaks of the pain Dante will feel to leave
behind him everything that he loved most dearly (*Paradiso*
XVII.55–56).

This time before his exile was cherished by Dante. In fact,
Dante's own memories of his youth could easily be transferred to
those of Cacciaguida, recalling a formerly virtuous society. Like
his ancestor, Dante could recall that "così bello/viver di
cittadini," that "così dolce ostello," into which he was born and
in which he grew up. [6] In the powerful proem to *Paradiso* XXV,

Dante declares his hope not to receive the laurel crown anywhere else but at the font where he was baptized and the sheepfold where he nestled as a lamb. The baptistry is the center of his life, just as it was for Cacciaguida ("nell'antico vostro Batisteo/insieme fui cristiano e Cacciaguida"—XV.134–35). In the *Convivio* Dante refers to Florence as that "most beautiful and famous daughter of Rome," from whose sweet bosom he has been cast out (I.iii).[7] And in *De Vulgari Eloquentia*, while Dante satirizes the pretentions of Florentines, he must admit that insofar as his own delight and personal comfort are concerned, "there exists no more agreeable place in the world than Florence."[8] The Florence of his youth was the mother of the warm embrace, and the city of the women who inspired their children by telling stories of Aeneas and the founding of Rome, and the Roman settlers in Florence (only after his exile was Florence to become like the cruel stepmother). Despite what happened later, perhaps because of what happened later, Dante's memories of his youth invariably were pleasant ones, and this bequest—almost in a Wordsworthian sense—remained with him the rest of his life. The happy nature of this experience is one to which he always returned—return, itself, being one of the dominant motifs of the *Commedia*. From this early experience one can see being shaped the Dante of confidence, energy, and public commitment, the poet who would never be content with less than the great hopes and fulfillment of the *Paradiso*.

But, as Dante was later to lament, this same period of growth and expansion introduced new forces that were quite inimical to the goals that inspired the universal Church and Empire. The latter was a world-ideal with roots in Roman history and the ideals of justice and civic dedication that evolved there. The Church was catholic, a spiritual union of all men, founded on the life, the teachings, and the sacrifice of Christ. Both institutions called for supreme devotion and self-sacrifice. Indeed they were complementarities: their very conflicts sprang from a common set of terms and common assumptions. So jointed were they that where one fell, it was not too long before the other collapsed. The image by which this relationship is to be understood is not that of the seesaw but rather of the raft: when one side goes down the other is soon to follow. After the death of Frederick in 1250 and the defeat of Manfred in 1266, it was not too long before the Guelph-Papal-Angevin alliance splintered, and the

more universal claims of the Church came to be regarded as a
threat to the autonomy of commune and nation. This is what
Pirenne meant when he wrote, "The Papacy was tottering . . .
on the ruins of the Imperial power which it had overthrown."[9]
And this was Dante's view of the subject as well.

Dante, who perceived this mutual relationship of the two
powers, also identified the new forces that were forming, forces
that did not acknowledge any of the supranational aims of
Church and Empire. The "new people" and the "fast money" of
the developing urban centers (*Inferno* XVI), on the one hand, and
the autonomous national state on the other, were indifferent if
not hostile to universal aspirations. The Florence that Dante
knew had benefited from the influx of new peoples from the
surrounding countryside; they followed the lure of economic
advancement offered by the industries that flourished in the
cities. The city wall ("cerchia antica"—*Paradiso* XV) that lent
containment to the energies of the people of Cacciaguida's time
was built in the ninth century; a second wall was constructed for
the growing population in 1172–74, and in 1284 even a third
wall was begun. Cacciaguida regrets this "confusion of people":
the new people did not share the Roman ideals of the old, and
their vision was much more restricted to their own interests.
Later Dante will be outraged that these Florentines would in the
name of this freedom dig in and oppose (successfully) the advent
of Henry VII, who represented the last opportunity for the
restoration of an imperial order.

Except for what he considered the deranged activities of the
Florentines, the political phenomenon that provoked Dante's
fiercest resentment was the rapid growth of the power of France,
particularly in the affairs of Italy. While England opposed
Boniface no less than France, the involvement of Valois in Italy
caused Dante more grief. This hostility to France, as well as his
contempt for Philip IV, blinded him to the remarkable achievements of French culture in the thirteenth century; for instance,
Hugh Capet's account (*Purgatorio* XX) of his descendants
contains no reference to the great Saint Louis. The house that
Hugh Capet helped to found existed modestly and peacefully
for centuries; in the thirteenth century this containment was
changed, and by a combination of military victories, marriages,
and, according to Dante, deceit, France became the most considerable power in Europe. The role of Charles of Valois in

1301–1302 helped reverse Dante's appreciation of Charles of Anjou, and Charles's treachery in regard to Florence was capped by the violence used against Pope Boniface at Anagni, where in 1303 the forces of the King of France took him prisoner. The history of these events is also told allegorically in the concluding lines of *Purgatorio* XXXII.

Surprisingly, from out of the events of his early life Dante tells us little about his immediate family. Zingarelli has written that Dante's father seems to have passed silently into history.[10] There is no mention of father or mother, or brother or sister in the *Commedia*. A sister is possibly referred to in the *Vita Nuova*, and his father is the subject of some insults by Forese Donati in sonnets addressed to Dante. In order to find a familial spirit congenial to his own lofty sense of himself Dante went back to his great-great-grandfather, Cacciaguida, a crusader and a martyr for the faith. Born at the end of the eleventh century—that is, in the misty past, when the new growth of the cities began to take place—Cacciaguida is spokesman for the spirit of Florentine history that Dante so willingly and eagerly imbibed. From the Cacciaguida cantos of the *Paradiso* we learn much of what we know about Dante's family history. Cacciaguida tells Dante indirectly that his family had Roman origins, and that the family name of Alighieri (there are many variant spellings) was derived from his wife, who had come from the Po valley. Cacciaguida's son, named Alighiero, by the year 1300 had already spent more than a hundred years on the terrace of pride in Purgatory. There is documentary evidence that this Alighieri had two sons, one named Bellincione and one Bello (we meet the incensed and injured Geri del Bello, the latter's son, in *Inferno* XXIX). Bellincione was the father of Dante's father.

While Farinata can say that Dante's ancestors were "fieramente" his adversaries and that they were exiled, he could not have been referring to Dante's immediate family, since Dante's birth took place in 1265, and the exiles did not return until later, in 1266. Dante himself tells us in the *Convivio* that he was born in Florence. All this can only mean that Dante's father was not a political figure considerable enough to warrant exile (and indeed, following 1260 many Guelphs did remain in Florence). Dante's mother died when he was young, certainly before he was fourteen. Her name was Bella, but of which family is unknown.

Dante's father remarried Lapa di Chiarissimo Cialuffi, and

evidently they produced another son, Francesco, and a daughter, Tana. Dante's father himself died prior to 1283, since at that time Dante, having come into his majority, was able as an orphan to sell a credit owned by his father. The elder Alighieri left his children a modest yet comfortable patrimony of property in Florence and in the country.

Of Dante's general culture, surviving documents tell us little. Far more important for our purposes than the kind of schooling he received were the figures who influenced him when he began to come into his own cultural majority, the models he chose to follow, his elected affinities. Dante himself tells us of the importance of two figures who stand out in his early cultural development. They were Brunetto Latini and Guido Cavalcanti, memorialized in cantos XV and X of the *Inferno*.

II   *Brunetto Latini*

In the pedagogic structure of *Inferno* XV, Dante presents the summary of the culture that he inherited in the person of Brunetto Latini (1220?–94). This is not to be regarded as an isolated meeting of one pupil with his master, but rather as the encounter of an entire generation with its intellectual mentor. Villani recognized well the role that Brunetto Latini played after 1266 in the formation of Florentine culture, in bringing together that particular blend of philosophy, rhetoric, and politics devoted to the service of the commune. In his portrait of Latini, Villani called him a "grande filosofo," and a master of rhetoric in the spoken and the written arts, that is, in oratory and in letter-writing. Latini produced a commentary upon Cicero's work of rhetoric, the *De Inventione*. He was the "dittatore" or secretary of the commune, and although he was a "worldly man" —Villani is referring to the vice of sodomy for which Dante finds his master in Hell—nevertheless he was the "beginner [cominciatore] and master in refining the Florentines and in teaching them how to speak well, and how to guide and rule our republic according to policy [la politica]." [11] According to Villani, Latini was the first to revive the study of classical rhetoric and politics, and he brought those arts for the refinement of the Florentines in the service of their commune. Like Villani, Dante had seen Latini as a "cominciatore." In fact, as Ms. Wieruszowski has written, it was the particular guidance of Brunetto Latini after his return from exile in 1266 "that opened up the world of the ancients to the Florentines and stirred their enthusiasm for classical authors." [12]

Returning from a political embassy to King Alfonso of Castille, he was informed of the stunning defeat administered to the Guelphs at Montaperti by the Ghibellines and their ally Manfred. Because of that defeat, Latini stayed in France for six years, only returning after the Ghibellines and Manfred were defeated in their turn by the forces of Charles of Anjou in league with the papacy and the Florentine Guelphs. In fact, Latini was already back in Florence within three weeks after that Guelph victory in February 1266. While in France he mainly wrote three interrelated works: *The Tresor* (*Li Livres dou Tresor*), written in French; the *Tesoretto*, written in Italian but modeled after the *Roman de la Rose* in its personifications; and his *Rhettorica* (or commentary upon Cicero's *De Inventione*). Upon his return he served the commune in a variety of ways: in 1273 he was secretary; in 1282, along with two other Florentines important to Dante's story (Guido Cavalcanti and Dino Compagni), he was a member of the podestà's council; and he was a prior in the August-October bimester of 1287. Here we can see some reasons Dante gave him such prominence in *Inferno* XV: the parallels in their careers were striking. Like Dante, Latini learned of defeat and exile while returning from an ambassadorial mission; like Dante he was an active public servant, and in him Dante could follow the pattern of the "philosopher-mediator," the student of philosophy and classical culture devoting himself in the service of ethics and politics.

Latini's *Tresor* is a compendium of classical culture, and a compilation of its philosophy.[13] The first part of Book Two contains one of the first translations in a modern European vernacular of Aristotle's *Ethics*. The *Tresor* was written in French because Latini was located in France when writing it and because the French language is the most delightful and international ("commune") of all the languages (I.1.7)—a recognition of the fact that French culture was the presiding culture of the thirteenth century (an item Dante was determined to alter).

Yet the culture of the *Tresor* is Dante's culture; it is a repository of classical citation. On almost every question or topic of philosophy, of ethics and politics, in Books Two and Three, Latini freely quotes from Cicero and Seneca. And almost as

frequently, when treating questions of government, he quotes
from the Book of Proverbs, as Dante will do. Aristotle, the study
of philosophy, and the method of systematically ordering the
discussion of topics, Cicero and Seneca, the Bible—these are
some mainstays of Dante's culture and they are fully represented
in Latini's works.

What we witness emerging in the works of Latini is the political and ethical culture of the city-state. Aristotle's *Ethics*,
recently rediscovered in the thirteenth century, were, as Hans
Baron tells us, "better understood than ever before in the sur-
roundings of the Italian Commune, the counterpart of the Greek
polis." [14] Like Dante, Latini adopted the basic principles of
Aristotle's political doctrine. Man is a social animal ("l'ome se
delite naturelement en compagnie"; man, Dante will say, is a
"compagnevole animal").[15] Human felicity resides in the exercise
of virtue (II.47.4), yet—since man is a rational animal—his
highest felicity is of an intellectual order. Hence the philosopher,
the lover of wisdom, enjoys the greatest felicity. This is what
Dante means when he writes in canto XV that from Latini he
learned how man makes himself eternal. Yet, the great aim of
philosophy, or of one of its practical branches, is government,
and, in this case, the government of cities, which he calls the
highest and noblest science and the noblest duty available to
man (III.73, and also II.3.1.). The efforts of philosophy are
directed toward the service of the state; the man of letters can
use his skills to help the orator in council, or he can be the
dittatore, the secretary, writing epistles or diplomatic messages
on behalf of the state.

Despite the heavy reliance upon quotations from Aristotle's
works, the fullest inspiration for this new ideal came from the
example of Rome. For this reason, Latini praises in Dante the
revival of the "holy seed" of those Roman veterans who chose to
remain in Tuscany. Consequently, the cult of Cicero began to
develop side by side with that of Aristotle, for Cicero "began
to be recognized as the most effective guide to the citizen's obli-
gations." [16] He, perhaps more than anyone else, is the model in
Latini's *Tresor* (as well as in Dante's *Convivio*). It was Cicero
who "set himself the task of adapting the Greek spirit of philosophical investigation to the needs of the Roman citizens, who
were not to turn away from their responsibility for the common
weal." [17]

And if there is one other Roman element in Brunetto Latini's total legacy that became an important part of Dante's culture it was the love of glory. Before taking leave of him (*Inferno* XV), Brunetto commends to Dante his *Tresor*, "nel qual io vivo ancora." This is a direct reference to the chapter on "gloire" (II.120), where Latini quotes Horace on the rewards of fame.

The role of Latini was influential enough to justify Dante's remembrance of his image as a "fatherly" one. The record is a remarkable one of indebtedness. But the pathos of Hell comes from the fact that not only must indebtedness be recorded but also supersession, transcendence. Dante found the model for the style of his philosophical prose in the *ars dictandi*, the stylistic and encyclopedic efforts of the Latin secretaries (the *dittatori*) of the thirteenth century. Yet this important background does not explain the great leap of the *Commedia*. In fact, Latini, who first showed the political dedication to the life of the commune on the part of the man of letters, remained essentially "municipal" in his literary and political interests. In *De Vulgari Eloquentia* I.13, Brunetto is listed among those poets whose style remained municipal (a reading of the *Tesoretto* will quickly confirm that judgment) and did not rise to the illustrious vernacular style. In canto XV, Dante has another guide, Virgil, who is also his poetic guide toward an integration of philosophical learning, history, and personal experience into a suitable aesthetic form. It was not through Latini's guidance, but rather through Virgil's, that Dante rose to the level of the epic. And, to look only at another item, Latini remained a Guelph, hostile to Frederick and his son Manfred, while Dante went on to become the great theorist of the universal Empire. In Latini we see embodied the culture that Dante acquired in the Florence of his youth (and this is all expressed in the magnificently synoptic and dramatic canto XV); in him we also see, moral and religious problems to one side, the limitation of the culture that he left behind.

III   Vita Nuova: *Moral Pattern*

Brunetto Latini was Dante's great predecessor in regard to civic culture, to the mediating role of philosophy and the uses of rhetoric for the public weal. When it comes to poetry, however, Dante had other models, for Latini was only "municipal" in his horizons. From the time that he sent out one of his first poems

when he was eighteen until the end of his life, Dante's major
study was always poetry. So evident is this that in *Convivio*
I.13, it does not require further testimony. And in *De Vulgari
Eloquentia* (I.xiii) he lists himself among a group of practicing
poets (including Guido Cavalcanti, Lapo Gianni, and Cino da
Pistoia), all of whom made excellent use of the vernacular,
eschewing the local Tuscan dialect.

Of this vernacular verse Dante made two collections, the first
being the *Vita Nuova* and the second the *Convivio* (although
the *Convivio*, with its extensive philosophical commentary, was
much more than a simple anthology). The earlier work summarized his poetic interests from before 1283 to roughly 1292–
93; the *Convivio*, a bulkier and more ambitious work, was to
contain the more important part of Dante's poetic compositions
from just prior to 1294 to the time of the *Commedia*. His other
verse has been gathered together by later generations and is
called more generally *Rime* (which is more appropriate than
Canzoniere). Both of Dante's collections are of the same form,
the *prosimetrum*. The most notable example of this form is
Boethius's *Consolation of Philosophy*, but there are many other
examples in Latin as well as in Provencal. (Latini's *Tesoretto*
was supposed to have a prose commentary more elaborately
filling out the meaning of his verse.) Obviously the form is not an
easy one; witness the fact that the *Convivio* was left incomplete.
The danger of the form seems to lie in unavoidable repetition
and in some discrepancies of sentiment if the prose commentary,
as is true in each of Dante's efforts, follows almost a decade later
than some of the verse.

The *Vita Nuova*, Dante's *libello*, or small book, is a remarkable work.[18] It contains forty-two brief chapters, with commentaries on twenty-five sonnets, one *ballata*, and four *canzoni;*
a fifth *canzone* is left dramatically interrupted by Beatrice's
death. In this first decade of Dante's poetic activity, obviously
the dominant form was the sonnet. This changes radically at the
start of his second period, which culminated in the *Convivio*,
when his major form will be the *canzone* (his theory of the
canzone will be elaborated in the closely related work *De
Vulgari Eloquentia*). In this earlier period, Dante's main subject
was love. This too will change by the time of the just-mentioned
later works, when, in addition to love, virtue and war will be the
main subjects of poetry, and Dante will refer to himself not as
the poet of love, but rather as the poet of rectitude.

The commentary for the poems selected in the *Vita Nuova* is surprisingly spare. It is definitely not a narrative, or if so, a most discontinuous one. It seems to proceed by anecdotal explanations, giving the origins and the circumstances of the poems. In it Dante seems to relive some of the incidents and emotions that first inspired the material of the poem (thus leading to some of the repetition). Much of the commentary is made up of very schematic analyses of the divisions of an individual poem. When it is, the prose serves as a very elementary guide, reminding us of how early an age in the development of the modern cycle of Western poetry Dante's must have been if his readership required such obvious explanations.

The prose commentary has also the purpose of providing the poems with a frame-story, one which does not seem to emerge sufficiently from the *rime* themselves (it is possible, of course, that some of the sonnets were written for different purposes from those alleged). The story is simple and well known: the first sight of Beatrice when both she and Dante were approximately nine years of age, her salutation when they were eighteen, Dante's expedient of the screen-woman, the crisis experienced when Beatrice withholds her greeting, Dante's anguish that she is making light of him, his determination to rise above anguish and sing only of his lady's virtues, many anticipations of her death (that of the young friend, her father, and Dante's dream), and finally the death of Beatrice, Dante's mourning, the temptation of the sympathetic *donna gentile*, Beatrice's triumph and apotheosis, and, in the last chapter, Dante's determination at some later date to write about her "that which has never been written of any other woman."

Yet with all this apparently autobiographical purpose, the *Vita Nuova* is strangely impersonal. The circumstances it sets down are markedly devoid of any historical facts or descriptive detail. In language as well the commentary adheres to a level of generality. Names are rarely used—Guido Cavalcanti is referred to three times simply as Dante's "best friend"; Dante's sister, who wakes him from his bad dream, is referred to as "she who was joined to me by the closest proximity of blood." On the one hand, Dante wishes to suggest the most significant stages of emotional experience, but on the other he seems to distance his descriptions from strong emotional reactions. In this work, despite its concern with important thresholds of experience—first revelations and then their aftermath—there is an absence of the "affective." When

Beatrice dies, Dante makes use of a powerful quotation from Jeremiah, suggesting the desolation implicit in such a death. He then lists three reasons why he cannot go into great detail about her death, and in the next chapter he further diverts the affective by showing how, according to the Arabic method of counting hours, and according to the Syrian method of counting months, she died on the ninth day of the ninth month (by the Roman calendar it was June 8, 1290). This movement toward generality has the obvious purpose of taking personal material and elevating it to the order of the universal and the typical. This would be consonant with Dante's later poetic as expressed in *De Vulgari Eloquentia*, where he advocates elevation in language, in sentiment, and in syntax. It is also, however, very far from the poetic of the *Commedia*, where Dante reaches typicality only through the deepest immersion in the particulars of place and time and character.

Dante's narrative does not have the normal continuities of a story; rather he chooses significant moments, those thresholds of experience that constitute stages in the development of a new life. In the first and second chapters he informs us of his intentions. Under the rubric *Incipit vita nova* he finds assembled the events of his life, which he intends to make into his book, giving at least their meaning ("almeno la loro sentenzia"). To fix on all the details of his love would surely appear to some a *parlare fabuloso*; consequently he will pass over these details and come to the parts that are written in his memory "sotto maggiori paragrafi." The essence, the major paragraphs of his life, these constitute the true literary material in the *Vita Nuova*. And he will deal with them under significant captions—frequently rubrics in Latin—as the first chapter announces.

Near the end of Dante's ninth year (chapter II) he sees the young girl whose name may not be Beatrice, but who is called that by all of those who do not know her name. She was just in the beginning of her ninth year, and thus is introduced the numerology of nine in the *Vita Nuova*, which is at the same time a formalizing and a distancing device. The coincidence of nines also lends greater significance to what is described. In the presence of this new experience that will give a basic definition to his personality Dante begins to tremble in all of his spirits. His vital spirits (located in his heart), his animal spirits (in his brain), and his natural spirits (in the liver) all shudder at the revolution.

The tumult into which these spirits have been thrown indicates that a basic revelation has taken place, a fundamental definition of personality: "from that time forward I must say that love ruled my soul, which was so readily joined to it."

The next significant encounter takes place nine years later, in the ninth hour of the day, when Beatrice not only appears to his sight, but actually greets him (Chapter III). The first vision was prepuberty; the second is postpuberty, and consequently assumes more of a physical dimension. Dante retires to his room to savor this special greeting and has a dream filled with a marvelous vision. Inside a cloud of fire there appeared the god of love, *di pauroso aspetto*. Of the words that this terrifying god spoke Dante only understood the rubric *Ego dominus tuus*. A woman, who turns out to be the *donna de la salute* (the lady of the greeting as well as the lady of salvation, or Beatrice), is sleeping in the arms of the God of love, and she is naked except for a rose-colored cloth in which she is wrapped. In his hand the God of love holds something that is all on fire, and this he informs Dante is his heart: "Vide cor tuum." He then wakens the sleeping woman and persuades her to eat the flaming heart, which she does reluctantly ("dubitosamente"). Shortly thereafter the happiness of the god of love changes to bitterest lament, and thus weeping he wraps his arms around the young woman and together they make their way toward heaven. This dream is the substance of the first sonnet in the *Vita Nuova*, A *ciascun'alma presa e gentil core*, which Dante tells us he sent out to many of the famous "trovatori" of his time asking their interpretation of the dream (we will return later to the poetic circumstances of the *Vita Nuova*). An age reared on Freudian interpretation need make no apology for responding to the very palpable sexual aspects of the dream. What is interesting is not the sexual overtones, but rather the reaction to them, the sense of regret, even lamentation, as if to have acquired body was an offensive thing, a limitation imposed upon the spirituality of idealistic love. We can also perceive how the episodes where thresholds of experience are crossed gain much of their momentousness from the conjunction of love with intimations of mortality.

We will skip over the chapters where Dante uses the screen-woman, that is, the substitute figure whom Dante feigns loving in order to conceal his real love for Beatrice. In chapter IX Dante is advised by the God of love, who appears to him in the disguise of a pilgrim to adopt a new defense, a new screen. In chapter X, he tells us that he succeeded so well in this ploy that it became part of common rumor, and Dante acquired such a reputation that Beatrice, upon passing him one day, withheld her greeting "in which lay all [his] bliss [beatitudine]." Chapter XI tells the reader of the significance of the greeting: it so fills him with the flame of charity that he has no enemies and pardons all offenses. Even when Dante senses the nearness of her greeting, all of his vital spirits are overwhelmed, her actual greeting is an "intolerable" beatitude. Obviously the greeting of Beatrice is akin to a creative inspiration that seems to take possession of all the vital activities of a being.

Overcome by sorrow at the denial of the greeting, Dante at length falls asleep and is visited by the figure of love, a young man dressed all in white (chapter XII). He informs Dante that it is time to give up the "screen-game." Dante recognizes the God of love as the figure of other dreams and is troubled that the young man seems to be weeping sadly. The present sadness helps to clarify the bitter lament of the earlier vision. The young man explains the cause of his tears obscurely (the difficulty does not only derive from the fact that he speaks in Latin, or under the rubric of significance): "Ego tamquam centrum circuli, cui simili modo se habent circumferentie partes; tu autem non sic" (I am as the center of a circle to which all points of the circumference are equidistant; you, however, are not so). When Dante asks the meaning of this utterance (which some critics have found close to the scholastic definition of God) the figure replies ominously that Dante should not demand to know more than what is useful. The meaning of the passage seems to imply that Dante, in particular, and, perhaps, by extension, mortal human nature, while experiencing the transcendence of love, cannot know its eternity since he is physically limited to a single being and a body.[19]

The next significant experience occurs in chapter XIV when Dante, present at a wedding reception, suddenly senses the closeness of Beatrice. He tries to distract himself by looking at the paintings that cover the walls of the house. Finally raising his eyes he sees Beatrice. At that sight all of his spirits are once again overwhelmed, which becomes apparent to those around him. Having after a while recovered himself Dante repeats one of those utterances that serve so much as captions to the fatal developments of the story: "I have moved my feet into that part of life beyond which it is impossible to go if I have any intention of ever returning." The style of the *Vita Nuova* involves such utterances that serve as captions to these significant compartments of experience (in fact, the suggestion of several Italian critics that in this regard the form of the *Vita Nuova* is based upon the medieval legends of saints' lives has much merit).[20]

As the small book proceeds, the line of fatality moves closer to Beatrice. In chapter VIII a young woman dies, the occasion of the famous sonnet *Piangete, amanti, poi che piange Amore.* In chapter XXII Beatrice's father dies. In chapter XXIII, Dante has fallen ill, and in the ninth day of his confinement the thought of mortality assails him. He thinks of Beatrice, and then he thinks of "the weakness of life and the brevity of its duration," and that causes him to weep. The thought inevitably leads to the conclusion: "Of necessity it must come to pass that Beatrice one day will die." This thought then induces a wild nightmare where disheveled women, like some fatal sisters, assault Dante with the thought, "Tu pur morrai" (You, too, shall die); "Tu se' morto" (You are dead). He then imagines that his lady joins the company of these disheveled women, weeping along the way. At this remarkable death the sun clouded over, birds fell dead from the air, and the earth shook (a similar pattern to the events that occurred at the death of Christ—which is not to say that Beatrice is Christ, or even like Christ, but rather that for the natural world her death is no less a catastrophe than Christ's). In the same vision, a friend of Dante comes to inform him of the news that Beatrice has died, so that Dante begins to weep even in his sleep. Dante seems to see Beatrice escorted gloriously into heaven by angels singing *Osanna in excelsis.* Dante now accepts the fact that Beatrice is dead. Even in death her face shows forth such beatitude that Dante himself wishes to die, at which point in the dream he sighs so uncontrollably that his sister, who has been attending him, begins to weep. This experience is the occasion of the splendid *canzone Donna pietosa e di novella etate.*

The next three chapters deflect the line of fatality (showing the love of variety which will be so prevalent in the *Commedia*): not until chapter XXVIII is Beatrice actually dead. The *canzone* of the previous chapter is interrupted and the Latin of Jeremiah is intoned, "Quomodo sedet sola civitas plena populo! facta est quasi vidua domina gentium." But here too the affective part is diluted by the degressions (already mentioned) in chapters XXVIII to XXX. It is only in XXXI that Dante speaks directly of the death of Beatrice, but mainly to sing her praises. "Departed has Beatrice for the lofty heaven / to the realm where the angels have peace." In fact, neither chills nor fever killed her, but rather the power of her humility that persuaded the Deity himself that this world was not worthy of so noble a thing. The rest of the verse praises her virtue and laments that the earth has lost so noble a being.

Chapters XXXV to XXXIX introduce a dramatic turn in the story. A young woman observes Dante's sorrow and pities him; in this show of pity he detects the traces of the love that he was lamenting. So moved is he by this show of compassion that he begins to take too much delight in seeing the young woman (XXXVII). In fact, he begins to regard her as a messenger of love, sent to bring him remedy for his distress. Other times he begins to consider her even more amorously (XXXVIII). He persuades himself that he should not resist the attraction since it derives from the same quality of Amor that his first love did, and writes the sonnet *Gentil pensero che parla di vui*. The prose addresses this passage, declaring that the thought was far from noble, but rather "vilissimo." In chapter XXXIX, Beatrice does return in a vision, at the hour of nine, and Dante realizes that he was being misled by an inferior emotion of pity that should not be compared with the more positive idea of Beatrice. Finally, in response to a demand made by two women, he sends them three sonnets, the *Deh peregrini* of chapter XL; another not printed, *Venite a intender*; and a third, *Oltre la spera che più larga gira!* This last sonnet is the most indicative of the future directions of Dante's thought. In it Dante's sorrow passes beyond the largest sphere, the Primum Mobile, and arrives at the Empyrean, where Beatrice now dwells. His sighs are motivated by the "new intelligence" that love has placed in him. In essence, then, the love he now knows is an intellectual virtue that is seeking its highest inspiration (hence the insufficiency in this work of the *donna gentile*). Of such splendor is the light that his pilgrim spirit gazes upon that it passes beyond his sense of comprehension. The prime conviction that he does bring away, however, is that all of his spirit's speech tells only of Beatrice.

IV Vita Nuova: *Poetic Circumstances*

Of late, American criticism has concerned itself chiefly with the moral and theological patterns of the *Vita Nuova* (what could be called ideal criticism). Yet, the *Vita Nuova* is a mine rich in suggestions about the poetic circumstances in which Dante wrote and about his own poetic development. We know that when he sent off the sonnet to the famous "trovatori," or poets, of his day, he had already taught himself the art of making verse (chapter III). We are also struck by the audacity of this young man, the sheer aesthetic self-confidence (similar to that of the young James Joyce, who at eighteen sent off a letter—in Norwegian—to Henrik Ibsen). We know of three responses to Dante's sonnet, from Guido Cavalcanti, Dante da Maiano, and, perhaps, from Cino da Pistoia. Dante himself informs us (without mentioning his name) that Guido responded with the sonnet *Vedeste, al mio parere, onne valore*. And this was the origin of their great friendship.

What we must imagine is a remarkably active poetic culture, with poems circulating among friends, or among well-known poets. Such a poetic culture flourished in Florence and throughout Tuscany not only in Dante's time but even earlier. Doctors, jurists, notaries, and merchants exchanged verse on all kinds of topics—political, moral, and satiric. For Dante, intent on emulating the linguistic refinements, the poetic resources, and the imaginative form of Latin poets, these earlier local versifiers suffered the limitations of being "municipal." The most typical of these municipal poets was Guittone d'Arezzo, who again and again is dismissed by Dante as an unworthy model. Nevertheless, Guittone, who was born around 1235–40 and died in 1294, was the dominant force in the poetry of central Italy for many years. In *De Vulgari Eloquentia* Dante rejects Guittone, Bonagiunta da Lucca, and others (including Brunetto Latini) for never having aimed at the lofty poetic style, the tragic style of the *canzone* (I.xiii). From their works one cannot derive a "courtly" poetic style but rather one that is "merely municipal." In other of his works (*De Vulgari Eloquentia* II.vi, the *Purgatorio* XXIV and XXVI), Dante will demean the poetic accomplishment of Guittone, in particular the reputation he enjoyed.[21]

The poet responsible for changing the dominant Guittonian

style and content of verse was Guido Guinizelli, whom Dante
praises in *De Vulgari Eloquentia* I.xv, and celebrates in his great
encounter with him in *Purgatorio* XXVI. We do not know when
Dante could have made contact with Guinizelli's verse (Guinizelli himself died in exile in 1276). In chapter IX of the *Vita
Nuova*, Dante indicates that he was compelled to travel in that
area where his screen-woman was living. In his poem *Non mi
poriano già mai fare ammenda* he mentions having seen the
leaning tower of Bologna, the Garisenda.[22] This poem was
transcribed in a work dated 1287. So it is clear that within a few
years after the earliest poem recorded in the *Vita Nuova* Dante
traveled to Bologna, where he could have learned of the poetry
of Guido Guinizelli. In any event, it was Guido's influence that
was responsible for the central declaration of the *Vita Nuova*,
its poetic turning-point, when in chapters xvii to xxi Dante came
to write poems in praise of his lady, especially the *canzone
Donne ch'avete intelletto d'amore*. This *canzone* is followed
immediately by the sonnet *Amore e 'l cor gentil sono una cosa*,
the first line of which is clearly an adaptation of the first line of
Guido's *canzone Al cor gentil ripara [reimpara] sempre amore*.

Guinizelli's verse conveys a fresh brightness, a memorable and
easy gracefulness (hence Dante can praise his *dolci detti*). In
such poems as *Io voglio del ver la mia donna laudare*,[23] he
provided what Cavalcanti and Dante needed: a remarkable
sense of joy contained in a refined and lucid aesthetic. What
increased the appeal of his poetry was that it had a discernible
intellectual (even philosophical) consistency. His poems were
written in praise of his lady and of the virtue, or *gentilezza*, that
she brought out in her admirer. The philosophy of love that he
extolled was part of a refined and noble sense of life.

It was probably Guinizelli's influence, direct, or indirect,
through Cavalcanti, that first led Dante on the road to becoming
a philosophic poet. Zingarelli has declared that Guinizelli renewed vernacular poetry by virtue of his philosophical studies.[24]
A contemporary witness, Bonagiunta da Lucca, declares the
same—but in a more critical sense—in the poem *Voi ch'avete
mutata la maniera*, where he declares that Guinizelli changed
the manner of the pleasant sayings of love by introducing
philosophical considerations, subtle speculations so obscure that
they elude comprehension. And even though, understandably

enough, coming from Bologna, Guinizelli is a philosopher, Bonagiunta concludes it is a mistake for him to fill his *canzoni* with such abstruse philosophical matters (II.481).

The *canzone Al cor gentil ripara sempre amore* is dense with philosophical speculation that seriously strains the reader's powers of comprehension; nevertheless it is a crucial statement for the new school of poetry and will even assume surprising importance in the intellectual system of Dante's *Commedia*. At first Guinizelli elaborates upon the inextricable unity of love and the noble heart: to separate them would be like separating light from the sun or heat from fire (stanza 1). This is the thought Dante reproduces in the sonnet *Amore e 'l cor gentil sono una cosa*, referring in the next line to Guinizelli himself as the "saggio," or wise man, responsible for it in his "dittare," or poetic saying. In Guinizelli's *canzone*, the second stanza, where he distinguishes between potency and act, is philosophically the most interesting. The natural development of a precious stone is the basis of comparison. Just as the stars and the sun combine to produce the gem's value so nature and the lady work to produce the noble heart: "Foco d'amore in gentil cor s'aprende / come vertute in petra preziosa. . . ." The conceit is elaborate. The sun first removes from the stone that which is "vile," thus disposing it to receive the actions of the stars which give it its peculiar virtue. The two stages of the process involve predisposition (or potency) and then achieved virtue (or act). Nature works in a manner similar to the sun's in that it "elects" the noble heart, which is then infused with the virtue of love by the lady, acting in the manner of the stars. One can see why Bonagiunta da Lucca thought such verse difficult to expound, saw it in fact as deriving from Bologna's philosophical schools. For Dante and his friends such verse showed the greater power of the vernacular to cope with difficult concepts and provided them with a new outlook on life and the powers of poetry.

The fourth stanza of Guinizelli's *canzone* has distinct social implications, and this may have been another appeal of his doctrine. If nobility is a predisposition of nature it is not bound up with line of descent, but is, rather, individual. This argument will comprise the Fourth Book of Dante's *Convivio*. For Guinizelli, that man is proud who declares, "Gentil per sclatta torno," that is, he is noble by virtue of his line of descent (his "schiatta"):

ché non dé dar om fé
che gentillezza sia fòr di coraggio
in degnità d'ere'
sed a vertute non ha gentil core. . . .

This passage can be loosely translated to mean: Man should not
believe that nobility resides in "inherited dignities" if he himself
does not have a noble heart disposed toward virtue. Inherited
dignities are like the mud that does not respond to the rays of the
sun, while the noble heart is like the translucent water.

Dante's earlier verse, even the *Donne ch'avete*, is not as complicated. It deals more with the relations and powers of the
donna angelicata rather than with the philosophical arguments
underlying these powers. His verse is more akin to Guinizelli's
sonnet, noted above, *Io voglio del ver la mia donna laudare*. He
is more content to praise her beauty as being the epitome of all
natural beauty and the source of virtue and lofty thoughts in
man. The new life involves a new style, and the *Donne ch'avete*
(*Vita Nuova* XVII) ushers in a new period in Dante's writing.

The three chapters (XIV to XVI) preceding this important
change were dominated by the anguish and inner combat felt by
Dante at his loss of vital spirits in the presence of Beatrice. In
chapter XVII, he tells us that he had therefore resolved to be
silent since he had made so much of his condition known. But
contrary to this design he was struck by new material that was
nobler than that of the past. The prose commentary provides the
background. Some ladies, knowing of his love for Beatrice, ask
him what is the end of his love. It must be a strange ("novissimo")
love indeed if he suffers torments in her presence. Dante replies
that the end of his love is her greeting, which has now been
denied him. That greeting is his beatitude, the end of his desires.
After some consultation among themselves they then ask him in
what his beatitude currently exists. He responds, "In those words
that praise my lady," thus explicitly linking Beatrice with the
poetic act itself.[25] The ladies then conclude that his earlier
sonnets describing his condition would seem to have had a
different intention. Rather than uttering those words of praise
his verse gave expression to his emotional anguish (in particular
imitation of Provençal poetry). Why, he asks, if there is so much
joy ("beatitudine") in writing the praises of his lady, should he
have written in a different way? Henceforth he will take for his

material only that which contributes to her praise. This change amounts to something of a self-definition, particularly in regard to the subject matter of Provençal poetry. From an Italian, Guinizelli, Dante (and before him Guido Cavalcanti) has found a more congenial poetic model, one better suited to his more positive sense of life's resources.

Despite the new resolution, the sweet style did not come easily, because Dante was intimidated by the material. It was too lofty, and as a consequence he was afraid to begin. Inspiration was lacking. Then one day, walking by a river (he tells us in chapter XIX), Dante began thinking of the "mode" of his poem (what we might call its "strategy") and decided that while describing Beatrice's virtues the poem would not be addressed to her, but rather to noble women (like those who directed him toward his true purpose). Once he hit upon the right mode, the words of *Donne ch'avete* came to him almost by themselves ("la mia lingua parlò quasi come per se stessa mossa"). Inevitably in the "sweet new style" there must be a sense of inspiration, of the words coming almost naturally and involuntarily out of the situation.

The first stanza of the *Donne ch'avete* again explains the mode. The poem commences with the problem of writing the poem, the choice of style, and the reader for whom it is intended. For fear of proving unworthy, Dante will not attempt to make his style equal to its source; he will write *leggeramente*, that is, easily, even lowly. The recipients of his poem are the gracious ladies who helped occasion it (in the envoy Dante will add to them the *omo cortese*, the noble man, who is himself aware of the ways of love), and consequently are in a position to receive his poem with understanding. Already we see that Dante's new style will not be of a kind to appeal to all readers but to a select few.

The body of the poem deals with the ideal virtues of the lady. Heaven's only defect is her absence. Dante will tell the ladies of her virtues that are so desired in heaven. Beatrice is the best that nature can produce; through her example one can know the true nature of beauty. In her salutation—her eyes and her words of greeting—are held salvation. Later Dante will give very specific allegorical meaning to the salutation. For the moment, fearing his inadequacy in regard to the lofty material (hence his *Donne ch'avete* is closer to Guinizelli's *Io voglio del ver* rather than to *Al cor gentil*), he avoids philosophical complications.

Something of the same disclaimer is implied in Dante's response to Bonagiunta in *Purgatorio* XXIV, where the Lucchese poet identifies Dante as the author of *Donne ch'avete*. Dante's response, the practical definition of the *dolce stil novo*, is in fact a correction. While the inspiration of the new vein of verse came from the Guinizellian school of philosophy, and all that Bologna represented, its poetic genius was in the fresh brightness, the positive idealism, and the grace of poems that, while possessing great meaning, were still faithful in their responses to their genuine inspiration.

I am one who, when love breathes in me, take note, and in that manner which he dictates within go on to set it forth.

Lacking this same directness was the real knot that prevented the poets of the Guittonian school from approaching the style introduced by Guinizelli. It was not that the new school was reliant on philosophy (which it was), but that this philosophy translated itself into a heightened sense of life, into a luminous kind of creativity that contrasted with the pedestrian, even prosaic, straightforwardness of the "municipal" poets.

When, of course, we speak of brightness we must consider the next figure, that of Dante's first friend, Guido Cavalcanti, who is primarily remembered by his father for his bright eyes: "non fiere li occhi suoi il dolce lume?" (*Inferno* X.69) The friendship with Cavalcanti, like all relationships between talented people, is a complicated one, and must be observed in all of its implications if we are fully to appreciate what a magnificent monument to Cavalcanti canto X of the *Inferno* really is. Though not physically present in the canto, he had been a constant presence in the life of Dante the man and the poet.

Like Dante, Cavalcanti was a true disciple of Brunetto Latini. He was a poet, philosopher, soldier, and political figure—a Florentine Philip Sidney, the representative of the resurrected Roman and Ciceronian ideal of the writer actively engaged in the life of the commune. His family was one of the most aristocratic and prominent in the city. At an early age, and in order to help alleviate the tensions following Benevento, Guido was married to Bice degli Uberti (the daughter of Farinata—another link bringing together that great gathering in *Inferno* X). Like Dante, he fought at Campaldino and was active in the subsequent decade of troubles, the 1290s. Dino Compagni has left us a strong picture of him: "A young man of gentle birth, named Guido (son of a noble knight, M. Cavalcante Cavalcanti), courteous and bold, but disdainful, solitary and intent on study, an enemy of M. Corso, had several times determined to attack him. M. Corso feared him greatly, because he knew him to be high-spirited." [26]

Boccaccio would adorn the picture (VI.IX): ". . . Guido, the son of Cavalcante de' Cavalcanti, a youth who, besides being one of the world's keenest logicians, and a great natural philosopher, . . . was a most gracious, accomplished, eloquent courtier, better versed in all that makes a gentleman than anyone of his day." [27] In this story, Boccaccio also turns to the legend that *Inferno* X may have originated: since Cavalcanti held "somewhat," as he declares, to the opinions of the Epicureans, the vulgar people, seeing him distracted, assumed that he was busy speculating on the nonexistence of God. One day a group of partygoers coming upon him by the sepulchers then near San Giovanni asked him of what value it would be if he ever did prove that God did not exist. Guido responded that in their own house they were free to say what they pleased. An instant later their leader, Betto Brunelleschi, interpreted his response, noting that they were in the middle of the houses of the dead, "which he says are our houses, in order to demonstrate that we and the other idiots and illiterates like us are in comparison to him and learned men ["scienziati"] worse than the dead." Whether true or not, this story suggests the haughty attitudes of the new young intellectuals such as Dante and Guido to the "nonletterati" and "nonscienziati."

Guido holds to something of the same loftiness in his conception of love, by which conception he interprets the first sonnet sent to him by Dante. Love holds court in the place of the intellect. And if this is the case, what Dante has dreamed is not cause of terror but for joy. "Vedeste, al mio parere, onne valore. . . ." If Dante has seen the lord of love then he has known all virtue, all pleasure, and all good that man can feel.[28] As Dante will do in his own poems in praise of Beatrice, Guido expounds the social and intellectual nobility of love. Not only is love lodged in the mind, but where it prevails all baseness dies. Dante's responsiveness to love passes the test of true nobility: love after all rules the world of honor. Up until the time of his own philosophical studies, Dante's conceptions of poetry and of love were guided by those of Guido Cavalcanti.

This idealized expression of love represents an internalized and heightened sense of creative existence. The love-elite is also a poetic coterie. Thus, sometime after they had become friends (notably now using the "tu" in contrast to Guido's use of the "voi" in his first response to Dante's sonnet), Dante addresses a famous sonnet to Cavalcanti: "Guido, i' vorrei che tu e Lapo ed io." His wish is that these devotees of the higher love—incidentally they, along with Cino da Pistoia, are mentioned in *De Vulgari Eloquentia* as being the only Tuscan poets to transcend their dialect and to aspire toward the courtly vernacular language—would set off in an enchanted vessel, like that which Merlin provided for Tristan and Iseult. This vessel, moving only to the will of those on board, would thus avoid "Fortuna od altro temp rio," the difficulties and tempests of life that afflict the lower forms of human existence. They would be joined by their respective ladies, and all together they would spend their time in "ragionar d' amore," in discoursing on love, and expressing the superior visons of their minds.[29]

A third poem, this from Guido complaining of Dante's dejection following the death of Beatrice, will further show the relationship between the two poets. The vibrant idealism of Dante's earlier life has been overcast by the loss of the vision that Beatrice represented. Guido's sonnet complains of such *invilamento*, this loss of spiritual courage. "I' vegno 'l giorno a te 'nfinite volte / e trovoti pensar troppo vilmente" (II. 548). An infinity of times during the day Guido thinks of Dante and his despondency. He regrets that Dante seems to have lost his nobility of mind ("la gentil tua mente") and his other virtues. This loss has brought about a change in Dante's habits. Formerly he used to despise the crowd (the "villana gente" of the *Donne ch'avete* who do not know the true directions of love). In fact, Guido's portrait of Dante suggests a likeness with himself (corroborating Dino Compagni's portrait, where Guido was called "disdainful and solitary, intent on his studies"). The *Vita Nuova* itself is the product of such a lofty and aloof personality, making no concessions to time or to place, confidently sketching in a refined and elusive manner the stages of a life. The Dante of the *Vita Nuova* is a close collaborator with Guido Cavalcanti. In the next two lines Guido acknowledges the same: in contrast to Dante's disdain for the ways of the crowd, he always wrote to Guido with affection ("coralemente") so that Guido gathered and kept all of Dante's poems ("che tutte le tue rime avie ricolte").

In this meeting of minds, the discoursing on love also involved talk of critical theory and practice, so that when we turn to the explanatory chapters of the *Vita Nuova*, XXV and XXX, we find Guido's presence there as well. To begin with the smallest section, chapter XXX, Dante tells us that it was through Guido's exhortations that he wrote the *Vita Nuova* in the vernacular Italian. This is by way of explaining why it was that he did not quote in full the subsequent lines from Jeremiah, but only the first lines, *Quomodo sedet sola civitas*. Later, in the *Convivio* (written in Italian) and in *De Vulgari Eloquentia* (written in Latin), Dante will make one of the first great Renaissance defenses of the vernacular. His later thinking on these matters grew out of his discussions with Guido Cavalcanti, who prevailed upon him to write only in the vernacular: "And I know that my best friend, for whom I write this book, shares my opinion: that it be written entirely in the vernacular." The passage shows explicitly that because of their similarity of views and close consultation, Dante dedicates the *Vita Nuova* to his "primo amico."

The longer critical section is chapter XXV, which while not a major statement is still of great interest as we follow the evolution of Dante's poetic theory and practice. In this section Dante defends his use of personification, that is, attributing to love properties of a body: motion, laughter, speech. (Dante's style at the beginning of this chapter is philosophical, and in fact he quotes Aristotle, whom, following medieval usage, he calls "lo Filosofo.") Again we can see how rudimentary Dante thought the sophistication of his readers to be if he needed to defend personification. We also notice that Dante does not yet make use of the term "allegory."

Here Dante shows his taste for the historical scholarship that will be so prominent in *De Vulgari Eloquentia* and the *Commedia*. In ancient times, love was not the subject for vernacular poetry but only for Latin poetry: "the only love poets ["dicitori d'amore"] were those writing in Latin ["certi poete in lingua latine"] . . .; it was not vernacular poets ["volgari"] but learned poets ["litterati poete"] who wrote about love." (We note the distinctions Dante makes between the *rimatori*, the *dicitori*, the *trovatori*, all those who wrote in the vernacular tongues, and the true, or regular poets, the "litterati poete" who wrote in Latin.) His evidence for this claim is dependent upon historical search: "if we look into the Provençal and the Italian literatures, we shall not find any poems written more than a hundred and fifty years

ago." Sometime in the early 1290s, Dante has already made a
survey of Provençal and Italian poetry back to the middle of the
twelfth century, prior to which time he finds no instances of
poetry in those vernaculars. This demonstrates that the treatment
of love in the vernacular was a relatively recent innovation. It
also indicates that the origins of vernacular poetry were closely
allied with matters of love, which, as Dante declares, argues
against those who choose subjects other than love for their verse.
This opinion will undergo radical changes in the course of
Dante's career.

Thus the use of love as the subject of poetry is defended. This
still leaves the question of personification. His argument derives
from classical practice. The poets were always accorded greater
rhetorical license than the prose writers ("li prosaici dittatori").
And since "dicitori per rima" are nothing other than "poete
volgari," the same license enjoyed by the regular poets should be
granted the vernacular poets. This passage shows us that while,
like Guido Cavalcanti, Dante was committed to the vernacular in
verse, he sought to elevate that poetic practice by imitating the
ancients, the Latin poets. This chapter is thus a brief summary,
ten or more years earlier, of the major statements of the *Convivio*
and *De Vulgari Eloquentia*.

So far we have followed Dante's own culture, his poetic practice and theory worked out in relation to his predecessors and
contemporaries, Brunetto Latini, Guinizelli, and Cavalcanti. But
if the *Commedia* is any guide—and clearly it is the most
authoritative—there was another element in Dante's culture that
separated him from his contemporaries, and this was his overwhelming devotion to the lesson and practice of the ancient poets.
After all, it is Virgil who is taking Dante beyond the levels of
both Cavalcanti in canto X and Brunetto Latini in canto XV.
In each instance, and this is somewhat surprising, the mainstays
of Florentine culture seem to have been either negligent or unin-
terested in the larger formal and aesthetic possibilities of classical culture. In this same chapter of the *Vita Nuova*, the poets
whom Dante cites to show their use of personification are the
same five who come together in *Inferno* IV: Virgil, Lucan, Horace,
and Ovid, with Homer being introduced indirectly by the means
of Horace's imitation of his verse. One of the resources to which
Dante evidently committed himself, unlike his illustrious contemporaries, was precisely this classical line, its vision, and its

poetic resources. And it was this commitment that allowed him to transcend the achievements of his contemporaries, to rise to the epic vision.

CHAPTER 2

La Donna Gentile:
Dante's Philosophical Growth and the Canzoni

I *New Public Life*

THE years before and after the *Vita Nuova* were for Dante a time of personal emergence and public recognition. In these years he not only achieved his identity as a poet, but committed himself to the larger life of the commune as well, serving in the cavalry at the battle of Campaldino in 1289. In a letter that Dante addressed to the Florentine commune when he was in exile and wishing to return, he reminds them, as we know from the summary of it in Leonardo Bruni's *Life*, of this service he performed at Campaldino.[1] In the opening lines of *Inferno* XXII Dante recalls this experience (with emphasis on personal testimony, "Io vidi già . . ."):

I have seen before now horsemen move camp, and open the attack, and make their muster, and at times go off in flight; and I have seen scouts over your land, Aretines. . . .

Following the battle at Campaldino the Guelph alliance retook the fortress at Caprona. Dante himself was part of this siege, and in *Inferno* XXI he tells how, as he moves toward Virgil past the line of devils, he is reminded of the scene of Caprona's surrender:

thus I once saw the soldiers that marched out of Caprona under treaty afraid at seeing themselves among so many enemies.

In the vibrant atmosphere of *Paradiso* VIII Dante gives us a glimpse of this early golden age when he as poet and citizen-

42

soldier was realizing his own powers. There the scene with Charles Martel bestows recognition upon Dante as the poet of the philosophical *Voi che 'ntendendo* (although Dante had just completed or was in the process of completing the prose commentary for the *Vita Nuova*, he is recognized as the author of the more philosophical *canzone*) and memorializes the larger identity of Dante in the Florentine community. In March 1294, Charles, the young Angevin prince and King of Hungary, came to Florence, where he was to meet his father, Charles II, returning from Provence. Dante may have been one of a contingent of Florentines sent to give special welcome to Charles and his 200 Provençal and French knights in Siena and to escort them back to Florence. Within the planet of Venus in *Paradiso* VIII, Dante recreates this mood of graciousness where all the souls wish to contribute to his own joy:

We are all ready at thy pleasure, that thou mayst have joy of us. We circle in one orbit, at one pace, with one thirst, along with the heavenly Princes whom thou didst once address thus from the world: *Voi che 'ntendendo il terzo ciel movete*; and we are so full of love that, to do thee pleasure, a little quiet will not be less sweet to us. (32–39)

The relationship was extremely cordial, as Dante has Charles declare, "Thou didst love me much, and hadst good cause." So bright and pleasing was Dante to Charles that the young monarch already showed him royal signs of favor, and had he lived longer (the scene is shrouded by the tragic sense that Charles Martel died prematurely at the age of twenty-four in 1295) he would have given Dante not only the buds of his friendship but the fruits of his patronage as well. In this atmosphere of love and cordiality, Charles discourses about good government and about virtue, so that it is hardly accidental that the poem he recalls is the one that announced Dante's new period of growth in philosophical speculation, the one introducing the decade which was to have been capped by the *Convivio*.

II *Philosophy and Allegory*

Voi che 'ntendendo marks the beginning of Dante's determination to base his life and poetry on the foundations of philosophical truth. It initiates a line of poems, where beauty and truth contend, and where the sweet old life of the *Vita Nuova* is shown to be struggling against the overpowering appeal of a rigorous and difficult new life. Of this next change in his life Dante has given us a full account in *Convivio* II.xii.[2] There he tells us that so profound was his sorrow after the death of Beatrice that neither he himself nor his friends could console him. Finally, he began to read Boethius's *De consolatione philosophiae*, in which the imprisoned Roman author recounts his own discovery of the resources of philosophy. Boethius's book, surprisingly said by Dante to be little known ("non conosciuto da molti"), was to have a remarkable following in fourteenth-century literature.

Along with Boethius's work Dante sought consolation in Cicero's *De Amicitia*, particularly in Laelius's words on the death of Scipio. Dante tells us that this was the first time he read these works and that at first he found their meaning difficult. Nevertheless, by the "arte di grammatica" (that is, instruction in Latin) he possessed and the exercise of his intelligence he succeeded in grasping their meaning. That Dante should have experienced such difficulty linguistically strikes us as surprising; his admission here is that reading the Latin poets did not necessarily prepare him for the Latin philosophers.

What was intended as temporary diversion soon led to greater things, the discovery that Philosophy—the "lady of these authors" —was the "somma cosa." The "donna gentile" of the *Vita Nuova*, chapters XXXV to XXXIX, is about to be transformed into Lady Philosophy. Not only did philosophy become the supreme thing, it soon became the only thing, occupying all of Dante's thought. He began frequenting those places where philosophy was taught truly, that is, "le scuole de li religiosi e . . . le disputazioni de li filosofanti." The religious schools at that time would have been the Dominican at Santa Maria Novella, the Franciscan at Santa Croce, and the Augustinian at Santo Spirito, and they offered "courses" which lay people could also attend. The "disputazioni" were more like large conferences, held several times a year, restricted or public, where particular problems were discussed by various specialists.[3] Commencing with this early taste of philosophy, Dante's development was such that, within a period of thirty months, "the love of her [philosophy] banished and destroyed every other thought. Wherefore feeling myself raised above the thought of the first love to the virtue of this one, almost as if wondering at myself, I opened my mouth in the words of the said *canzone*, setting forth my condition under the figure of other things. . . ." The time is roughly clear: including the one year after the death of Beatrice in June 1290, the two and a half years, or thirty months, of philosophical studies would place the *canzone Voi che 'ntendendo*, sometime in late 1293 or early 1294, that is, shortly before the arrival of Charles Martel in Florence in March 1294.

This period of marked change in Dante's thought and intellectual commitments was to culminate in the *Convivio*, that ambitious project of philosophical commentary that was begun after Dante's exile and left incomplete. From the changed circumstances of that later time, Dante, looking back at the period of the *Vita Nuova*, had several major concerns. One was to place that earlier work in the perspective of his youthful age with all of its passions. Nevertheless, he was still somewhat reluctant to repudiate that work and cut himself off, as it were, from the earliest sources of his inspiration (a tendency we shall see present in the cantos immediately preceding his arrival at the Earthly Paradise in the *Purgatorio*). So, even while emphasizing how different in style and matter are the *Convivio* and the *Vita Nuova*, he still must acknowledge that, almost as in a dream, the *Vita Nuova*, in its vague outline, anticipated some of his later, more specifically philosophical, positions (and this might be the most important gloss of that earlier work—II.xii). However, given his needs at the time (see Chapter 4), Dante's greater concern was to separate himself from his youthful love poetry. This second concern of establishing his later and more mature philosophical seriousness has the fundamental consequence of dethroning Beatrice and of elevating to superiority in the new *canzoni* and *Convivio* the previously superseded "donna gentile" of the *Vita Nuova*. If the *Vita Nuova* is to be relegated to an earlier period of lesser importance, the reigning lady of that work must also be demoted.[4]

In a way similar to the *Donne ch'avete*, the poem commencing this new period does not present us with Dante's conclusions but rather with the situation out of which the poem arose. *Voi che 'ntendendo* is a poem of struggle and debate. The new *donna gentile* does not represent the compassionate but decidedly inferior woman of the *Vita Nuova*, but rather a stern and rigorous dedication to the study of philosophy, in contrast to which Beatrice represents the harmony and grace of Dante's aesthetic period. The combat could be described as being a struggle between the rational soul and the sensitive soul.

The heart that is "sorrowful" and the soul that laments are the sensitive parts of the body most troubled by the new rigorous study. Formerly their lives had been made up of the "soave penser":

The life of my sorrowing heart used to be a gentle thought which would often take its way to the feet of our Lord, where it saw a lady in glory of whom it would speak to me so sweetly that my soul would declare, "I wish to go there too." (Foster and Boyde, p. 101) [5]

The description of this former inspiration that is now being challenged recalls the apotheosis of Beatrice in *Oltre la spera*. In contrast with this smoothness and sweetness, the new force that has overtaken Dante fills him with trembling. Its command is forbidding:

Let him who would see bliss [*salute*] gaze into this lady's eyes, provided he does not shrink from grievous sighing.

In the remarkably detailed allegorical exposition of these passages in the *Convivio*, we learn that the eyes of the new lady are philosophical demonstrations, the subject matter of the philosophical study in which Dante was engaged. The "grievous sighing" which the resolute rational soul must not fear derives from the difficulties that such a life requires.

The weeping soul regrets the intervention of this new force and blames the eyes for ever seeing "la donna gentile." But the voice of philosophical reason—"uno spirtel d'amor gentile"—informs the sensitive soul that it is not dead, merely confused. The new philosophical spirit has in fact transformed a life that had been getting faint-hearted, "vile." The new lady is "pietosa e umile, / saggia e cortese" in her greatness. These are her true attributes which the slothful life of the sensitive soul has failed to recognize, and this is the cause of its fear. In fact—and these are the issues with which a whole series of poems concern themselves—this philosophical truth and wisdom are the bases of beauty as well as of virtuous conduct. [6]

New critical concerns are involved in this change in Dante's subject matter and style. In the *Convivio*, Dante tells us of the origins of the *Voi che 'ntendendo* and that he had decided to describe his condition "under the figure of another thing." Where the poetry of the *Vita Nuova* was literàl, Dante's new philosoph- ical love poetry makes use of allegory. The adoption of allegory calls for a special chapter in *Convivio* II.1, where the term is defined and its various uses explained. After the "sweet new style," with its "soave penser," Dante now is writing verse that is labored and difficult. Its meaning is hard to construe, requiring special signals, even (as in the *Convivio*) copious commentary. This means, of course, that Dante's poetry, never intended for the "villan gente" but only for those gentle hearts capable of understanding love, will have an even more restricted reader- ship. The envoy to the *Voi che 'ntendendo* makes this apology:

My song, I think they will be few who clearly understand your mean- ing, so intricate and difficult is your speech. (Foster and Boyde, I.103)

And in the *Amor che ne la mente* Dante introduces another element not present in his previous poetry but noticeable in the *Commedia*, particularly the *Paradiso*, that is, the inexpressibility of his subject matter. So overwhelming is the new experience of philosophy that Dante's weak intellect ("debole intelletto") cannot comprehend all of its power, nor can human speech ("il parlar nostro") express what he does understand.

Another sonnet, and a famous one, presides, in a way, over this poetic dilemma. The *Due donne* represents the reconciliation of the implied and overt issues and conflicting demands of this early cycle of poems (Foster and Boyde, I.146). Does the study of philosophy mean that one is no longer a devotee of beauty, or that one can no longer afford a civic commitment? In short, had his study cut him off from the major interests of his past life? The *Due donne*, instead, suggests an integration of these forces. One of the ladies shows "beauty and lovely charm" ("bellezza e vaga leggiadria"); the other "cortesia e valore, / prudenza e onestà. . . ." The one lady enjoys beauty, the other virtuous con- duct, and yet they both have their roots in the study of philoso- phy. Thus it is that philosophy, "the source of noble speech," can effect the reconciliation that comes from the love of wisdom: "ch'amar si può bellezza per diletto / e puossi amar virtù per operare." It is possible to love beauty for the delight it brings and to love virtue for its works.

III · *The Moral* Canzoni

We have perhaps as many as nine of Dante's *canzoni* that would in due time have formed the subjects of commentaries in the *Convivio*. Not all of them were love allegories, treating in veiled terms the difficulties or pleasures of his philosophical engagement. Four—and there are critics who hold them to be the best of the *canzoni*—show Dante's renewed interest in the moral issues of his day. Two of them—*Le dolci rime d'amor* and *Poscia ch'Amor*—seem to have been written prior to 1300, while two others—*Tre donne* and *Doglia me reca ne lo core ardire*—were clearly written after the poet's banishment from Florence in 1302. These *canzoni* derive from the position at which Dante's previous poems had arrived and are expressions of his decision (made in 1295) to involve himself actively in the political life of the commune. The resolution of the *Due donne* was one that Dante personally implemented: he continued to write poetry and at the same time to offer his services to his city-state. In fact, the point must be insisted upon that each of these functions legitimately derives from his commitment to philosophy. Henceforth Dante would be the philosopher-mediator—and this is the role that Brunetto Latini fostered—the person who discusses social issues from the light of basic principles. The fuller expression of this chosen role will be made in the *Convivio*, and it, of course, will attain its fullest range and power in the *Commedia*. Other alterations, of course, will occur in Dante's evolution, but it is in this period of philosophical study and the *canzoni* that were its products that Dante's thought takes quite a new direction. Well before 1304–1305, or the period of the *Convivio*, even before 1300, Dante had made the great leap beyond the *Vita Nuova*. Here we begin to recognize the issues of the *Commedia*.[7]

The moral *canzoni* address misconceptions about the nature of nobility, courtliness (*leggiadria*), liberality, and justice. They are moral epistles, addressed to them who live in error (*contra li erranti*). Quite obviously in these poems Dante assumes a public voice, but it is still the voice of the philosopher-mediator, even when he maintains as he does in both *Le dolci rime d'amor* and *Poscia ch'Amor* that he is on leave from strict philosophy.

Dante's discussion of *Le dolci rime* in Book Four of the *Convivio* is his largest and most ambitious effort prior to the

Monarchia and the *Commedia*, and consequently it will merit special attention later. Here it will suffice merely to point out a pattern that it shares with *Poscia ch'Amor*. In the *Convivio* (IV.i) Dante tells us what problem it was that made his lady appear scornful and fierce toward him in *Le dolci rime* ("atti disdegnosi e feri"): he could not resolve the question debated in the schools at the time whether God could know the "prima materia." [8] Because of this problem Dante will lay down the "soave stile" that he used in poems praising Lady Philosophy, and instead he will turn to moral problems that show a confusion of popular thinking:

and I will speak instead in harsh and subtle rhymes concerning the quality by which man is truly noble; refuting the false and base opinion of those who hold that nobility depends on wealth. (Foster and Boyde, I.131)

While Dante is not writing a poem in strict praise of philosophy, still in the final lines of the first stanza he must involve his lady's lord, and that is truth (*Convivio* IV.ii).

And at the outset I invoke that Lord who dwells in my lady's eyes, and thus makes her in love with herself.

The meaning is that Dante will still be making use of philosophy in order to correct current opinion. And in the envoy, Dante sends off his *canzoni* to where his lady resides with the message that it should not be silent about its mission, but instead should express the true relationship existing between philosophical truth and ethical concerns by declaring that the subject of his verse is a friend, "Io vo parlando de l'amica vostra." To discuss the real meaning of nobility is to engage in a labor congenial to philosophy.

The first strophe of the *Poscia ch'Amor* shows the same turn of thought. Love has abandoned Dante not because of his volition but because she has taken pity on his complaints (caused by the difficulties of philosophical inquiry). Because of this avoidance Dante will turn to another moral issue, that of *leggiadria*, or courtliness:

I will direct my song, thus devoid of love as I am, against the error which has arisen amongst us of misnaming something which is base

and boorish by giving it a name connoting goodness, that is by calling
it Charm. (Foster and Boyde, I.139) [9]

In the confusion of the times bad habits are given names of
virtues. In another age the *Poscia ch'Amor* would have been a
canzoni of etiquette, but Dante is very far from the etiquette
books of the sixteenth century, as far from Giovanni della Casa
as he is from Castiglione. Dante does not advocate coolness or
insincerity, but rather philosophical integrity and personal
simplicity, the pursuit of wisdom and virtuous actions. By
correctly defining the true qualities of *leggiadria* Dante will
ingratiate himself with Lady Philosophy. In short, the aesthetic
impression of courtliness can only depend upon virtue and truth.

Nevertheless, in order to be well thought of the deceived
engage in showy expenditures. This does not bring them the
good report they pursue, since after their death the good find
shelter in the minds of those who have understanding. This is the
first (in the second strophe) of a series of declamations against
showy investments that are separated from simple intelligence.

For the wise do not esteem a man for his clothes, which are outward
adornments, but for intelligence and nobility of heart.

The third stanza attacks the same need to make a false impression, this time by words and deeds. The eternal persiflage
and witticisms of the courtly style and the use of high-sounding
words seem empty to Dante. Nevertheless, these courtiers are
content to be admired only from a distance. Nor do their *amours*
produce any results ("non sono innamorati / mai di donna
amorosa"), but instead they pursue their gross pleasure ("villan
diletto") the way a thief goes about his work. In all of this they
appear to be animals without intelligence. The *canzone* reveals
a morally serious Dante, with a powerful dedication to sincerity
and personal integrity.

Clearly an unhappy configuration of the stars is responsible
for the degeneration of *leggiadria* (which, Dante declares, is
even worse than he suggests). Nevertheless, because of "una
gentile" Dante is aware of the true nature of courtliness and will
use the remainder of the *canzone* to explain its positive qualities.
Stanza four contains the turning-point of the poem, after which
his verse will be even more "sottile," or given over to more

philosophical reasoning. As they were conjoined in the first stanza so here and in what follows the aesthetic appeal of courtliness is linked indissolubly with virtuous action and philosophical truth. There can be no beauty separate from these qualities.

I swear by him who is called Love and who abounds in perfection, that no one can win true praise without practicing virtue.

In the fifth strophe Dante shows that *leggiadria* is not a pure virtue since it is only appropriate for some; one would not find fault with a religious person or a scholar for being without courtliness, whereas everyone without exception is obliged to acquire "pure virtue." *Leggiadria*, moreover, cannot stand alone, but gives its pleasure in conjunction with the other virtues ("Amore e l'opera perfetta"). These form a triad similar to the way the sun is made up of heat and light and its "bella figura."

The analogy with the sun continues into the sixth strophe, by far the most important and philosophically most complex of the poem. Just as the sun ripens and matures things according to their natures ("sì com'è disposta"), so *leggiadria*, scorning those who only appear to be virtuous (whose fruit, or actions, do not correspond to their leaves, or appearance), helps bring out the virtues of the "cor gentil." We see, then, that the center of Dante's philosophical development has a strong consistency. The notions of potency and act, of development of the properly disposed, of the *cor gentil*, all of these notions that provide the material of Dante's philosophical *canzoni* and were derived from Guido Guinizelli's *Al cor gentil*, and were represented in the *Donne ch'avete* and more explicitly in the *Amore e'l cor gentil*, continue to dominate his *canzoni* of more ethical concern. These ideas are more fully treated in the commentary on *Le dolci rime* in *Convivio* IV, particularly chapters XXI to XXII.[10]

CHAPTER 3

Peregrino, quasi mendicando: *Exile, the* Convivio, *and* De Vulgari Eloquentia

I *The Divided City*

DANTE'S growth toward the *Commedia* can be represented by his search for the form to encompass his remarkably varied experience. The philosophical directions of that poem were determined by the new period of intense study following the death of Beatrice; its political directions, in the years 1295–1302, when Dante, benefiting from a relaxed provision of regulations, enrolled as a member of the Guild of Physicians and Apothecaries (to which philosophers could belong) and began taking a more active part in the political life of the commune. This led to his priorate of June-August 1300, which he laments in the letter that Leonardo Bruni saw as the origin and cause of all his troubles.

After Campaldino the victorious Guelphs themselves broke apart. Florence was a city once again divided between the *magnati* and the *popolani*, and, within the aristocratic circles, between the intransigent and conciliatory. This is the very period that is covered in the first encounter with a Florentine in the *Inferno*, when Dante asks what will happen to the "città partita," the divided city. Ciacco's answer (VI.64–73), rendered as of the spring of 1300, looks backward and forward, from the time of long-standing tension to the eventual expulsion of the White Guelphs, the faction to which Dante adhered, in 1302. The primacy of this period in Dante's life is reflected in the fact that this is the first news of Florence that he receives in his poem. For all of these events that form the imaginative and historical center of Dante's poem, we are extremely fortunate in having extant from those years the remarkable *Chronicle* of Dino Compagni.[1] His unfailingly accurate account makes us virtual contemporaries to the events that led to Dante's exile.

Following the victory at Campaldino the overbearing behavior of the aristocrats called into being a retaliatory popular regime. This new government enacted the Ordinances of Justice that were severe in excluding the *grandi* from public offices and harsh in determinations of justice. This popular regime did not last long. By the intrigue of Corso Donati (I.16) an outrageous judgment was rendered, one that even involved some alteration of testimony. The uprising that followed brought down the government and led in 1295 to the relaxation of the Ordinances of Justice. Public office was now opened not only to those who were active in one of the guilds, but also to those who were merely enrolled on the books, thus including the more conciliatory of the noblemen, Dante among them.

While this tactical move weakened the cohesion of the *magnati*, it also left them prey to the more headstrong members of their party, to men like Corso Donati. As Dino Compagni tells us in the crucial chapters 20 to 23 of Book I, the city that was poorly governed because of its ordinances now became bitterly divided. He traces in great detail the events that transformed the triumphant Guelph party into the Blacks, led by Corso Donati, and the Whites, led by Veri de' Cerchi and his family. The nature of the rivalry between the two figures goes far back into the past and deep into the sociological matrix of Florence, with the Donati representing a financially weakened knightly warrior class, and the Cerchi, a newly enriched merchant family.

Compagni lists the series of events leading up to May Day 1300, when a clash occurred between young members of the rival families. Ever looking for decisive events, Compagni saw it as the cause of the ultimate destruction of Florence, for that minor clash was followed by a major one on the feast of St. John, the city's patron saint, for which a number of the Blacks, including Corso Donati, were restricted to a castle near Perugia, and a number of Whites, including Guido Cavalcanti, were similarly banished to Sarzana, where Guido contracted malaria and died in late August. These events give another twist to the complicated history of the relations between Dante and Guido since it was under Dante's priorate that Guido was sentenced.

Since the revision of the Ordinances of Justice in 1295, Dante had become very active in politics. In fact, the *Codice diplomatico dantesco* gives us a considerable amount of information about Dante's political activities from 1295 on.[2] From the *Codice* we learn, for instance, that in May 1300 Dante had been part of an important embassy to San Gimignano. Since the purpose of that mission was to solidify the Guelph league of Tuscan cities against the advancing ambitions of Pope Boniface VIII, presumably Dante was elected to the priorate in 1300 as a spokesman for the commune's determined opposition to the Pontiff's policies.

The fall of 1301 was a time of crisis for the commune of Florence. In September Boniface had named Charles of Valois to be his peacemaker ("paciaro") in Tuscany. Ironically, the great alliance of papacy and France that had helped the Florentine Guelphs defeat the Ghibellines was now turned against the White Guelphs. In the midst of the turmoil, Dante's voice was outspoken against the papal threat. On June 19, 1301, in two sessions of the council, the issue debated was whether to extend the service of 100 soldiers provided by Florence to Boniface. According to the *Codice*, in the first session Dante was the spokesman for those who were willing to let the commission lapse, thus denying the Pope's petition. Deliberations were suspended and the issue was taken up by the Council of One Hundred the same day. Again Dante was the only recorded speaker against the proposal.

The approach of Charles of Valois created grave concern among the citizens of Florence. Among the many measures adopted by the commune one was to send three ambassadors to treat with the Pope in Rome; Dante was one of the three and is said to have expressed his own quandary this way, "If I go, who remains; if I remain, who goes?"[3] According to Compagni, Boniface protested the suspicions of the Florentines and denied that his intentions in regard to the city were anything but peaceful (II.4). He then dismissed two of the ambassadors, sending them back to Florence with this assurance, but he detained Dante in Rome. By this move it would appear that Boniface had out-maneuvered the commune, depriving them of one of the likely strong voices against Charles of Valois. His subtlety succeeded in isolating Dante from the events that would overwhelm Florence.

Dino Compagni himself was a member of the priorate of October 15–December 15 that permitted Charles of Valois to enter the city on November 4 (it did require a solemn declaration from Charles that he would in no way claim sovereignty over the city nor interfere with its laws or practices). That very night the exiled

Blacks and their leader, Corso Donati, also entered Florence surreptitiously, and there followed a six-day reign of terror. These are the events to which Ciacco refers as leading to the defeat and exile of the White Guelphs. From these events Dino Compagni derived the sobering moral that "good-will is helpless against great evil."

Leonardo Bruni tells us that Dante learned of his troubles at first in Rome and then more definitely in Siena.[4] He was called before the new government in January 1302 and, failing to appear, was condemned along with three other former priors for crimes they had never committed. Again failing to appear to pay the fine levied or to defend themselves, on March 10, 1302, Dante and some fourteen other Whites were condemned to be burned to death (Piattoli, 90, 91). Thus Dante suffered the most decisive reverse in his life, one that he would speak of so frequently and so powerfully in the great poem that would make him the most famous exile in history. This rupture in his life is the central dramatic act of the *Commedia*, one to which an entire string of prophecies point. But the aim of the poem is not only to show this deep cut in Dante's existence, but also to show how Dante learned to cope with his exile, to transcend it, to turn its force into something fortunate. But in the early months of 1302 Dante was one of some 600 Florentine exiles, who, as Compagni tells us, "wandered about the world in need, some in one place and some in another."

II   *Exile and the* Convivio

Information about Dante's early years of exile remains fragmentary at best—in many cases the flowering of legend around this famous man has led to suppositions that are flatly contradictory. Nevertheless, the larger outline of the events of Dante's life during this period is stable and clear. At first Dante was actively involved in the attempts of the banished Whites to win their way back into Florence by military force; eventually, and following a series of bitter defeats, Dante split with his White allies, and, in the language of Cacciaguida in *Paradiso* XVII.69, became a party of one. Thirdly, the most difficult period of Dante's life occurred after this bitter episode, when, lacking in means and tired of being an alien, he yearned to return to Florence and his family. It is to these circumstances that the major works of this period, the *Convivio* and *De Vulgari Eloquentia*, owe their origin.[5]

Dante's desire to reinstate himself after his break with the

Whites was the dominant motive in his early years of exile. The letter beginning "Popule mee, quid feci tibi?", which Leonardo Bruni saw, shows this need. At this time, according to Bruni, Dante tried through "good deeds" and "good conduct" to have his sentence completely revoked.[6] The famous *canzone Tre donne intorno al cor mi son venute* expresses this same change of heart. It is close in spirit to Book One of the *Convivio*, and, in fact, it probably was intended to provide the subject matter of the fourteenth book, justice. In the rhetorical fiction of the poem Dante is approached by three ladies (allegorically, they are, as Pietro di Dante informs us, three forms of justice: *ius divinum et naturale*, or divine and natural law, *ius gentium sive ius humanum*, the law of peoples or human law, and simple *lex*, or positive law).[7] Each of the ladies is sorrowing and disheveled,

like those driven from home and weary, abandoned by all, their virtue and their beauty being of no avail. (Foster and Boyde, I.177)

There was a time when they were made much of, but now they only suffer scorn or indifference. Thus outcast they have come to Dante as to the house of a friend, since they recognize that Dante can speak of their lot from personal knowledge.

Conscious as he is of his isolation, Dante is equally conscious of his self-worth. He was exiled because he served justice, and since the personifications of law are also rejected, he can take pride in such loyal companions: exile he considers a mark of honor. This affirmation, however, is immediately followed by a wish for reconciliation. Florence, the object of his mind's eye, has been denied him; except for this, his exile would be a light thing to endure. Missing Florence weighs him down so much that he fears it will be the cause of his death. The final three lines of the stanza contain an admission of some guilt as well as the wish for pardon because of his repentance.

Even if I were to blame for it, the sun has now circled for several moons since that was cancelled, if blame dies through repentance. (Foster and Boyde, I.181)

The culpability referred to is not the action that led to exile, but rather those maneuvers subsequent to that event, that is, most probably his participation in the military league against Florence.

In the second envoy to the poem, Dante sends out his *canzone* to "hawk" with the White Guelphs and to "hound" with the Blacks ("neri veltri"). At one time it suited Dante to flee from these very Blacks, but now they have the power to bequeath him peace, or pardon. More than likely the Black is Moroello Malaspina, from whom Dante once fled, but from whom he later received shelter and pardon. His final plea is for reconciliation: "a wise man will not lock the chamber of forgiveness; for to forgive is fine victory in war" (Foster and Boyde, I.181).

From this same desire for reconciliation, the *Convivio* takes its origins and essential purpose. The key passage occurs in I.iii, where Dante is describing his life as an exile:

Since it pleased the citizens of the fairest and most famous daughter of Rome, Florence, to cast me forth from her most sweet bosom (where I was born and nourished up to the apex of my life, and wherein, by their good leave, I long with all my heart to rest my weary soul, and to end the days allotted to me) through almost every part where her language is spoken I have wandered, a pilgrim, almost a beggar, displaying against my will the wounds of fortune. . . .[8]

This passage explains the absence in the *Convivio* of any invectives directed against Florence like those we find in the *Commedia*. Marked by disillusionment and the clear consciousness of approaching age, the earlier prose work was written in the hope of a pardon and a peaceful return to his native city.

There is every indication that as he began writing the *Convivio* Dante was committing himself to a major undertaking. He projected a work of great length, fifteen books, fourteen of which would be commentaries upon different *canzoni*. He only completed four of the books, but we know from internal reference that the seventh book was at least in part to be devoted to temperance; the fourteenth, to a commentary on the *canzone* of justice (most probably the *Tre donne*); and the last, to liberality (probably the *canzone Doglia mi reca ne lo core ardire*). These commentaries in many instances go beyond the requirements of the poem, becoming in a way a compendium of instruction, with a random display of the learning of an amateur in philosophy. It is this and yet more. Dante's intention is to place the challenging ethical issues, or topics, of his day into a suitable metaphysical and theological frame. The *Convivio* is not an original work; rather it is a large work of integration, in which Dante shows the uses of philosophy in the principled conduct of civic life. It was intended to be, as it were, a *summa* of civic life. What Cicero had meant for Rome, or Brunetto Latini for Florence, so Dante was to mean for his own time. Following Brunetto Latini, Dante presents himself as one of the new type of lay intellectuals, the philosopher, whose broad vision and specific training allow him to analyze problems and to understand them in relation to a coherent whole. The relative novelty of Dante's position is clear from Villani's description of him: "Questi fue grande letterato quasi in ogni scienza, tutto fosse laico." [9] *Although a lay person*, Dante was still deeply read, or at least proficient, in almost every field of knowledge.

In the *Convivio* the intellectual system of the *Commedia* is largely complete. In fact, it is a pivotal work that makes Dante's evolution understandable; without it, despite its philosophical consistency with the *Rime*, the passage from the *Vita Nuova* to the *Commedia* would be even harder to imagine. Like the *Commedia* the *Convivio* is ethical and educational in purpose. And in it we find elaborated the graduated universe that Dante inherited, his sense of heroic human development, his psychology of positive attachment and his belief in human freedom. In Book IV, xxi and xxii, Dante develops his sense of the *intelletto possibile* and the appetite, or *horme*, that returns man to God. These might very well be the two most important philosophical conceptions in his poem. Finally, it is in the *Convivio* that he seeks to establish his own role as a philosopher-mediator, a role that he will continue in the *Commedia*, using logical analysis and metaphysical speculation toward the clarification of broadly ethical ends.

In this sense Dante is a "popularizer" of philosophy placed in a moral setting. He is conscious of his audiences. The first is all those who are prevented from enjoying the delights of philosophy because they do not have the leisure: they are occupied by familial and civic responsibilities. He is writing in Italian, and not Latin, because the vernacular will reach more people, particularly the nobility, who have neglected the knowledge of their own heroic history and have allowed literature—here Dante means Latin—to become the monopoly of those who use it for professional reasons. Dante himself, then, is a mediator between those few who sit at the table where the bread of the angels is eaten and those who simply do not have the time or the means for such study (I.i). The food of the angels is the manna rained down in Psalm 78.24–25. By it Dante means the goal of philosophy, or wisdom. Interestingly enough, in the *Convivio* Dante does not regard himself as occupying the happy seat; he is not an Aquinas or an Albertus Magnus. Still he has by means of philosophy attempted to flee from "the pasture of the herd" and at the feet of the true philosophers to gather up these crumbs of moral philosophy. His *canzoni,* which already for some time have been available to the public, are the products of these philosophical remnants (I.i). Now he intends to prepare a general banquet, with meat and bread, the meat of philosophy turned into poetry, that is, the *canzoni* and the accompanying bread provided by the commentary. Thus his general reader will not only relish the superficial beauty, but will also benefit from the truth from which it takes its form—the meaning.

One of the constant features of Dante's work is his aesthetic self-consciousness, the way he takes his bearings in regard to his earlier works. As he wrote the *Convivio,* the work against which he measured his effort was the *Vita Nuova* (I.i). While not exactly disowned, the earlier work he saw as belonging to a different phase of his life, when he was less serious. The one was written at the entrance to young manhood, and as such was fervent and passionate; the other was written after he had passed through that same phase, and accordingly is more temperate and virile (that is, his matter is more serious and is treated in a sober and reasoned way).

The *Convivio* is first devoted to a defense of just such personal references to his work and to his exile. For this defense Dante relies on the examples of Boethius and Augustine (I.ii). From the former he knows that it is justifiable to write of oneself in order to remove undeserved blame, for Boethius's *Consolation* is really a self-defense. And from the *Confessions* he knows that it it is legitimate to write of oneself in order to communicate useful moral instruction. Both of these purposes are Dante's own as he attempts to alter the false impressions people will receive not only from the public accusations but also from his own poetic career that on the surface, at least, shows fickleness and change of heart. The allegorical exposition of Dante's commentary will show that the ideal cause of his new love was not passion but virtue.

But mainly Dante writes of himself because he is a proud man. He had been a diplomat, a political leader, and a poet, and as a consequence people had certain expectations of a man of his reputation. Now when they see him in his impoverished condition as an exile, they vilify not only the man but all his past works as well. It is, then, because he must present himself as a person of great seriousness, as a philosopher, that he painstakingly devotes himself to removing all possibilities of misunderstanding (hence the critical problem of the lengthy disgressions) and indulges in his great show of learning. And for that same reason the *Convivio* is designed to be a work of considerable magnitude. Dante has presented himself to almost all Italians in a state of poverty that belies his great reputation. He must consequently recoup that reputation by writing a work of great seriousness (I.iv).

When it comes to his defense of his use of Italian there is no such need of apology. The final nine chapters of Book One of the *Convivio* form a major document in the development of a poetic and literary renaissance. They should be considered in tandem with Dante's *De Vulgari Eloquentia*.

He begins his defense of the vernacular by acknowledging the superiority of Latin. The reason Dante does not use Latin in his commentary is that it is a sovereign language and thus would be inappropriately used in a servant's role of commenting upon vernacular poetry. Latin is a superior language for many reasons, but mainly because it seems unchanging, and in this it contrasts starkly with the instability of the vernacular. The language of the ancient Latin comedies and tragedies does not alter, whereas the vernacular, with its great variety of dialects, can never attain stability.

For we see in the cities of Italy, if we take notice of the past fifty years, how many words have been lost, or invented, or altered; therefore, if a short time can work such changes, how much more can a longer period effect! So that I think, should they who departed this life a thousand years ago return to their cities, they would believe them to be occupied by a foreign people, so different would the language be from theirs. (I.v)

A reflection of the enormous increase in energy and mobility within the late thirteenth and fourteenth centuries is the volatile state of the language in which the first Italian classics were written (if we think of Chaucer's envoy to the *Troilus and Criseyde*, we can say the same for the literature of England). Beset by this specter of change and acknowledging the unchanging quality of Latin—a grammatical language with rules—Dante was determined to bestow upon the vernacular Italian a similar stability. Consequently, as he declares in the same chapter V, he intends to write a small book, *di Volgare Eloquenza*.

After giving other reasons why Latin could not rightfully be made a servant of the lowly vernacular, Dante, in chapter VIII, commences his more positive defense of the vernacular, which he does by explaining why he has such an eager willingness ("una pronta liberalitade"), a natural and native urge, to use it. The first reasons are more practical: the vernacular will reach more people (including the nobility) and it will also be more useful to them, leading them to "scienza e virtu."

In all of these proceedings, one notices the logical rigor, or at least structural symmetry, of Dante's design: there are three reasons why Latin will not do and three why the vernacular will; and then in chapter X his third reason for writing in the vernacular—"the natural love of my own language"—has three subdivisions. The first is his desire to *magnificare* the Italian language. Almost literally Dante's desire is the same as DuBellay's in his *Défense et illustration de la langue française*, in the sixteenth century, and what we can imagine Edmund Spenser's to have been in his now-lost *English Poet*. All three of these works can be seen as ushering in a great age of national poetry. The defense of the language is a major effort in that enterprise. Like DuBellay Dante will magnify his language, exalt it, and make it illustrious. Of course, Dante is speaking about prose, but the same impulse will dominate his efforts on behalf of poetry in the *De Vulgari Eloquentia*. Dante will claim grandeur for his language by making manifest its theretofore hidden capacities for expressing conceptual thought. The loftiest and newest thoughts—and we may think of those regarding the immortality of the soul, the origin and the growth of the human fetus and its capacity to realize the *intelletto possibile*, the historic development of the Roman Empire—the vernacular can express easily, sufficently, and gracefully, almost as well as the Latin (I.x).

Perhaps even more interesting is chapter XI, where Dante inveighs against its detractors. Some of them disparage it from simple lack of discernment. People will follow the "grido," the general cry, and that cry has it that the vernacular is an insufficient language. Others who detract from the native language are the would-be poets ("dicitori") who place the blame for their own failures on the inadequacies of the language. Somehow, they claim, the *langue d'oc* is a better instrument for poetry. Like Petrarch in his letter to King Robert of Sicily prior to the coronation (*Fam.* IV.7), Dante invokes the parallel situation of Latin vis-à-vis Greek literature, arguing that if the Romans had acquiesced to the claims of the natural superiority advanced for the Greek tongue then there would have been no Latin literature.[10] Implicit in this argument (as it was explicit in Petrarch's letter) is a spirited faith in the capacities of the present language to express sophisticated thought, in the validity of the experience of his time, and in the poetic skills of Dante and some of his contemporaries and followers.

The analysis is a remarkable one, in many of its points contending with problems that later Renaissance writers would encounter as they struggled to assert the validity of their experience. Because his defense of the language is in fact a self-defense, his argument becomes personal. The *volgare* has become a necessary part of his being, well suited to the task of expressing his own thoughts. This it is that makes Dante its advocate. Even more than its advocate, he becomes its first great promoter, as in the final sentence of Book One, where he not only anticipates but accurately predicts its glorious future:

This shall be the new light, the new sun, which shall rise when the worn-out one shall set, and shall give light to them who are in shadow and in darkness because of the old sun, which does not enlighten them.

The sociological implications of this statement are no less astonishing than the literary. The vernacular is in the ascendant and Latin, the language of the clerisy, is setting. This means that a new lettered class is emerging, and Dante, the mediating philosopher, places himself at the head of those who, to change the convivial metaphor, will bring light to the larger numbers of people for whom Latin has no meaning. As the above quotation shows, the language of renewal is inescapable at this moment.

The revolution he describes is a major one: the twilight of Latin culture and the emergence of a lay, urban literacy. Dante sees himself as the philosopher-mediator between the two movements, helping to create the new classics for a newly enfranchised public readership. The Italian literature that Dante announces was soon to become the leading literary language of Europe and would continue to be that for close to three centuries. Its own masterpieces would be translated and imitated, and when the time came for the other national vernaculars to assert their own independence, they would knowingly or perhaps even unknowingly adopt the energetic and heroic tone and arguments with which Dante vindicates his own language and enterprise. As in this first book of the *Convivio*, the real proem to a poetic renaissance, the defense of the self and its experiences and the defense of language will go together.

III   De Vulgari Eloquentia

In the *Convivio* (I.v) Dante discloses his intention to write a "Volgare Eloquenza." In the same work (I.xiii) he declares that his life's purpose—one that should be evident to everybody since he had made his first reputation as a poet—was to bring stability to vernacular poetry. And since it contains a reference to Marquis John of Montferrat, who died in February 1305, the work must have been written shortly before that time. This makes it plausible to assume that *De Vulgari Eloquentia* was composed immediately after Book One of the *Convivio*. In any event, dating to one side, the *De Vulgari Eloquentia* is the logical complement to that work.

There are paradoxes, of course. In the *Convivio*, a more popular work, written in Italian, Latin is acknowledged to be a superior language. The *De Vulgari Eloquentia*, although written in Latin for specialists, adds to the arguments in the other work in favor of the vernacular. The native tongue is nobler, Dante now declares, because (1) of course, the first language employed by the human race was without rules, (2) the entire world uses its variants, and (3) it is more natural, whereas the learned language is more artificial (I.i).

Nevertheless, while granting the natural superiority of

the vulgar tongue, the *De Vulgari Eloquentia* is in fact a poetic, a treatise on the doctrine of vernacular poetry. It is an attempt to elevate the vernacular to the position where it too can become a literary language, using conscious techniques and rules. One reason for this is simply ascribable to Dante's extraordinary consciousness of change. Given his sense of linguistic mutability (already made known in the *Convivio*), Dante's response is to build order and stability into the rapidly changing vernacular. Hence his need to transform the vernacular dependent upon use into a *grammatica*, "which is nothing else but a kind of unchangeable identity of speech in different times and places." This grammar (here he means the literary languages, Latin and Greek) was evolved from the "common consent of many peoples," and in this way was spared the idiosyncracies and arbitrariness of any one of them (I.ix). In short, one aspires toward a literary language in order to be understood not only in one's own time and place but in other times and places. Dante could not tolerate the simple anarchy of the vernacular, no more than he could tolerate any lack of order in the universe.

The way to achieve this regularity is by imitation. By this method the vernacular poet is transformed into a great poet. In Book II.iv Dante gives the name of poet to those who write in the vernacular. He even defends his practice, arguing that "they are in fact poets, if we take a right view of poetry, which is nothing else but a rhetorical fiction set to music ("que nichil aliud est quam fictio rhetorica versificata in musicaque posita"). By this definition all writers of verse in the vernacular are poets. Dante, however, also employs the term in a grander sense. The simple practitioners differ from the great poets—and these are the Latin poets—since the procedures of the latter are regular and according to art, while the others proceed by chance. This is one of the most important passages in the *De Vulgari Eloquentia* and summarizes the whole purpose of the book. In order to become like the regular poets, those who write in the vernacular must abandon chance and acquire doctrine, a poetic, which Dante is supplying. And they do this primarily by imitating the ancients: "quantum illos proximius imitemur, tantum rectius poetemur." The more closely we imitate them the better poets we become.

The *De Vulgari Eloquentia* was planned to contain at least four books. Like the *Convivio*, it was to be a large undertaking, and like the *Convivio* it was left incomplete. We have only Book One and a portion of Book Two. The second book treats the *canzone*, while other lesser forms and the comic style were to be discussed in the projected fourth book (II.iv; viii). The first book could be called a survey of linguistic geography and the second a progress of poesie. Dante's survey of the Italian dialects, which utilizes all the linguistic knowledge he gathered during his enforced travels, is a stunning performance. His object is nothing less than a new language composed of the best elements of a great variety of dialects, a new language to serve the vehicle of a new literature. There is this connection between the two books. Dante needs to sort out the bases for a literary vernacular before he can indicate the means for its improvement. And in his second book, filled with the examples from the literatures he knew—French, Provençal, Sicilian, and central Italian—we witness Dante's own historical consciousness, his first major attempt, repeated several times in the *Commedia*, primarily in the *Purgatorio* (cantos XXI, XXII, XXIV, and XXVI), to place his poetic theory and practice in an historical perspective, to give his sense of what was available to him and where he stood in relation to it. It is a fact, however, that his knowledge of the poetry that preceded him was already evident in *Vita Nuova* XXV.

Before Dante can discuss the divisions of language current in his own day (or at least those of the Romance languages that concern him most), he must deal with an issue that he will confront once more in the *Inferno* and finally in the *Paradiso*. In Book One, chapters IV to VII, where he speculates about the origin of language and the cause of the diffusion of tongues, Dante anticipates the sublime meeting with Adam, the first father, in *Paradiso* XXVI: Adam, not Eve, must have been the first speaker in Paradise, and obviously the first sound he uttered was *El*, or God (IV). Linguistic differentiation was a direct consequence of Nimrod's sinful presumption in building a Tower of Babel (VI, VII). This account of the variety of tongues is found in Augustine (who will be followed by Milton).[11] Dante, for his part, repeats it in the *Inferno* XXXI.77–78, where he names Nimrod as the man "through whose wicked device the world

is not of one speech." In the *Paradiso*, however, with its
much longer perspective, this view is directly contradicted
by Adam himself, who declares that even in his own lifetime
the word for God changed several times, with the obvious
implication that there is no immutable language, not
Hebrew, not Latin, but they are all subject to change.

Dante quickly settles on the three variants within the
Romance family: the language of *oui*, or French; the language of *oc*, or Provençal (he calls both Catalan and
Provençal Spanish since both areas were ruled by the house
of Aragon), and the peninsular language of *si*, or Italian. Provençal has claim to being the first language of
poetry among the vernaculars—it being a "more finished
and sweeter tongue." The superiority of Italian is two-fold:
"the sweetest and most subtle poets who have written in
the vernacular are its intimate friends" (Dante refers to
Cino da Pistoia and himself) and it seems to be the most
grammatical of the three languages, "and this appears to be a
very weighty argument to those who examine the argument in
a rational way" (I.x).

Dante then proceeds with his survey of the various Italian dialects (lending linguistic proof to his claim in *Convivio*
I.iii that exile had led him through practically all the
parts of the land where the Italian language reaches).
It is a remarkable performance: some fourteen to seven-
teen (counts will vary) dialects are discussed, and the discussion is illuminated with some thirty specimens of the various
dialects. In this survey the most important chapters deal with
the great centers of Italian poetry, Sicily, Florence, and Bologna
(XII, XIII, XV).

Of all the municipal dialects, that of Bologna seems
the most satisfactory, and the reason for this is revealing
(I.xv). The Bolognese dialect is an amalgam which borrows, and as it borrows it tempers the individual qualities
of the neighboring dialects, those of Imola, Ferrara, and
Modena. Accordingly, from Imola it takes "smoothness
and softness"; from Ferrara and Modena, the "tang of
sharpness characteristic of the Lombards"; and "by this mixture
of opposites [it is] tempered to a praiseworthy sweetness."
Despite these qualities Dante does not find the Bolognese dialect
to be the ideal he is seeking, as witnessed by the fact that the

major writers of that city, preeminently Guido Guinizelli, departed from the local speech.

It sounds very much as if Dante, in his quest, is resorting to the method of a common denominator, choosing those words that while known to all regions of Italy are particular to no part (xvi). This would be a mistaken view; for while he is engaged in a rational survey, he never fails to defer to the practice of the proven poets. In fact, the *De Vulgari Eloquentia,* rather than being a literary projection (Dante, we must remember, is never utopian), is a defense of a program of practices already established in the works of a few poets in the court of Sicily, by the Florentine writers, and by Guido Guinizelli (a list that will be lengthened by the addition of the French and Provençal poets in Book Two). And the modern poetic associations here delineated are not much different (including rejections) from those drawn in the *Purgatorio.* How much of Dante's thought, in prose and poetry, is devoted to describing the literary situation, with its traditions, its needs, and its discards! In this sense, the *De Vulgari Eloquentia* needs to be allied with the *Convivio,* inasmuch as both are alive with the sense of new possibilities in literature. Dante sees the Italian language in his time as ready to rise beyond its dialectical idiosyncracies and to emulate and even surpass French and Provençal. In this sense the first book, the linguistic survey, is proemial; it is the basis for a larger poetic.

In the final chapters (XVI to XIX) Dante describes the positive requirements and the virtues of a literary vernacular. It must be illustrious, cardinal, courtly (*aulicum*), and curial. That which is illustrious is exalted and also exalts. It is exalted by the training of its practitioners who have weeded out the rougher elements of the dialects (as examples Dante refers to his *canzoni* and those of Cino). The vernacular is also exalted by virtue of its powers of persuasion, of altering wills. And it exalts by virtue of its power to confer honor and glory, honor on those recipients of poetic praise (witness Dante's celebration of the Malaspina, the della Scala) and glory on the writers themselves. And in a highly personal passage, Dante acknowledges the sweetness of this glory, since for its sweetness he is willing to disregard his exile. In this work, as distinguished from the early *Convivio,* we witness Dante's changed attitudes toward exile. As he writes about poets and poetry his own courage revives.

The illustrious vernacular is also cardinal, since upon it depends the municipal dialects. Being a cultural elitist Dante holds that popular art derives from high art. The writers in the literary vernacular are the arbiters of taste; they "purify the dialect of the tribe," weeding out rough words and adding new ones. The true locus of this litera.y language is the court. Dante's poetic as well as his political experiences make him see the need for such a center in every state (see the passage describing the Sicilian court in I.xii). Without it, without an institution where the illustrious vernacular is in daily use, "the illustrious language wanders about like a wayfarer and is welcomed in humble shelters." In the absence of a court, language and poetry suffer.

Because the illustrious vernacular requires a just balance, it is termed curial—after the imperial courts of justice. Here, too, Dante's language is highly personal, uniting social and poetic issues with his own experience. Although Dante regrets the absence of a true imperial court in Italy, he and his friends can still bring judgment under the "gracious light of Reason." Like the poet who is a citizen of the world, so the philosopher in Dante finds a support against the disordered conditions of Italy.

The last chapter of Book One looks ahead to the books that follow, where Dante will treat in order such questions as who ought to use the illustrious vernacular; for what subjects; how, where, when it should be used; and to whom it ought to be addressed. Although the illustrious vernacular is common to all the realm, not all ought to aspire to use it. Since it is the best language only those poets who have "ingenium et scientia" are equal to it (II.i). As for the subject matter, since man has a three-fold nature (vegetable, animal, and rational) the subjects of poetry ought to correspond to the highest workings of these three interests. The vegetable seeks that which is useful, and since the height of utility is safety, one subject of poetry deals with war. The animal seeks that which is pleasurable; and, since the highest pleasure is love, love is another subject. Lastly, since the rational seeks that which is just or right, the third subject concerns these matters, or virtue. Turning back to the poetics of the *Vita Nuova* (XXV), we notice the expansion of interest in the subject matter of poetry beyond that of love.

Furthermore, Dante in his examples uses Italians along with the illustrious writers in Provençal: Bertran de Born stands out as the poet of war; Cino da Pistoia is ranked with Arnaut Daniel as a poet of love; and Dante himself stands with Giraut de Borneil as a poet of righteousness (and as an example from his own verse he cites *Doglia mi reca nello core ardire*, probably intended to be the last *canzone* in the *Convivio*).[12]

Reflecting his own current poetic practice Dante, in chapter III, concludes that the *canzone* is the noblest poetic form. It is more self-sufficient than the *ballata*, which requires other performers, and it seems to be able to do all that the slighter sonnet can, and more. The rest of the *De Vulgari Eloquentia* details shop-talk, such as the number of syllables per line, the kind of words allowed, and stanza-form. Of these matters we can single out chapter VI, where Dante treats of poetic syntax and periphrasis. The illustrious vernacular should avoid the straightforward primer-sentence construction; it requires a syntax that has flavor and grace, not to mention a diction that is imaginative and allusive. His crowning example reveals a nature still sensitive to his personal fortunes: "Having cast the greatest part of the flowers out of thy bosom, O Florence, the second Totila went fruitlessly to Trinacria." The reference is to Charles of Valois, who like the Hun Totila was responsible for the destruction of Florence by causing the exile of the Whites. Such phrasing, while not to modern taste, figures prominently in Dante's great poem. This periphrasis will also be called for in DuBellay's *Défense et illustration*, and will be present in much of Elizabethan literature, including Shakespeare's dramatic verse. In the general movement of Renaissance poetics, the great and evident need was to introduce to the vernacular poetry more of the resources of classical Latin poetry. Supporting his doctrine with example, Dante quotes from ten vernacular poets who make use of the elaborate classical syntax. He could have added copious listings from the regular, or classical, poets (as well as writers in prose) whom he has been reading in his enforced leisure—he calls it "friendly solitude." To the names given here (Virgil, Ovid, Statius, and Lucan), the poetic pantheon of *Inferno* IV will only add Homer (from whom Dante obviously could not give examples in the original) and Horace (Statius, mentioned here, will wait until the upper reaches of the *Purgatorio*). Dante's epic line is essentially that of *Vita Nuova* XXV. The poetic action of the *Purgatorio* is here suggested when Dante again wonders in amazement (in some anticipation of canto XXVI) how followers of ignorance can praise Guittone d'Arezzo and others "who have never got out of the habit of being plebeian in words and in construction."

IV   Convivio: *Allegory in Book Two*

While much has been said about allegory, only in Book Two does Dante introduce the reader to this crucial methodology, one that lent philosophical justification to the surface passion of his *canzoni*. This discussion ought to be compared with another exposition of allegory written some fifteen years later in the famous letter addressed to Can Grande della Scala, to whom he dedicates the *Paradiso* and to whom he had been sending completed portions of the last *cantica*.[13]

The four ways of reading a work of poetry are the literal, the allegorical, the moral, and the anagogical. While the term allegory refers specifically to one kind of reading, it also covers all three of the supraliteral methods of interpretation. The literal interpretation confines itself to the letter of the fiction, to what in fact happens. As we shall see, Dante regards a correct understanding of this level as the basis for all further readings. A true hold on the literal happenings serves as a control on interpretative arbitrariness (a practical concern of Dante's in Book Three of the *De Monarchia*). The first of the "mystical" readings is allegory itself—the allegory of the poets, or that of the theologians.[14] Here in the *Convivio* he adheres to that of the poets, using as his example Ovid's Orpheus, who tamed the beasts with his lyre and made the stones and the trees move. According to Dante's allegorical interpretation this means that the wise man with the instrument of his voice can tame wild and cruel hearts.

Moral interpretation involves ethical instruction; it does not tell us what has happened, but how we ought to behave. When the Gospel recounts that Christ took with him to the mountain of transfiguration only Peter, James, and John (that is, only three of the twelve disciples; those, incidentally, who come to examine Dante in Paradise on faith, hope, and charity), it is advising us that in the most sacred and important matters we should have few companions.

The fourth, or anagogical method, comes close to what we could call *figura*.[15] In this reading both the literal and the allegorical are true. This is evidenced by the opening lines of Psalm 114, "When Israel went out of Egypt," which is not a fiction, but true historically, according to the letter. It is also true spiritually, when taken to apply to the soul liberated from sin. This Psalm is sung by the souls in the boat that brings them to the shores of salvation in *Purgatorio* II; these souls literally are being released from sin. Anagogically the passage refers to all souls alive who are striving for the same liberation.

Two points stand out in this simple recitation of Dante's views in the *Convivio*: (1) that a different example is used for each of the spiritual interpretations, and (2) that Dante insists on the primacy of the literal reading, as his commentaries throughout the *Convivio* make clear. In fact, the exposition in these three books as well as in Book Three of the *De Monarchia* is our best practical guide to Dante's understanding of allegory. When we come to the letter to Can Grande, however, one passage, the verses from Psalm 114, is subjected to all three interpretative methods. In this letter expounding the *Paradiso*, Dante, understandably enough, refers to the allegory of the theologians and not of the poets; accordingly, the allegorical meaning of the passage is said to be the redemption brought by Christ. The moral interpretation does not seem to imply ethical exhortation (as it does consistently in the *Convivio*), although the anagogic sense is roughly the same. All in all, it is the *Convivio* and not the epistle to Can Grande that squares with Dante's practice.

The subject of exegesis in Book Two is the *canzone Voi che 'ntendendo il terzo ciel movete*, written, as we are told, about thirty months after the death of Beatrice. It is a poem that announces Dante's own struggle, as he leaves behind the *soave penser* of aesthetic dedication typical of the *dolce stil novo* and is drawn unavoidably toward the arduousness of philosophical speculation. In this poem the

alluring *donna gentile* of the *Vita Nuova* has been transformed into Lady Philosophy. After the introductory first
chapter (explaining allegory), chapters II to XII are devoted to the divisions and the subdivisions that make up the
literal readings of the poem and XIII to XVI present the
allegorical interpretation.

The commentary immediately presents a critical problem, one that might prove to be central to the nature of
Dante's work. Representing the interests and growth of
Dante after 1304, the commentary is cumbersome and weighty
in its service to a *canzone* written at least ten years earlier.
It is discursive and digressive in its show of learning. In fact, at
times the lines that inspired the comment seem to have been
lost from sight, as Dante, far beyond necessity, explains the nature of the angels and their hierarchies and orders (IV to V),
attempts to prove the immortality of the soul (VIII), and shows
the correspondence among all the ten heavens and the seven
liberal arts, metaphysics, moral philosophy, and theology (XIV
to XV). Where one aspect of an argument is relevant, Dante will
mount the entire system. And while the digressions are interesting in themselves, or for an understanding of Dante's total
thought, their presence in the *Convivio* works to destroy its
dramatic economy. And in this Book Two is not the worst
offender. The *Convivio* is a failed work not because Dante
left it incomplete but because it represents an inadequate
amalgamation of contrary interests. Dante's need is to
prove to his fellow Florentines and the people who have seen
him as an exile that he is a man of learning, a philosopher who has written a major work of ethical usefulness
for his community. These extraliterary motives put insupport-
able pressures on the *canzoni*, and as a result the entire
work breaks down. Nevertheless, when Dante evolved the
system of thought of the *Convivio*, he was putting together
the moral universe that would enjoy a better form in the
Commedia.

Dante begins the allegorical exposition in chapter XIII,
which   follows   the   valuable   biographical   material
about his conversion to philosophy after the death of Beatrice. He then turns to the very elaborate series of correspondences between the ten heavens and the ten areas of learning. We get some sense of the nature of the comparisons when

we read that Venus represents rhetoric because of her clarity and because she is both an evening and a morning star. Since the aim of rhetoric is to persuade, it is the "clearest" of all the disciplines, and hence comparable to Venus. The rhetorician, too, is like the morning star when he speaks to his audience, and like the evening star when he addresses them in a letter or other work from a distance. Since the other correspondences are hardly more compelling, it is fortunate that as yet no convincing case has been made for Dante's use of these correspondences in the *Paradiso*.

The allegorical application of this system of comparisons (certainly out of proportion to the actual need) is made in the last chapter. It is interesting to note how sparse the actual allegorical applications are throughout this book, and that for many sections of the poem Dante declares the literal exposition to be sufficient. Allegorically understood, the moving intelligences of the celestial spheres to which the poem refers are the writers Boethius and Cicero, whose rhetorical skills entice the reader into philosophy. Their works are the real stars radiating light. The new lady upon whom they direct Dante's attention is Philosphy, and her eyes that promise salvation are the demonstrations of philosophical truths (both of these notions will be more amply treated in Book Three). But his promise only holds for those who have no fear of the difficulties of philosophical study. Final beatitude is attained through this heroic struggle of doubt (in the *Paradiso* IV.130–32, Beatrice will praise this struggle from which emerges truth).

V Convivio: *Philosophy in Book Three*

In the second book, Dante identified the *donna gentile* as philosophy; in the orderly progression of Dante's work (and the *Convivio* does have these internal guidelines and order) Book Three is devoted to explaining more about the nature of philosophy. In order to do so, Dante uses as the object of commentary, one of his most beautiful *canzone*, *Amor che ne la mente mi ragiona*. From *Purgatorio* II, we learn that this song used to be sung by Casella. Its date of composition has been placed between 1294 and 1298, in any event prior to 1300.

In chapter I Dante tells of the biographical circumstances of the *canzone*. Not only was he consumed by the
desire to be in the company of this lady, but also in that of
"all persons that had any closeness to her at all, whether
friends or relatives." (Here Dante obviously means students
of philosophy, and philosophers themselves, or their works.)
"Oh, how many were the nights when the eyes of others were
closed in sleep, that mine were gazing fixedly on the habitation
of my love!" Later, at the end of chapter IX, he will tell us that
his study was so intense that he damaged his eyesight, and that
only by rest was his vision restored.

By way of showing that this love that resides in the mind
is the noblest of human occupations, Dante must again
digress. As he will elsewhere in his work, Dante assumes a
graduated chain of being made up of simple elements
(fire and earth), compound elements (minerals, etc.),
plants, animals, and human beings. To each of these
a basic movement belongs. Dante calls this basic movement *amore* (as he will, with some distinctions, in *Purgatorio*
XVII). This essential love assumes for each level a
basic proclivity. Dante then ascends the chain until he
reaches humankind, who possess a particular love for
"perfect and virtuous things." Moreover, man within his own
nature subsumes the essential interests of the lower gradi-
ents, so that he possesses the love of downward motion
shared with the simple elements, the brute nature of the
animals, and finally his rational nature, which makes him human
("or better yet, angelic"). For these reasons Dante can regard
this special love as part of the mind, and begin his *canzone*,
"Amor che ne la mente mi ragiona. . . ."

In the literal exposition of the *canzone*, the *donna gentile*
is an example and a model. She is an example of the
divine intent, and as such is an aid to faith and a
model for human conduct. In expounding the lines of Italian
poetry (chapter VI), Dante begins to make use of some of
the concepts that will be relied upon in the *Commedia*; he
begins to construct the positive philosophical background for
his ethical considerations. The world-view that Dante
develops is animated, graduated, heroic, and intensely
dramatic, extending from Heaven to Hell, from Heaven,
where man preserves his divine similitude, to Hell, where he

has lost that good completely. This system is based upon God's creative love communicating his intentions through the celestial intelligences, as secondary agents, who complete the form of these instructions in matter. These intelligences are the intermediaries between the divine intent and human reality. They know what is above them as their cause [God], and what is below them as their effect [humankind]. They know humankind in its divine purpose and intent. If reality does not measure up to the original plan, this is not the example's fault, but rather due to a defect in matter. Thus communication descends down to man, but the system also works the other way, when man acts upon his great desire to return to his source—in fact, to regain his original likeness. And until he recovers the perfection of that original likeness he is condemned to great restlessness (witness the *Inferno*). There are examples along the way, however, of creatures so perfectly realized that they represent the perfection after which people strive, and in comparison to which all other gratifications are found wanting. The *donna gentile*, in the literal interpretation, is an example of such perfected humankind, and she satisfies all who love her and who share in her nature.

One key idea in this system is that of *similitudine*, or conformable likeness, whereby the creature assumes many of the attributes of the creator.[16] Since the *donna gentile* is a high example of such "likeness," she is able to represent to other mortals the qualities of the "divine virtue."

The divine goodness descends into her in the same way as into an angel that sees Him; and let any noble lady who does not believe this keep her company and contemplate her bearing. (Foster and Boyde, I.109)

When Dante proceeds to the allegorical interpretation (XI to XV) the idea of likeness will again be used in reference to these lines.

In chapter XI he tells us of the history of the term philosopher and that since the *donna gentile* is philosophy the satisfactions she affords are those that derive from the loving use of wisdom in the act of speculation (XII, XIII). Since wisdom exists in God, divine philosophy is part of the divine essence itself (XII). By virtue of this exercise of the loving use of wisdom, or philosophy, man partakes of some of the attri-

butes of divinity—that is, he realizes full peace and satisfaction of his desires. In chapter XIV, relying on the idea of
comformable likenesses in relation to the passage just
quoted above, Dante explains how this principle operates:

Here we must observe that for the virtue of one thing to descend upon
another, that other thing must be brought to the first one's likeness. . . .
So we see the sun, that, sending his rays here below, makes all things
to resemble his own brightness, as far as they are, of their own nature,
capable of receiving light. Thus I say that God brings this love to his
own likeness, insofar as it is possible for it to resemble him.

And since this divine love is eternal it makes eternal
those things that love its wisdom.

The pleasures of Paradise appear in the face of the
donna gentile and in chapter XV Dante tells us specifically what they are. Her eyes are the philosophical
demonstrations, "through which truth is seen most certainly."
Going beyond the material of Book Two, Dante adds that
her smiles are the "persuasions"—the other evidence that
leads to certainty. These demonstrations and persuasions
constitute the heights of beatitude, "which pleasure
cannot be had here below, except in regarding those eyes
and that smile." From this we understand why in Paradise
so much is communicated by the eyes and the smile of Beatrice. Because man is principally a rational creature
and can only find perfection by developing this nature, his
beatitude can only lie in the resources of wisdom, the eyes
and the smiles of the Lady Philosophy.

Dante makes it as clear as he possibly can that
there is no contradiction between this view of the great role
of philosophy and that of religion or ethics. While leading
to beatitude, or the full satisfaction of desires in this life,
philosophy, nevertheless, can only approach an understanding of God, eternity, the primal matter—those things
that will be understood better after death—by means of
negation. It can only say what they are not. This
means, of course, that the perfection attained in this life
is a limited but fully satisfying one. Philosophy can satisfy
us according to the limits of our natures. The answer that
Dante proposes to this dilemma is the one that he will

utilize in the *Paradiso*, effecting the reconciliation between unity and diversity that is so crucial for his poem:

And this is the reason why the saints have no envy one of the other, because each attains the fulfillment of his desire, which desire is proportioned to the natural goodness of each. (chapter XV)

Far from being hostile to the *Paradiso*, the *Convivio* enunciates one of its primary tenets.

Nor is philosophy subversive to ethics. In the allegorical exposition Dante explores the meaning of the poetic line "Her beauty rains down small flames of fire. . . ." These flames coming from wisdom are the flames of right appetite, providing true moral direction. This exemplary power cannot only correct vices of habit, it can also redirect those of temperament ("connaturali"). Throughout these pages Dante's primary source is Solomon's Book of Proverbs. The object of philosophy is Wisdom, that which existed before the creation of the world and is the basis of all moral principles. Wisdom is synonymous with the Logos, which itself entered human existence after the Fall in the person of Christ, our likeness, "nostra similitudine" (XV), in order to lend direction to humankind. Not only does this inspired final chapter of the third book of the *Convivio* provide the tenets of the *Paradiso*, it also instructs us in its procedures. Dante urges those who do not sit at the table where the bread of the angels is served to honor the friends of wisdom and to follow them. Again, Dante refers to Solomon: "But the path of the just is as the shining light, that shineth more and more unto the perfect day" (IV.18). The way to beatitude is not only made up of doctrines and principles, but also of people, people embodying principles, the heroes and the saints, the one leading to the other. Just as Dante follows the light of Virgil that leads to Beatrice, so he follows the light radiated by the other just, those heroic recipients of virtue along the graduated way to beatitude, who make up the substance of his poem. As Dante does in his poem, so we should follow behind them, "witnessing their works ["operazioni"] that should shine as a light . . . along the path of this most brief life." Man acquires light by philosophy, or doctrine, and by personal imitation—the two major procedures of the *Commedia*. And each of these procedures has a common source in the Logos and in "our likeness" that Christ assumed. The principle of the *Commedia*'s unity, so sought after by twentieth-century critics, is here approached.

VI The Major Effort: Convivio, Book Four

There is every indication that the fourth book of the *Convivio* is the largest and most important work that Dante—ever growing in ambition and scope—had yet attempted. Just as Book Three amplifies the issues presented in the previous book, so Book Four looks more closely at the meaning of *gentilezza* (after all his lady is *la donna gentile*): what is the nature of its origin in man, and given this origin how can it have ethical implications? Dante's theme is the great one of his age. "Dirò del valore/per lo qual veramente omo è gentile." He will speak of the virtue ("valore") by which man is truly noble and in so doing he sees himself as addressing an issue of ultimate ethical significance. False opinions in the matter of true nobility have had disastrous consequences, as when virtuous men have been condemned and dishonest men praised, "which confusion was the worst in the world." To such an extent is this the case that he must leave behind the "dolci rime d'amor" that used to occupy his thought and confront the moral issue directly. This means because of the urgency of the problem he also will relinquish his allegorical method and write as directly as possible (IV.i). This book might be subtitled An Address to the Italian Nobility, warning it against reliance on false attitudes. It is the necessary prelude to cantos XV to XVII of the *Paradiso*, most particularly to canto XVI, where Cacciaguida recites that moving survey of the fallen Florentine houses. It is the crucial gloss to the opening exclamation of *Paradiso* XVI, where Dante urges the need for some response to the destruction of time: "O our poor nobility of blood. . . ."

Dante is convinced that he is addressing a question of ultimate importance for his society, and moreover one that has been little studied. "Oh, how great is my undertaking in this *canzone*, in wishing now to weed so overgrown a field as is that of common opinion, so long left without any tillage whatever" (vii). And because the misconception is so basic, and what he is attempting is to restructure thought, he will need skills in philosophical procedure and rational analysis. The reader will have to tolerate his procedural commitment to philosophical distinction. Even the major disgressions take on a new seriousness, evidence as to how much Dante's mind as represented by the interests of the prose commentary had grown beyond the poetry of the earlier *canzoni.* While we might regard this as a critical problem, a failure in the fusion of poetry and structure, or in finding a form suitable to his philosophical, encyclopedic, and moral interests, for Dante himself these disgressions are an indication of the importance of his theme. He must take great pains—since he attempts to refute his "ultimo imperadore" Frederick and, along the way, Aristotle—that no one misunderstand the great esteem he holds for each. In the process of refuting Frederick's definition of nobility, Dante defends, in chapters IV and V, imperial legitimacy, his first major statement of political theory.

Chapter IV does not begin as a continuation; rather it has all the earmarks of an insertion of a powerful and fully developed argument. The prose is authoritative: "Lo fondamento radicale de la imperiale maiestade . . . è la necessita de la umana civilitade . . ." (The radical foundation of the imperial majesty . . . is the necessity of human society . . .). It is as simple and as basic as that. Man is a *compagnevole animale,* a social being; he enjoys a complexity of relationships and a diversity of interests. These relationships and interests expand and involve him in family, neighborhood, city, kingdom, all of which are framed to promote his happiness. The end of this human society is *la vita felice* (how far we are from Rousseau!). But this same diversity of interests can be a tragic principle since it contains the basis of competing and hostile ambitions. In order to prevent this, a universal monarch is needed, an emperor who, possessing all things, requires no more. Men's desire to achieve perfection can thus be restrained by superior rule even when it becomes misdirected by *cupiditas.* The emperor restrains the rulers within his own territory, who in turn restrain their subordinates, and thus man lives happily in social peace, "which is that for which he was born." Dante then argues by analogy that since all other enterprises directed toward a single end (a ship, an army) require a single ruler so, too, does human society.

But Dante's primary interest is not just with any emperor, but rather with an emperor whose historical connections, whose place of residence and whose high ideals, are Roman. This conception of the mission of Rome brings the fire of historical and poetic vision to Dante's political thought. That Rome did not conquer by force is the new conclusion he has come to (formerly, he tells us in the *De Monarchia* II.i, he had believed that Rome had conquered by might). In pursuing its great mission Rome was fulfilling the role that divine providence had ordained for it. Force may have been the material cause ("cagione instrumentale"), but it was not the efficient cause ("cagione movente"). The active cause was the superior character, virtue, and sense of justice of the Romans themselves, their skill in acquiring and their wisdom in maintaining their empire—all of these virtues operating under a divine plan. From here on Dante's thought is Romanocentric (as it was when, as a youth, he heard the tales spun by the women about the early Roman origins of Florence).

This chapter shows another important milestone in Dante's development: Virgil has become his guide to the superior mission of Rome. Of course, he quotes from Aristotle, and his recounting of historical events derives from Livy, but his understanding of the historical destiny of Rome comes from Virgil. Dante concludes that divine providence prevailed in the triumph of Rome, "and with this Virgil agrees, when in the first of the *Aeneid*, where he says, speaking in the person of God, 'To them . . . I have set no limit of things nor of time; to them I have given an empire without end' " ("Imperium sine fine dedi"). And thus the prophecy of the *Aeneid* caught fire in the imagination of Dante more than thirteen centuries later to provide him with his new vision into the divine basis of the secular mission of Rome (the great spectacle of human history under the banner of the Roman eagle, worked out by Justinian in *Paradiso* VI, has its roots in this chapter of the *Convivio*). Already in the *Convivio* Virgil is more than the one who showed the way to Dante's *bello stile*: he is the poet-prophet of the Empire, an Empire that will have one of its last wholehearted defenders in Dante.

In order to defend his sense of the divine mission of the Empire Dante cites the circumstances surrounding the birth ("nascimento") of Rome and the course ("processo") of its history. Under the birth he is struck by two "coincidences." The first was the birth of Christ under Roman rule. This he regards as a divine source of Rome's authority, for it establishes as an indisputable fact that the Incarnation of the word of God, who in due time made it possible once again for man to regain his likeness to God ("a se reconformare"), occurred in a Roman province under the authority of Rome. The highest intervention of the divine power seemed to require the best disposition of the secular world, and this was provided by the period of peace under Augustan rule. The interconnection between these two Dante emphasizes in the *De Monarchia* (I.16; II.11) and in the *Paradiso* (VI and VII).

Not only did these two world-moments converge, but the second coincidence is that these events of salvation history and Roman history were contemporaneous in their origin. David, from whom Christ's line descended, was born at the time that Aeneas came to Italy. As he does in regard to cosmological matters, so in relation to human history Dante can only marvel at this temporal conjunction in the history of the two most precious legacies known to him.

As Dante recounts the great events of Roman history and calls the roll of its illustrious heroes, he concludes that the course of Roman history was shaped by the divine will. As in the *Commedia*, he seems to be returning, thanks to Virgil, to an earlier faith, to a faith, as he will explain in the *De Monarchia*, that had been lost. A new note of identifiable heroism enters his work, one that is based upon this rediscovery of the role of ideal principle in human history. And in all of the Roman heroes whom he invokes we observe a love for principle and for law, and a kind of rugged primitivism associated with the renunciation of ambition. Behind the fervor of these portrayals lies Dante's own growing identification with models of asceticism and virtue. Moreover, they seem to anticipate the self-sacrifice and suprapersonal dedication that Dante will associate with the calling of the Christian saints in the *Paradiso*.

Small wonder then if Rome, for Dante, is the holy city, "la santa cittade," the "loco santo," to whose very site reverence is due. Dante's fervor rises as he praises the stones of Rome (as Petrarch and other Rome-centered humanists will do):

And certainly I am of the firm opinion that the stones which form her walls are worthy of reverence; and the ground on which she stands is worthy beyond all that has been praised and approved by men.

Dante's list of Roman miracles and martyrs shows the divine part of its history and supports his argument that the Empire is the legitimate secular expression of the providential intent. This argument will be more fully developed in the *Monarchia* II and in the *Paradiso* VI. The difference is that in the later works Dante will centrally confront the rival claims of the papacy. Here, in the *Convivio*, just as Dante refrains from attacking Florence so he avoids denouncing papal policy. Nevertheless, the gist of Dante's political thought is delivered here in the deliberately unpolemical pages of the *Convivio*. In his later works the ideas here expressed will receive further development but will not be contradicted.

Following another digression, where he must clarify a statement by Aristotle, the next six chapters (X to XV) deal directly with the popular transformation of Frederick's definition of nobility. Where Frederick regarded nobility as being due to the ancient possession of riches accompanied by "reggimenti belli" or "belli costumi," the people forgot the phrases touching on behavior and made nobility simply dependent upon long-standing riches. Thus Dante's subject in these chapters will be riches and time and whether nobility can have any integral relation with either.

With one startling exception, the pages on riches bring us close to the motives of the *Commedia*. Here the she-wolf of avarice (the major obstacle of *Inferno* I) raises her head, and we begin to get Dante's tremendous sense of the motivating power of appetite. This *cupiditas* needs to be placed in the larger context of Dante's philosophy of positive attachment, one of the key principles in the poem. It is the misbegotten product of the fundamental desire to return to God (which motivating power will be more fully explained here in chapter XXII). Riches cannot satisfy this desire; in fact, they only produce greater restlessness. When Dante discusses the difficulties brought on by the need to acquire more riches, the language is particularly close to that of the *Commedia*. Wealth is traitorous, promising one thing and producing another, and in the process delivering the human will into the grip of avarice. These are the false goods of the *Purgatorio* that do not live up to their promises. Avarice and the rampageous need of the vulnerable human will are the great subjects of this chapter, as they are of the *Commedia*. In this chapter Dante's quotations from the classical authors, Cicero, Seneca, Horace, Juvenal, and Boethius form a small topical essay on the subject of insatiable greed.

But Dante's own generous nature and his philosophical vision enable him to place this "anthropology of desire" within the frame of a larger psychology of positive attachment. Some of its lines were suggested earlier in III.vi, for instance. All things desire a return to the source of their being. Man, who came from the hand of God, desires to return to that source. Motivated by this strong desire and yet "neither experienced nor properly instructed" the young soul is like a pilgrim in a new city, searching for his promised place of rest, and mistaking each new place he comes upon as the right location. Thus the soul in search of the highest good (the "sommo bene") thinks every pleasing object is that good. "And because his knowledge is at first imperfect, because he is neither experienced nor properly instructed, small goods appear to be great things, and this is the origin of desire" (IV.xii).

This is the beginning of the terrible search that for so many ends in Hell. And this is why Dante's *Commedia* is a great world on the move, and is populated by so many beings whose endings are tragic since they have been misled by "goods" that do not lead to the highest good. Indeed, the passage that follows in chapter XII is a direct anticipation of the memorable speech of Marco Lombardo in *Purgatorio* XVI ("Esce di mano a lui che la vaggheggia . . ."). The young soul moves through a series of desires, none of which leads to satisfaction. At first a fruit, then a small bird, then rich clothing, and then a horse, and then a woman, and then moderate riches, and then great riches, and then "more and more." It is caught in the syndrome of constantly accelerating desire. And this is because, Dante concludes, in none of those things that it meets does the soul find that for which it is seeking, and thinks to find it further on.

The question still remains, however, as to the positive nature and origin of nobility. This work is done in chapters XVI to XXII. The modern reader can have some problems here. He might not be surprised to read that "gentilezza" is found wherever virtue is present. What is surprising is the philosophical system that follows and its basic assumptions. Where he might expect to read that nobility is dependent upon virtuous behavior, the reverse is in fact true. The virtuous man is one who is noble by nature. It is not virtue that is the cause of nobility, but rather nobility that is the precondition of virtue.

Nobility, simply put in the *canzone* and its commentary, is a given, a gift of God, and it is the seed of the virtues, whose exercise results in human felicity. Dante's biblical source is the Epistle of James (I.17): "Every good gift and every perfect gift is from above, and cometh down from the Father of lights. . . ." Therefore—and this is where the other arguments lead—nobility cannot reside in a familial line of descent but rather in individuals who have been endowed with it by God. Let not the Uberti of Florence or the Visconti of Milan say (chapter XX), " 'Because I

am of such a family I am noble,' for the divine seed does not fall
upon a family, that is, a race, but upon individuals; and, as will
be proved hereafter, the race does not ennoble the individuals but
the individuals ennoble the race." This is the lesson that needs to
be learned in the Valley of the Negligent Princes and that is
summarized so powerfully and memorably for Dante by Sordello
(*Purgatorio* VII, 121–23).

Dante's thought in these pages returns us to the *dolce stil novo*.
In fact he quotes the motto of that school, the first line of Guido
Guinizelli's *Al cor gentil ripara sempre Amore*. The heart already
"gentil," or noble, is the one disposed to receive love. In the
Convivio Dante's thought has greater profundity and larger social
importance. This idea of nobility transcends the aesthetic
dedication to love and ideal beauty so typical of the *dolce stil
novo*; it extends to the values upon which a society models itself.
As an indication of the deep interconnections of this thought and
Dante's career as a poet it should be noted that *Purgatorio* XXV,
where the thought of these chapters is virtually duplicated, occurs
between the definition of the *dolce stil novo* in the encounter
with Bonagiunta da Lucca and the meeting with Guido Guinizelli
himself in canto XXVI.

Chapter XXI is a "special chapter" and chapter XXII is its
continuation in which Dante explains, first by means of natural
reason, or philosophy, and then "in the theological way" what is
the principle of all good, called nobility, and how it "descends"
into man. In these chapters we see that the intellectual system of
the *Commedia* is largely present in the *Convivio*, and that the
great poem's dramatic philosophy of human freedom, its combined emphasis on divine nature and human conduct is here first
expounded.

Dante's viewpoint in chapter XXI emerges from between
several opposed theories. The first is that of the Arabic philosophers Avicenna and Algazel, whose notions Dante was able to
read in Albertus Magnus's summary. They held that the soul was
noble or base by nature and from its very beginning (just as he
rejected the aristocratic notion of unchanging nobility, so
he must object to this denial of development and change). Dante
then refers to the opinion of Plato and others that the soul is good
or bad according to its astral influences (a kind of determinism he
must refute in *Paradiso* VIII). Dante's own opinion, heavily indebted to Aristotle and Aquinas's commentaries upon Aristotle,

is that while possessing some truth neither of these opinions is the true one. His solution is more of a synthesis, involving a "given" nature, the "complexion" of the body, education and ethical practice. This position might be summarized by the Thomistic sentence, "Moral virtue is not given to us at birth, or by nature, nor is it imposed upon us *contra naturam*, from outside." [17] Dante combines geneticist arguments with environmentalist, positing innate capacities whose proper development depends upon external influences.

The biological system of growth and development described in chapter XXI is the same as that rendered in verse in canto XXV (although in this latter Dante makes a polemical discrimination not present in the earlier work). In each he traces the growth of the human fetus after the impregnation of the female by the male sperm. The semen carries with it the "vertù" of the father, or the "anima generativa" (or "generante"), the "vertù" of the heavens presiding over the conception, and the vertù of the "elementi legati, cioè la complessione" (the particular combination of characteristics). These elements are brought together and developed by the "vertù formativa" (the organizing principle of development in the fetus—the DNA) which derives from the male seed ("anima generante"). This "vertù formativa," or inherent principle of development, produces the "anima in vita" or the sensitive soul. Instantly as this potentiality is realized the *anima in vita* receives from God "lo intelletto possibile." And this possible intellect has the capacity when developed to understand the universal forms as they are present in the mind of its "producer," or God, and as little or as much of the universal forms as it is distant from God himself, or the first Intelligence. [18] What this all comes down to is a capacity within the human organism to develop a mind that can comprehend the universal forms, but that this capacity varies according to its distance from the First Intelligence. This means then that there are many "possible intellects" and that they themselves can constitute the same hierarchy as the angelic intelligences. There is not one world-soul separate from the individual souls. Dante's needs are several: to achieve unity but not at the expense of diversity. He cannot do away with his sense of individual richness, and of the many roads leading to salvation, and yet these many different energies need to

be harmonized. The basis of the varied, graduated, yet
concordant life of Paradise is this conception of the *intelletto
possibile* that allows for many individual realizations of the
universal forms, according to their essential distance from the
primal intelligence.

Dante is a pure intellectual. Nobility is not in race, nor
in money, not even in long-standing practices, but rather
in the mind of man, that gift of the *intelletto possibile* which
allows him to perceive the universal forms according to his
proportion. The true nobleman is the philosopher, and it is
his contemplation that produces the satisfaction of beatitude. Hence the paradisal condition, which is a figure of
this beatitude, contains many different souls who have
their special peace. There is no envy in heaven. All wills
move with the divine will when they perceive the forms of their
own individual beings.

This is what can be said by the natural reason. The
last paragraph of chapter XXI and the rest of chapter
XXII deal with the question of nobility by way of theology.
These two chapters summarize in prose the central theoretical discussions of the *Purgatorio*, whose canto XXV is
based upon chapter XXI and whose cantos XVI and
XVII are closely related to chapter XXII. Dante lists the
seven gifts of the Holy Spirit; six of them are found in
Isaiah: wisdom and understanding, counsel and might,
knowledge and fear of the Lord (the church added a
seventh by dividing the last into two, fear of the Lord and
piety). These are the excellent seeds of the divine sower who
plants them as soon as the human person is ready to
receive them. And of these seeds the noblest shoot is *horme*,
which is an essential appetite by which man is disposed
to search out God. It is called by Dante *appetito de
l'animo* (Augustine called it an "impetus," or *appetitus actionis*).
This impetus is at the basis of Dante's animated universe, where
man and things are not stationary but are filled with desire to
move toward all that appears to be good. But the *horme* involves
both appetite and reason, the appetite that desires and the
rational intellect that judges. It is, in the language of Ambrose,
who is evidently following Cicero, a twin power, one of appetite
and the other of the restraining reason, or judgment ("una
in appetitu, altera in ratione posita, quae appetitum

refraenet et sibi obedientem praestet et ducat quo velit . . ."). Aquinas, from whose commentary, as verbal echoes show, Dante's own position derives, believes man to possess this instinct for good by virtue of divine grace ("Et ex hoc homines vere sunt bene fortunati, quod per divinam causam inclinentur ad bonum . . .").[19]

In his letter to Can Grande, Dante declares that the speculation in the *Commedia* is undertaken with ethical results in view; in the *Convivio*, a similar aim is apparent as this metaphysical system leads toward questions of education.[20] After all, the section of Aristotle's *Ethics* upon which Aquinas is commenting deals with the education of the youth. This natural instinct, or *horme*, Dante holds, is not sufficient by itself. The shoot requires good cultivation and virtuous practice (it must be "bene culto" and "sostenuto dritto, per buona consuetudine"). Its cultivation is provided by good doctrine and its uprightness is sustained by the formation of good habits. In these words we can see the basis of the educational and ethical goals of the *Commedia*.

Man has had placed upon him a terrible burden that he cannot ignore. Despite the presence of Purgatory there is no middle ground in Dante's world. Dante's world is divided into extremes, because the very basis of bliss carries with it the equally real possibility of damnation. The uncontrolled or misdirected appetite careens headlong, eternally diseased and damned. Despite the *horme*, or really because of it, Dante's injunction is still ethical and educational:

And if this [*horme*] be not well cultivated and kept upright by good habits, the seed is worth little, and had better never have been sown.

Better not to have been born, is the true motto of Hell. Even to have been born in a time of confusion does not absolve one from this terrible responsibility. Just as there are some who have misdirected a true impulse so there are those who, born in a bad time, can graft onto their natures the practice of more successful natures. "And therefore there is no excuse for any, for if man does not bear this seed on his own stock, he can easily obtain it by grafting" (IV.xxii).

The great difference between the *Convivio* and the *Com-*

media is that in the earlier prose work Dante does not give a specific historical setting to the great personal issues of salvation and damnation. The *Convivio* has the same intellectual system, the same ethical and educational purpose, but it does not have the historical dimension. In the *Commedia* the word is made flesh; ideas become historical things and persons and events. But the *Convivio* cannot be said for that reason to deal with a different order of ideas. The *Convivio* and the *Commedia* grow out of a single system of ideas; the intellectual system of the *Convivio* is recognizably the staging ground for the *Commedia*.

CHAPTER 4

The Five-Year Drama of Henry VII: Dante's De Monarchia and the Political Epistles

I   The Great Redeemer

IN November 1308, Henry, the Count of Luxembourg, was elected emperor, and on July 20, 1309, Clement V, through whose maneuvering the election turned out as it did, declared him to be the "rex Romanorum" and invited him to Rome, where in time he would be crowned in the Basilica of St. Peter. The Pope and the new emperor had enjoyed cordial relations since Clement's consecration in 1305; Henry himself was French in culture, and he seemed a natural ally of the Pope, who was determined to offset the dominance of Philip of France. The choice seems to have been a spectacular one. Henry VII declared his subordination to the "greater light" of the spiritual authority, vowed a Crusade, and, pledging to restore peace, directed his attention toward Italy. In the spring and summer of 1310, in the midst of preparations for his peninsular descent, he dispatched emissaries to the Italian cities, and in September 1310 an encyclical from Clement glowingly welcomed him to the divided land. In October, Henry crossed the Alps (with 5,000 troops) and entered Turin. All in all, it was an exciting time. Finally an emperor was coming into Italy, one who was prepared to cooperate with the Pope.

As we know from the *Purgatorio* VI and VII, Dante's complaints were many against the Hapsburgs, Rudolph and Albert, by whose neglect Italy had become wild and savage. Now, at last, in 1310 a new Caesar has appeared. Dante, in his exultation, has recourse to the myth of the Golden Age (as well as many another expression of messianic fervor). *Ecce nunc tempus acceptabile*—the divine moment has arrived, he writes in a letter addressed to the kings of Italy, to her civil leaders, to the dukes, marquises, counts, and peoples.[1] The letter was written after Clement's words of benediction, and perhaps before Henry's actual arrival in Italy. It is directed to these important people by "the humble Italian Dante Alighieri, Florentine, exiled counter to his deserts. . . ."

Italy is at last emerging from the long night of horror. The bridegroom Caesar is coming, and Italy who was pitied even by the Saracens, will soon be the envy of the world. Henry is another Moses, leading his people out of captivity "into the land that flowed with milk and honey." In a letter (VII) written some six months later, Dante, beginning to be anxious at Henry's delays in the north of Italy, recalls this exciting time, when "the new hope of a better age flashed upon Latium. Then many a one, anticipating in his joy the wishes of his heart, sang with Virgil of the kingdom of Saturn and of the returning Virgin." Dante recalls that he, too, hastened to pay homage to the new emperor. He saw him, he heard his words of clemency, and he kissed his feet. "Then did my spirit exult in thee, and I spoke silently with myself, 'Behold the Lamb of God! Behold him who hath taken away the sins of the world!' " (pp. 324–25.)

These political letters are marked by such fervent language, which in the Gospels is used only of Christ. Yet in all three there is also a consistent doctrine, making these letters a useful bridge between the political thought of the *Convivio* and that of the *De Monarchia*. The consistent doctrinal point that Dante makes is that of the Empire's independent authority, which he holds to have been derived from God himself. This is one of the reasons for his use of religious language to celebrate Henry's arrival.

Within a short time after his arrival, however, Henry's bright appeal began to fade. The returned exiles in the northern cities created havoc in some of them. A challenger (Robert of Sicily, who had actually been a contender for the imperial crown) entered the arena. And behind all the machinations against Henry and in the front ranks of the military opposition to his progress, Dante could see—as he feared he would—the arrogant leaders of his own Florence. Their response was bullish (but memorable) in denying Henry's request that they desist in their belligerency against Arezzo. Dino Compagni records that Betto Brunelleschi, asserting his city's ancient rights, declared that

Florence never had lowered its horns for any Lord ("mai per niuno Signore i Fiorentini inchinarono le corna"—III.xxxv). In early February 1311, they decided to make military preparations and to fortify their walls. All of this seemed mad to Dante, who responded with a letter addressed to the "infamous Florentines within the city" (VI. p. 316).

The letter to the Florentines begins by declaring that the Empire was ordained by divine providence to be the guardian of civic life. Beyond the two forms of evidence presented earlier— the words of Christ in the Gospels and the history of Roman antiquity—Dante sees a third "and no small confirmation" in the consequences of the emperor's absence: "When the throne of Augustus is vacant all the world turneth out of its course, the helmsman and rowers in the ship of Peter slumber, and wretched Italy, deserted, and abandoned to private caprices, destitute of all public guidance, is tossed with such battling of winds and waves as words may not express . . ." (p. 316). As he will in the *Commedia,* so here Dante must look at the practical results of the imperial absence.

With all this evidence, moral and pragmatic, Dante can only condemn as perverse the Florentines' insistence on their native liberties. Though he himself once proudly defied the demands of Pope Boniface, he now condemns the stubborn willfulness of the Florentines, who seem now to be avoiding the "yoke" of true liberty. Rational liberty for Dante is not absolute freedom, but doing the right as it is revealed by the nature of things. It means voluntary obedience to the "sacred laws that copy the image of natural justice; the observance whereof it it be joyous, if it be free, is not only proved to be no slavery, but to him who looketh clearly is seen itself to be true liberty." Florence is making a show of its defense of liberty, yet it is acting in violation of "universal law" as well as against the "prince of law" (pp. 320–21). Dante will continue the same thought in *De Monarchia* (I.xii). It must further be said, however, that much of the letter is filled with images of horrible destruction that Dante conjures up to give the Florentines some sense of their impending doom. Nothing of the sort happened. The military preparations (aided by diplomatic cunning) paid off, and the Florentines were able to withstand an ineffectual siege of their city with impunity.

Two weeks later, again writing from the Casentino, Dante addresses an epistle (VII) to Henry exhorting him to move against

Florence, the pin holding together the entire Guelph League. It is the real center of resistance, and without it, the proliferating rebellion in the north would cease. Dante is worried that Henry may have a narrower conception of the Empire, one limited to Lombardy, and he must remind him, quoting from the *Aeneid*, that just as the Empire is without temporal end so it knows no earthly bounds. These political letters occasioned by the advent of Henry VII are written in a masterful Latin, and contain most of the general ideas of Dante's political thought. They are classics of political polemic and should be known by all students of Dante, not only for the thought but for the style, which shows the power of the "regular" writing which Dante advocated in the *De Vulgari Eloquentia* and in the *Convivio*.

In the spring of 1312, Henry sailed from Genoa and debarked at friendly Pisa, whence he marched on Rome. What he met there instead of the friendly welcome promised by Clement was an armed camp, with Robert of Sicily and the Roman noble families, the Caetani and the Orsini, blocking his way. Almost literally Henry's men had to fight their way to St. John Lateran, where, instead of at St. Peter's, as Clement had promised, Henry VII was crowned. The "deceit" of the Gascon Clement, to which Dante refers in *Paradiso* XVII.82, was made known when a papal epistle overtook Henry soon after he departed from Rome and ordered him to leave at once the lands of the Church, to refrain from attacking Naples, and to make a truce with Robert of Sicily. This turnabout took Henry by surprise, but he responded with a strong defense of the emperor's independence from religious authority. Into this debate Dante stepped with his *De Monarchia*.

II *Dante's Response:* De Monarchia

The *De Monarchia* was probably written after Henry's coronation in Rome since, at the start of Book Two, Dante (in imitation of Psalms 2.2) grieves at the sight of the kings and princes who can only agree in opposing the "lord, and his anointed, the Roman prince." [2] In the meantime, of course, Henry launched his futile attack upon Florence, withdrew, and then wintered at Poggibonsi, near Siena. He was preparing a campaign against Robert of Sicily, when in June 1313 Clement threatened him with excommunication. (However, in the midst of a campaign launched against Pisa, Henry, already ill, died near Siena in August of the same year.) Only in these times, when the break with Clement became open, could Dante have written the *De Monarchia*, where, especially in Book Three, specific arguments of papal apologists are directly confronted.

Like Dante's other major works, the *De Monarchia* has an ethical purpose, but one which because of the historical situation is far more practically urgent. Nevertheless, Dante continues to use his resources as a philosopher to provide principles for political conduct. Since the distinguishing feature of man is the capacity for cognition by means of the *intellet to possibile*, the purpose of the state Dante argues in *De Monarchia* I.3 is to provide for this intellectual growth by means of peace, and the best way of attaining peace is through the universal monarchy or Empire (I.iv, v).[3] As he proceeds Dante will have recourse to various kinds of argumentation: rational proofs through the aid of logical analysis, citation of authorities whose utterances constitute evidence (the Bible, Virgil), what he calls "memorable experience," or history, and finally, a look at historical consequences. Italy itself is tragically torn apart because the secular power that is the guardian of the peace has been either neglectful (the Hapsburgs) or hobbled (Frederick and Henry VII) by papal policy. Plain to any clear mind must be the need for the emperor as a guarantor of peace. In fact, so obvious is the point that after patiently presenting all of his arguments in III.13 Dante can only break out in soul-felt exasperation, "Oh, how tiresome it is to construct proofs, when the matter is so very clear."

Book One of the *De Monarchia* goes well beyond *Convivio* IV.iv in defending the advantages of unity in rule. Proceeding by analogy in chapters VI, VII, VIII, and IX, Dante argues that, since parts themselves operate best when given a single direction, so this must be true of the whole, or the universal monarchy. But the human totality is part of a larger entity, whose principal source is God. Therefore the human enterprise ought best to imitate the larger whole, and like it, have a single head. In chapters X to XV, Dante offers more practical arguments.

Book Two of the *De Monarchia* takes its essential argument from *Convivio* IV.v, its purpose being to show that Rome acquired its power not only by might but by right as well. Nature provided

the means and divine providence the direction for Roman rule.
In his preliminary chapter II, Dante acknowledges that his
argument is not as direct as he would like it, but that our expectations of certainty must be adjusted to the nature of the material.
Here Dante is dealing with historical evidence: as in Epistle V
he is looking at visible effects in order to determine invisible
causes. He must look to the "evidence of clear signs and the
authority of the wise." Throughout, his assumption is that God's
hand operates in human history, and where we see an imprint
we must assume a cause, just as when the wax bears the sign of
the seal, one assumes the existence of a seal although one does
not see it. With greater elaboration than in the *Convivio*, these
are Dante's assumptions as he searches for God's hand in human
history.

III   Book Three: The Great Argument

In Book Three Dante enters into the most polemical part of
his treatise: he shows that the authority of the Roman Emperor,
the *de jure* ruler of the world, derives directly from God and not
by way of the spiritual ruler. Because in his arguments he might
prove offensive to religious and political leaders, Dante affirms
his own righteousness, and supports his affirmation with quotations from the Old and New Testaments and from Aristotle. God,
he asserts, has shut up the mouths of the lions because He has
found justice in him. And he takes comfort in David. The just
will always be remembered, and he will have nothing to fear
from detractors (Psalm 112.7). More and more we hear in Dante
the voice of the inspired prophet, who already in *Convivio* IV.v
urged all to listen, "for I will speak of excellent things."

Dante's philosophic commitment and learning and his return
to the authentic sources of the Old and New Testaments and the
Church Fathers have put him at odds with the decretalists. The
decretalists were the commentators on the accumulated body of
papal decrees that formed the basis of canon law. In Epistle
VIII he blames the churchmen for pursuing only studies that
promise·to serve their avarice while neglecting Gregory, Ambrose, and Augustine. The loving use of wisdom, or true philosophical commitment, requires other less selfish motives than
those which inspire the study of ecclesiastical decrees. Dante
introduces the decretalists here in order to dismiss them as serious

intellectual opponents—because their authority is a derivative one. The Church does not, as they would maintain, derive its authority from its traditions; rather the traditions—while worthy of serious respect—are subordinate to the more authentic testimony of the Scriptures. Consequently, Dante, in disputing this matter of temporal authority, can rely on the older documents (chapter III).

In chapters IV to XI Dante refutes specific papal arguments which include allegorical interpretations of the Old and New Testaments, the Donation of Constantine, and rational, philosophic proofs. In chapters IV to IX he deals with "mystical" readings and provides us with a remarkable lesson in allegorical interpretation, one that ought to be considered along with *Convivio* II.i and the letter to Can Grande. Through this performance we become aware of how fine a tool logic had become in Dante's hands, the practical rewards of his philosophic training. His exposition is a caveat to modern allegorists, since he subjects fallacious uses of the method to rigorous rational tests. In establishing restrictions he follows the model of Augustine. The first lesson is of course that not all matters in the literal level are significant (as we saw in the practical commentaries on his *canzoni* in the *Convivio*); secondly he introduces some means of limiting arbitrariness. What limits or restraints exist on mystical interpretations? The limits are, as indicated already in the *Convivio*, a firm understanding of the literal level, followed by rigorous proceedings when it comes to drawing analogies.

Using the analogy of the sun and the moon, papal apologists argued that since the moon derives its light from the sun, the sun is the superior light; upon this analogy they then argue the superiority of the greater light, or the sun, of the spiritual power. Dante shows that this analogy includes an inadmissible transfer from the relations of two physical bodies to the relations of two forms of government. All analogy, of course, involves such transfer; but this one is inadmissible because it violates the letter of the text. The lights God made on the fourth day; man he made on the sixth and he made him innocent. What would be the need of having these lessons in government before man was made and especially before man fell ("for such devices as government are remedies for the infirmity of sin")? Further, he argues—in discussing their functions—that though the moon might derive its light from the sun, its being and its function are surely independent of the sun. "In like manner," Dante concludes, "temporal power receives from spiritual power neither its being, nor its power or authority, nor even its functioning, strictly speaking, but what it receives is the light of grace, which God in heaven and the Pope's blessing on earth cause to shine on it in order that it may work more effectively." We notice Dante's clear insistence on the separation of powers, but we also notice his sense of the need for some contact however indefinable it might be.

This remarkable method of analysis continues in chapters V, VI, and VII, where Dante dissects the analogical appropriateness of Levi and Judah, Samuel and Saul, the Magis' offering of gold and incense to the infant Christ. A major text for the proponents of superior papal authority is Matthew 16:19, where Christ leaves to Peter the keys to the Kingdom of heaven; "and whatsoever thou shalt bind on earth shall be bound in heaven; and whatsoever thou shalt loose on earth shall be loosed in heaven." For the defenders of papal power this meant that the Pope can loosen the decrees of the emperor, and can bind the emperor with laws and decrees. Dante's attention is directed toward the phrase "whatsoever" ("quodcunque"); does this mean everything, all things, or only those things pertaining to the spiritual life? If it means all things then the Pope can also absolve from sin even though the sinner is not penitent (and here we see the great relevance of the dramatic passage in *Inferno* XXVII, where Boniface absolves Guido of Montefeltro of his future sin). Can the Pope loosen one man's wife and bind her to another? Clearly there is a problem with "whatsoever." In order to clear up the difficulty Dante again refers to the text: the keys that are bestowed are those to the kingdom of heaven, for which Peter is the gatekeeper. With this literal guidance, Dante can conclude that the "whatsoever" of Peter's office (and that of his successors) refers to all those things that are part of his spiritual power of showing the way to salvation.

In his papal bull *Unam Sanctam* Boniface made much of a passage in Luke (22:38), where Peter responds to Christ's warnings that after his death the apostles will have need of a sword by saying, "Here are two swords." Boniface argued that the two swords are the spiritual and the temporal powers and that they belonged to Peter and as a consequence are inherently the properties of Peter's successors.[4] Dante then goes on to prove that the response, in context, was not an intelligible one; rather it showed Peter's zeal as well as his "natural innocence and simplicity"(IX). In short, Peter frequently (and Dante, in a great display of close reading, cites more than a dozen instances from the Gospels where this is the case) spoke or acted before he thought. The sword that Christ intended, Dante argues, was the sword to which Matthew refers (10:34): the spiritual commitment and conviction that will set a man at variance with the earthly connections of family and friends (as we shall see, this was a sword that Dante well understood).

After refuting papal claims derived from the so-called Donation of Constantine (X) and conclusions drawn from the fact that Pope Leo III crowned Charlemagne, Dante turns in the final sections of Book Three to the positive arguments for imperial independence. In chapter XII, he argues that since the Empire existed before the papacy it is not possible that its prerogatives are derivable from the papacy. In chapter XIII, neither natural law nor Scripture can support the papal arguments, since the Church is not the creation of nature, but of supernature, and a close scrutiny of the revealed scripture, although with minor complications, gives predominancy to those arguments that would preclude clerical possession of power. And this is the way it must be (XIV), since the form of the Church is the life of Christ. All of its actions and the guidance it offers must be in imitation of that pattern. Indeed, in the *Paradiso*, this doctrine of evangelical asceticism emerges as one of the most powerful forces in the poem. And Boniface VIII is shown in a favorable light only once, and that is when (in Hugh Capet's account—*Purgatorio* XX. 85–90) he is humiliated by the soldiers of Philip of France at Anagni, and repeats, in his own way, the ordeal of the Crucifixion.

The most powerful chapter in the *De Monarchia* is the last, where Dante argues that the authority of the Empire derives directly from God and that the Empire possesses the right to function independently of the papacy. The argument is fairly simple: all things have distinct natures and all natures have specific ends. Man, however, has two natures, one physical and the other spiritual. The body being perishable has for its end the "bliss of this life," while the soul being immortal has for its end the bliss of eternal life. The passage is an important one, since it helps us to read more accurately the allegory of the *Commedia*, to which it is clearly relevant.

Twofold therefore are the ends which unerring Providence has ordained for man: the bliss of this life ["beatitudinem . . . huius vitae"] which consists in the functioning of his own powers, and which is typified by the earthly Paradise ["et per terrestrem paradisum figuratur"]; and the bliss of eternal life, which consists in the enjoyment of that divine vision to which he cannot attain by his own powers, except they be aided by the divine light, and this state is made intelligible by the celestial Paradise ["que per paradisum celestum intelligi datur"].

At the top of the mount of Purgatory, where Dante the pilgrim enters into the Earthly Paradise, the scene amounts to a figure, as here suggested, of individual and social life in its highest attainable form. Paradise is also a figure, as Dante takes pains to tell us more than once, showing the bliss of those who enjoy the benefits of divine grace.

These different ends require different means. We come to the one by means of philosophy ("per phylosophica documenta") and according to our moral and intellectual capacities, and we come to the other by spiritual teachings and by the exercise of the theological virtues of faith, hope, and charity. The one way is within nature; the other, like the foundation of the Church in the life of Christ, is outside of nature. Yet man, because of his sinful nature, requires reinforcements in these capacities; they are provided by the institutions of the Church and the Empire that serve as guides to direct him and to keep him in rein, to check his greed (*cupiditas*). ("The bit and bridle" of control is quoted from Psalm 32.8–9.) The goal of temporal felicity is in the hands of the emperor, whose constant aim must be peace (the argument of I.iv), for no one, or at most very few, can reach this goal of felicity (because of *cupiditas*) unless humankind enjoys peace. Consequently, the role of the emperor is vital to human well-being and must not be hindered.

In the concluding passage of the *De Monarchia*, Dante takes pains to emphasize that while advocating separate and independent missions and hence authorities his ideal of human society is not a secular one. Dante does not mean to imply by his carefully worded argument "that the Roman government is in no way subject to the Roman pontificate, for in some ways our mortal happiness is ordered for the sake of immortal happiness." And throughout the history of the relations between papacy and Empire, Dante can point with approval to the good intentions of Constantine that derived from gratitude to Pope Sylvester, or the protective attitude of Charlemagne toward the Church, or the indebtedness of Justinian to Pope Agapetus—these are the examples showing the pious reverence which the firstborn (hence favored) son pays to the father, and that Caesar should rightly pay to Peter. Disagreement stems from the force of the phrase *quodammodo* ("in some ways"). The exact meaning of the phrase is hard to express. But impossible though it may be to define it as a concept, it is not impossible to express in a metaphor or to point to a specific historical event as illustration (such as the examples above that Dante will allude to in the *Commedia*). The fact remains that there is no contradiction between the political thought of Dante in the *De Monarchia* and the *Commedia*, and these works (except for the new polemical attitude toward the Church, which may be found by implication in the *Convivio*) are direct extensions of chapters IV and V, Book Four, of the earlier work. There is expansion, amplification, but no contradiction.

And while in the *Commedia* Dante's religious attraction will become stronger and stronger toward those models of ascetic renunciation and even of martyrdom, in these earlier works there is no indication of any difficulty on Dante's part in yoking together his Christian interests and his philosophical and political ones. The philosophical mode and the theological mode are complementary. Man requires grace and faith for salvation; some passages of *De Monarchia* III.xv read like a confession of faith. The Church is rebuked for failing in its institutional structures to live up to the evangelical and ascetic model of Christ. More importantly, in his integrated vision of politics and morality, Dante's models go beyond Aristotle to the Psalms and the Book of Proverbs; and these sources are powerful even in the *Convivio*. In the *Convivio* the intellectual system of the *Commedia* is complete, and in the *De Monarchia* we come even closer to the personal needs and resonances of that great poem. The attempt to posit a major doctrinal conversion, which would set the author of the *Commedia* apart from the author of the earlier works, is clearly misguided; after the experiences of 1300–1302 what we witness is not so much an intellectual conversion or contradiction of previous views (except in a few cases) but rather a development and an intensification.

CHAPTER 5

Commedia: Inferno

I *Introduction*

THE argument of this book has insisted on the essential consistency of Dante's political and philosophical thought. In his declarations to the Florentine Council in 1301 (and perhaps as early as his priorate of 1300) Dante's anti-Bonifacian line was clear. Just when he came to see that the Roman rule could justly lay claim to divine sanction is not clear (perhaps his visit to Rome in the Jubilee year of 1300 helped inspire that revision in his thinking); yet the fact remains that after *Convivio* IV.iv–v, his defense of imperial autonomy was unflagging and was not to be contradicted by anything in the *Commedia*. Philosophically, despite minor alterations of opinion, Dante's position as well as his chosen role of philosopher-mediator was set by 1294, and to such an extent that the *Convivio* could serve as commentary for those philosophical allegories and moral *canzoni* written as much as ten years earlier. There is nothing in the philosophical and political ideas of the *Commedia* that could surprise the student who has followed the development of Dante's thought.

The same cannot be said of his poetry. There is little in Dante's poetic practice or theory to prepare us for the *Commedia*. The *Commedia* has all the striking unpredictability of a work of genius. The leap to the *Commedia* seems even greater than that from the *Portrait of the Artist* to *Ulysses*. Like Milton, Dante began his great epic late (at age forty-three or thereabouts, in 1307–1308), but there is no indication that he was long in choosing his subject. Milton was committed to writing a great epic from the time he was a young man. Dante still held the *canzone* in the tragic style to be the highest poetic achievement as late as the *Convivio*. To be sure, the classical poets who meet him in *Inferno* IV are the same as those named in *Vita Nuova* XXV and in the *De Vulgari Eloquentia* II.vi, but there is no indication that Dante would aspire to their great scope and vision, that he would place historical figures in a rhetorical fiction that would contain the great issues of his time, that he would become the poet whom Yeats called "the chief imagination of Christendom."

While we can see the great vision developed in *Convivio* IV as the staging-ground of the *Commedia,* still that work of poetry and prose must be put down as a failure. Its original design seemed to lead inevitably to repetition (what more could Dante have possibly written in regard to the *Amor che movi* that had not already been used in relation to the other *canzoni?*), and the frequent use of digressions tells how much Dante's current interests had gone beyond the *canzoni.* In short, the *Convivio* lacks formal and imaginative integration; and this had been the fault of much of Dante's earlier work which, autobiographical as it may have been, contained so little reference to his own political activities, and was, in effect, so distant, despite its ultimate reference, from his own experiences and that of his time.[1] It would be hard to know from the prose of the *Vita Nuova* that Dante had fought at Campaldino, or from the *canzoni* that he had taken an active part in Florentine political life. Then, again, despite his role as philosopher-mediator Dante had not yet, even in the *Convivio,* made the connection between his philosophical vision and his personal experience. Before the *Commedia,* in fact, he had not made the connection between his theories and attitudes—his animated view of the universe, his psychology of positive attachment, the need for education and practice if the soul is to reach its fullest development—and his own personal experiences as exile in the midst of a disintegrating social order brought about by the failures of Church and State.

The sense of urgency in the poem derives from the fact that Dante finally brought together his speculative system and his personal and public experiences. If the right direction of the *horme* still depends upon education and ethics, or good models and virtuous practice, then Dante has within his reach an understanding of why the breakdown of the relations of Church and State should have had such disastrous consequences. The Church after all was supposed to provide guidance and direction to the will, and the emperor's function was to serve as a restraint to the wild ambitions of his subjects. Dante finally came to understand, by virtue of his speculative system, that the chaos of his time into which he was inevitably drawn was due to the confusion of their roles. We can see how cantos XVI, XVII, and XVIII of the *Purgatorio*, the central theoretical cantos in the entire poem, bring together the two elements that had been treated separately in the *Convivio*. The *Commedia* is a great poem because it shows the coincidence of these aspects of Dante's life, the integration of his philosophy and his experience into a coherent, imaginative whole. His philosophical speculations were finally given a definite historical focus and a distinct location.

With the *Commedia* Dante enters into history. He made that poem out of his most intense personal experiences and knowledge of his times. This is what E. R. Curtius meant when he wrote that the *Commedia* represents the "explosive eruption of subjectively experienced history into the cultural world of the Latin Middle Ages." [2] "Explosive" is the right word, since it suggests the urgency with which Dante tried to understand the crisis through which he had survived. He is no longer concerned merely to trace the itinerary of a mind through an ideal landscape; his task is now to represent historical characters in all their earthly reality. Starting with Virgil in the very first canto, all of his characters present themselves as historical personages.

My parents were Lombards, both Mantuan by birth. I was born *sub Julio*, though late in his time, and I lived at Rome under the good Augustus, in the time of the false and lying gods. (*Inferno* I.68–72)

(We may recall by way of contrast the lack of specificity in the references to people and friends in the *Vita Nuova*.) Here Virgil is not content to give a simple historical account; in his self-representation he marks significant history. He must tell that he was born under Julius Caesar, perhaps suggesting the crisis of civil war that ended with the final victory of Augustus. And while Augustus was "good," still he lived at a time when all men worshiped false and lying gods. History for Dante is real and is filled with "turning-points," with decisive junctures in time, whereby what follows is critically altered from what preceded such a time of change. Moreover, temporal references are usually quite specific (if elaborately rendered). We are clearly given to understand that the ideal date of the poem is 1300, the year of the first Jubilee. This is also the year of Dante's priorate, which he later regarded as being the origin of all his troubles.

The reality of historical change also implies the reality of places and of things. The "where" of man's origins is as important as the "when." Dante chooses to give specific geographic locations to the great stories of Francis and Dominic and of Damian and Benedict in the *Paradiso* (as these transcendent figures become their offices so they seem to merge with the nature of their places). Almost because of its other-worldly setting the *Commedia* must be filled with references to the cities and landmarks and things of this world. The *Inferno* in particular is filled with such references, as Dante by use of simile links poetic event with the known world, emphasizing the connections between what he is describing and real existence. These are just a few of the resources that make the world of the *Commedia* so real.

Surprisingly enough, given Dante's own strong instinct toward self-representation and the many biographical suggestions in the poem, we actually know almost nothing concerning the circumstances and genesis of the *Commedia*. We know, often by Dante's own words, the situation that gave rise to almost every other major work of Dante, and yet we have no such information in regard to the *Commedia*. We do not directly know how he hit on the scheme of a fictional journey to the other world, nor do we know when or why this inspiration struck him. If we take Dante's own dramatic word for it, clearly the new motives are involved with Virgil, and a rediscovery of that Latin genius and the large poem. Like the other Florentines of his time Dante had become so involved in the events of his day that he lost that large and encompassing imagination, that poetic distance that is able to see things in their stable and enduring forms. While he had been "reared" on the stories of Troy and Aeneas and the ancient Romans, somewhere he had lost the faith in their great mission. Yet when we come to *Convivio* IV we see that Virgil's poetry is highly instrumental ("'Imperium sine fine dedi'") in Dante's renewed conviction of Roman legitimacy. Thirdly, Dante may have received the inspiration to place himself and his own times in the great epic tradition from the sixth book of the *Aeneid*, where Virgil calls the roll of Roman history. Furthermore, when Virgil introduces himself in *Inferno* I, we see that his theme is Dante's:

I was a poet and sang of that just son of Anchises who came from Troy after proud Ilium was burned. (73–75)

In the literal story of the *Aeneid* Dante found a parallel account within an imaginative frame for his own exile and wandering. Even if we remember that Ilium is merely "proud" and not quite deserving, as was Florence, of its ultimate destruction, nevertheless both Aeneas's and Dante's stories are those of wanderers, of exiles (however different the circumstances of their leaving). Moreover, the outer dimensions of each of the works is the city, one abandoned and one promised, even if for Dante the ultimate destination is not Rome but the city of God.

In the early twentieth century this "structure" that Dante hit upon of a visit to a strictly compartmentalized world beyond the grave was regarded as a liability, something in despite of which the poetry of individual sections was achieved. We, however, may better regard it as a "permitting device" and appreciate it for the opportunities it does allow its inventor. Within the vast but relatively simple frame of his imaginative world Dante was able to realize his tremendous sense of the varieties of experience. Each of the *cantiche*, the *Inferno*, the *Purgatorio*, and the *Paradiso*, is after all a version of life. And within each we find different types of people, all with their distinct personalities (a distinctness, if we think back to the *Convivio*, that Dante's own metaphysics insisted upon). The amount of freedom that Dante's structure allowed must be acknowledged. Closer to Dante's own time, Leonardo Bruni doubted that anyone else ever "took a larger and more fertile subject by which to deliver the mind of all its conceptions through the different spirits who discourse on diverse causes of things, on different countries, and on the various chances of fortune." [3]

II   Inferno: *New Directions*

The direction that Dante takes in Hell is opposite to that taken in either of the other two realms. The visit to the underworld seems to say that, in the pattern of Christ, ascent first requires descent, a deeper understanding of the possibilities of degradation and of demeaned actuality before consciousness can be converted to conviction. Dante's journey to Hell represents the elementary spiritual act of dying to the world, and hence it coincides with the season of Christ's own death. The placement of Hell in the structure of the poem shows how truly complex is the dynamic of Dante's evolution. Almost literally the first step of his pilgrimage is to alter the direction that he had been taking. Under the surer and more alert moral guidance of Virgil Dante must retrace his steps so that he can come to understand where it was that he went wrong. The purpose of Hell is to explain the causes of his own inability to ascend the mountain. He must recognize the values responsible for his first missteps. Hell is the place of disaffection, where many false commitments must be "unlearned." Since Hell is a place of avoidance, in any positive dynamic it must naturally precede the fuller realizations of commitment.

This can be seen by comparing Dante's journey to the underworld with that of his classical prototypes, the sublime Book XI of the *Odyssey*, which he did not know, and Book VI of the *Aeneid*, to which so much of the *Commedia* is indebted. The visit to the land of the dead is an essential motif in the classical epic because there basic values are discovered. Dante seems to be following that precedent and adopting that convention. Yet in absorbing he also transforms. In both position and purpose, Dante's *Inferno* differs from its classical predecessors. Since in both the *Odyssey* and the *Aeneid* major revelations occur in the underworld, both accounts of the journey there are located at the center of each poem. In the land of the dead both Odysseus and Aeneas learn the purposes of their lives; in hell they receive the definitions of their beings.

Dante's itinerary suggests a different purpose. In Hell he receives the opposite of any self-definition; he experiences separation from what had been false gods, and falsely based attachments. The doctrines and beliefs that had captured his attentions and his commitment and those of the men like him in his time are rigorously scrutinized in Hell and shown to be insufficient. Consequently, Dante's experience in Hell is dominated by supersession. Dante leaves behind the Guinizellian–courtly love doctrines of his young manhood, so beautifully represented by Francesca; the values of his fellow Florentines Farinata, Guido Cavalcanti, and Brunetto Latini; and the higher commitments to energy and experience found in Ulysses. Dante's Hell confirms Freud's view that in it are placed the superseded powers of creation, those forces and individuals that no longer serve. In this sense supersession of Cavalcanti and Latini is aesthetic as well as moral: Dante's new guide is Virgil, who has brought with him all the imaginative possibilities of the classical epic, a scope and a form that transcended the limited perspectives of the local and in Latini's case "municipal" style. They are the discards of Dante's own "overgoing" ambition and his restless search for perfection.

In Hell the positive working of Dante's model system breaks down. The representative figures he meets there do not lead to higher goods, but rather to the bottom of the universe and to Satan, the author of all evil. Restraint, distance, and hidden agenda are the products of the infernal meetings, not uplift, openness, and identification. Meetings do not end satisfactorily—witness the strange look with which Ciacco gazes upon Dante before resuming his position on the ground (VI.91–93); the quarrel that results from the meeting with Farinata (X); and the chastened moral purpose which Dante the author derives from the mere memory of the condition of Ulysses (XXVI.19–24). In fact the very conditions for "modeling" are reversed, with the supposed objects of value existing on a lower plane than Dante, the apparent apprentice. The most notable instance of this is in the episode with Brunetto Latini, where the pedagogic pattern is reversed and Dante the student walks with head bowed while actually being in a physically superior position to Latini, and it is the former teacher who must keep restlessly moving, unable to satisfy the student's request that they sit still.

The visit to Hell is, as both Virgil and later Beatrice explain, an extreme measure, a painful act of surgery before the real plan of rehabilitation can begin. This explains why the *Inferno* is both aesthetically and theologically incomplete and why, unlike its two precedent models from Greek and Latin antiquity, the visit to the land of the dead is only an initial step. Hell begins with an anti-Romance and it ends with an anticlimax. Students who first come upon the description of Satan in canto XXXIV frequently express disappointment at the lack of dramatic or emotional power in that final encounter, and yet Dante's instinct is correct. Since the *Inferno* signifies primarily a process of separation it cannot end on an upbeat, or produce a grand finale, but must terminate rather with distinct feelings of being let down. In a way this is inevitable, because the final revelation of Satan can have nothing new to show: we have already experienced his works in human history through the extent of the *Inferno*. Virgil's last words on the subject are resonant in their understatement. After identifying the figures in Dis's jaws he abruptly announces that night is coming and that it is time for them to be gone, "chè tutto avem veduto" (for we have seen all). The weariness of the phrase summarizes their emotional condition. No outrage or anger is expressed, for it might be too volatile, part of the love-hate equivalency, and too prone to lapse into its opposite. Far more reliable is the sense of disgust, which the penultimate episodes with Bocca degli Abati and Ugolino combine to produce.

III   *Cantos I and II*

The point of the *Inferno* is to explain why Dante was unable to climb the mountain from which at the outset in canto I he was turned back, to expose what allegiances and traits of character kept him from going forward. To succeed Dante does not so much need new sponsorship as a return to old faiths and old sources of inspiration. This explains why Virgil comes to his rescue, the very Virgil whose voice is weak because he has been silent for so long. Cantos I and II, the prologue to the poem, reestablish in the persons of Virgil and Beatrice the classical and Christian bases to Dante's undertaking—and it is revealing that they must do so. This need grows out of Dante's condition, where as an outsider and an exile he seems to be rejecting the wisdom and the standards of his day. Consequently he must show his true supports; he must defend himself against the charge of *follia*—that word so important throughout the *Commedia*, where it means not only folly but a kind of hubris, a deficiency in the fear of God. Is Dante only an overreacher, a Phaeton, an Icarus, who is fatally deluded into thinking that outside of his old commune he can find real peace and understanding and that by going beyond the practices of his own time he can write a poem worthy of a place in the line of the great masterpieces of antiquity? He is not Aeneas; he is not Paul. Who is he to risk such an adventure? What results from his journey will justify it? Virgil correctly identifies the source of the questioning as *viltà*, that cowardice whose unenterprising dimensions Dante explored in *Convivio* I. Although he does not say so at the moment, Dante's journey is intimately connected with the products of the journeys of those earlier heroes Aeneas and Paul—the Roman Empire and the Roman Church, each of which in Dante's day seems to have lost its true direction. One of the purposes of Dante's poem is to restore them to their proper roles by showing how much of the contemporary chaos is the result of their confused roles. In this sense, then, Dante is attempting a journey that is as significant as that of the greatest models of the past. Moreover, if the end of the pilgrimage is redemption, Dante as a contemporary Christian has as many resources as had any of the heroes of antiquity. Poetically, the same applies to the poet as well as to the wayfarer. As prologues, cantos I and II justify the poem as well as the journey. The message is complementary in each case: from the midst of contemporary life, with all the misgivings and the doubts there involved, a poet has emerged who has found the form and the language to express the highest values of a Christian civilization. His theme is a lofty one, and thus it is that despite the fact that the first canticle will take him through all sorts of horrors and degradation, Dante invokes the Muses and his own lofty intelligence that this experience might be faithfully recorded—here his mind will be given a chance to show its nobility.

Virgil is the first figure of support for Dante, and we must understand that he represents much more than reason (if he were only that Aristotle, upon whom Dante was so dependent in the *Convivio*, "il maestro di color che sanno," would have been a better guide). In more than one way Virgil is Dante's master and his author (Moore has counted at least eighty-four references, echoes, and resonances taken from the *Aeneid* in the *Inferno* alone).[4] When Virgil, who unlike Aristotle was a poet, returns from his long silence (a time coincidental with Dante's lost period in the dark wood, where the sun was silent) he brings back the scope, the hopes, and the aspirations of the great epic *Aeneid*. He also represents the wisdom and the spiritual yearnings of the classical world at a specific historical moment—just prior to the advent of Christianity. For these reasons, Virgil is more than just an exponent of reason; he is also an emissary of grace prompted by Beatrice. He can lead Dante to that of which he only knows the need; he can inform Dante of greater supports than he himself has the power to provide. As the guide to Hell, where avoidance is required, Virgil is largely cautionary, prohibitive. Yet, given Dante the author's positive psychology of attachment, his sense of transcendent heroism, such restraint is obviously not enough. Consequently canto II opens with a beautiful image of twilight where all the animals of the earth are ceasing from their labors, preparing for rest, while only Dante must gird himself for a terrible, solitary journey ("io sol uno, m'apparecchiava a sostener la guerra sì dell'cammino sì della pietate"). In order to complete this undertaking Dante will require more than a policy of avoidance; he will require positive idealism and inspiration, some force that moves him on. Consequently, to allay his fears and doubts, Virgil reminds him of the solicitations on his behalf by a trinity of blessed ladies. In Virgil's sudden reappearance there was more than just a coincidence, there was a kind of concern, which could be regarded as a favoring and fortunate quality in life itself. We shall see again and again how Dante's poem is motivated by this sense of return. Now, not only does he experience the return of Virgil but also that of the presiding spirit that dominated his early age of poetry, Beatrice herself. She has lost none of her exemplarity. Virgil tells how he addressed her with these words:

O lady of virtue, through whom alone the human kind surpasses everything within the smallest circle of the heavens. . . . (76–78)

On the level of allegory, the three ladies represent different forms of grace (Mary, prevenient grace; Lucy, illuminating grace; and Beatrice, efficient grace), and they are the ones who stirred Virgil to move from Limbo in Dante's behalf. Hearing of their concern and interest, Dante is like a flower suddenly revived by the warm rays of the morning sun. The twilight time of doubt and fear has been metaphorically dispelled. This procedure at the verge of Hell will be repeated when Dante, finding Virgil's exhortations inadequate, will only require the suggestion of Beatrice's name to pass through the fire of the final terrace of Purgatory.

Among the other general characteristics of the *Inferno* is its obvious pluralism. There is little connection among the many individuals. If Paradise is based upon the concord made of diverse individuals, the *Inferno* reminds us that in the *De Monarchia* I.xv Dante thought that to scorn unity and hence to proceed toward pluralism was sinful. This is the case in the *Inferno*, where no larger principles, such as are guiding Dante,

seem to guide conduct, and where, as a consequence, its atomism
is merely antagonistic. There are no large vistas in the *Inferno*,
no great metaphysical discussions, nor even theoretical ones
(with one exception). Those in Hell have lost the "good of the
intellect"; they have lost any sense of the workings of higher
principle either in the public life or in their private lives. They
embrace no large ideals, or if they do so, they have come to no
understanding in regard to their private selves.

Despite this absence of connections or any larger understanding, there are some principles at work in the background of the
Inferno that encourage us to make connections between individual cantos. Some of these connections are thematic, bringing to
our attention recurrences and developments. Others are structural, whereby we might pair cantos, or group them, or align
them in a series. These are elements in the architectonics of
the poem, and an important part of Dante's artistry and of the
aesthetic pleasure his imaginative skill affords us. When we
proceed higher and are able to comprehend the other books in
relation to the preceding, and his enormous system of correspondences becomes apparent, there will be even more pleasing proof of the fusing power of Dante's imagination and of how
difficult it is to separate structure from poetry in Dante's higher
vision.

Thematically, since the journey to Hell is made on Good
Friday the pattern involved is not only that of Aeneas's visit
to Avernus but Christ's death and harrowing of Hell. Dante's
own experience of exile participates almost unconsciously in
Christ's own separation and death to the world. And while Dante
cannot literally follow in Christ's steps, since Christ only advanced as far as Limbo (from which he rescued the Old Testament figures), still this basic event serves as a pattern and support for Dante's journey. Dante's passage through the gates of
Dis is justified by what Christ did to the larger gates of Hell
(*Inferno* IX.124–26). But even before that triumphant action,
the earthquake that attended the death of Christ so shook the
structure of Hell that the rocks it tumbled provided means of
descent for Dante. Again and again he will rely upon these
rocks, clinging to them tightly in canto XXVI, where he learns
of the fate of Ulysses, or using them as his means of moving
down. Dante does not know it at the time, but the agony of
separation and exile that he undergoes participates in the pattern

of Christ's own death. By such indirect ways and with remarkable aesthetic confidence, Dante depends upon the reader to connect these incidents that are so separated in the poem.

While this pattern is kept mainly in the background (without, however, diminishing its importance), the other pattern of irrational challenge to Dante is much more in the foreground. It is fitting that in Hell the threatening forces are much more immediately apparent than are the saving graces. Mainly the challenges come from classical figures derived from the *Aeneid:* from Charon, Minos, Cerberus, Plutus, and Phlegyas. In each of these instances Virgil's response is roughly the same: he reminds them of the divine sanction for Dante's "fatale andare." It is decreed that these powers of evil yield to the superior sanctions behind Dante's progress and development. However, the kind of doubt and fear that was aroused in canto II persists and reaches a climax in cantos VIII and IX when Dante and Virgil are not only challenged by the classical forces of irrationality (whom Virgil knew well) but by the apostate angels. They guard the walls of the city of Dis (Virgil refers sardonically to its "grave citizens and great garrison"), perhaps lending some support to associating this opposition that Dante encounters with the "madness" of his former fellow citizens in Florence.

Virgil's response to Plutus in canto VII prepares us for the dimensions of this later confrontation. He informs the enraged guardian of the third circle that Dante's descent to the bottom is not without reason: it is willed on high, there where St. Michael first routed the rebellious angels (7–11). These fallen angels have become the demons that guard the wall of Dis (IX.91–97) and they were, as we saw above, the same forces of opposition that tried to block Christ's advance. Dante's own drama has already been fought out on the divine plane, to the pattern of which it reaches for help. Virgil himself is stymied by these new forces of perversity (while the allegorical interpretations of each are quite specific, generally the demons, in combination with the Harpies and Medusa, represent a loss of courage, a despair at sinfulness, for which the only remedy is grace). The demons warn that Dante should return by his "folle strada," VIII.89–91, reproaching him for the kind of presumptuousness that he had so feared at the outset of the poem. In a way the incident is summary of the many doubts that may have beset Dante during his own pilgrimage, doubts about the rightness of his course when his past actions swarmed at him, and he saw his native city turn hostile. But Dante has the capacity of intellect, and the favoring supports, to overcome these momentary doubts and to see his own trials as existing within larger patterns of order. His fight with the obstinate city, or that of Henry VII, is part of the same pattern as that which occurred in the heavens when the proud angels fell and recurred at the Crucifixion and continues to recur whenever forces of light are challenged by those of darkness.

IV   Cantos III to XVII

Cantos III and IV, and V and VI show the resources available to Dante when he juxtaposes, or pairs, cantos. The materials of cantos III and IV are juxtaposed because they show two groups of people who while damned are still set apart from the rest of Hell: the neutrals, who are not good enough to be placed below, and the virtuous pagans, who are too good. With dramatic abruptness, with no narrative preparation at all, the reader is confronted with the famous inscription over the gate of Hell (in imitation of the inscriptions placed over the gates of many medieval towns). It explains that Hell is a city ("città dolente"), that it lasts forever (io etterno duro"), and that it is inhabited by the lost people ("la perduta gente"). Dante confesses that he finds the meaning of the inscription "hard"—that is, not difficult to understand but rather terrifying. As we saw in *Convivio* IV.xxi–xxii, the instinct to return to God is also a terrible burden. That man has the freedom to pass from time to eternity also means that his random and thoughtless choices can harden into the finality of Hell.

With Virgil's comforting guidance Dante has his first experience of Hell: the sighs, the shrieks, the strange tongues and the horrible outcries, the pain, the anger, the hands futilely slapping at wasps. Virgil explains that these sounds come from those who lived without praise or blame. They too have their heavenly prototypes in the angels who in the war in heaven were neither loyal to God nor his enemies but were only for themselves. Dante, naturally enough, must have felt great contempt for those who would not take sides in the issues of his city, but would be there to benefit with the winners. So ignominious are they that, should they be placed in Hell, their presence would give comfort to the outright sinners, who would be able to say that at least they took a chance. Dante knew too well the modern refrain that Hell is preferable to nothingness. From out of the large number of the unwanted and the unnamed Dante does recognize one person, "him who through cowardice made the great refusal." This is the hermit Pietro da Morrone, who five months after becoming Pope Celestine V renounced his office. In the very first canto where the personages of Hell are presented, Dante introduces his political theme. By virtue of Celestine's abdication, Boniface VIII became Pope. When Dante enters the world of the *Inferno* he is indeed entering the world of history where not only bad actions, but inaction, the refusal to assume moral responsibility for issues of power, can have terrible consequences.

Canto III ends with an earthquake (the day is, after all, Good Friday, and Dante will himself later be helped by the ruins caused by the prototype of this tremor at the Crucifixion), at which Dante falls into a faint. On the other side of the river, Dante, at the beginning of canto IV, is awakened by the sound of thunder which is the effect of the lamentation coming from the abyss at whose edge he and Virgil now stand. The limbo of virtuous pagans occupies the first circle of Hell, but its quiet dignity separates it from the horrors below. It is indeed an enclave, a special preserve of nobility. The deliberate gravity of the classical figures contrasts with the hectic actions and emotional obsessions of Hell: "they spoke seldom, [but with] gentle voices" (114). Virgil must first explain that these figures are in Hell not because of guilty actions but because they lived too early to know Christ: in all of their works there is no sign of the great hope that inspired Christianity, and yet in their sighs they seem to be yearning for a Redeemer.

Dante not only shows us the classical world, but also indicates the proper reaction to these great pagan exemplars. By the very sight of them he feels himself exalted (118–20), as the spirit surges to become like that which it admires. Nevertheless, the picture of Limbo is still tragic. The poets still live within a dark world, within which their own illuminations have created a small hemisphere of light (67–69). It is in relation to these brave figures that Dante defines himself. They represent the best of the classical world and are so privileged in Hell because of the honor (a word that within the space of some thirty lines occurs seven times) due their great accomplishments. This section could serve as another preface to the poem, an aesthetic one, where Dante's remarkable self-consciousness defines itself in relation to its antecedents, and in so doing marks a new page in our cultural history. At its most audacious this cultural self-consciousness is an expression of Dante's great aesthetic confidence. Not only does he look back and take his own historical bearings, but in effect he dramatically announces a new poetic renaissance. After a long silence, the great poem of the classical age, the epic, is returning, and Dante is next in the line of Homer, Virgil, Horace, Ovid, and Lucan (later Statius will be included, an important Christian link). There are no other representatives from the intervening "middle" age great enough to be mentioned with this group. History has become culturally tripartite, consisting of the great classical age and an intervening middle period over which the new age jumps in order to return to its primary inspiration. When Petrarch came to write his *Coronation Oration*, that other central manifesto of a poetic renaissance, there was little that he could add that was not already present in canto IV of Dante's *Inferno*.

Cantos V and VI, despite the vast differences in their subject matter, can be treated jointly because in them, at the outset of the painful approaches to Hell itself, Dante confronts two of the great forces that attracted his youthful imagination, courtly love and attachment to his city. To show what misdirections can afflict each of these great forces is a preliminary duty for Dante in the *Commedia*. In Francesca, we meet the first of Dante's contemporaries to rise to the level of exemplarity. Here, in the initial meeting of Hell, Dante encounters the first and noblest error of his culture. He brings under review the great assumptions of the courtly love ethic of his day, one to which in his youth and in his poetry he evidently gave his full allegiance. Just as in the doctrine of courtly love it was the woman who set the tone, it is Francesca and not her lover who tells their story. In fact she is the only woman heard in the entire *Inferno*. This encounter will be compared with those of two other women who occupy similar positions in their respective books, La Pia in the *Purgatorio* and Piccarda in the *Paradiso*. Just as Francesca is the first speaker in the *Inferno*, Beatrice is the last in the *Purgatorio*. The first sin which Dante must understand in the *Inferno* is the last from which he must be purged in the *Purgatorio*. Indeed, so prominent is Francesca's presentation and so challenging that Dante will feel the need to answer it at important later moments in his *Commedia*.

Francesca is a spokeswoman for the tragic power of love. Love pervades her first discourse, anaphorically introducing three consecutive tercets. "Amor . . . Amor . . . Amor." Crucially, Francesca links love with the noble heart, "Amor ch' al cor gentil ratto s'apprende . . ." (love which is quickly kindled in the gentle heart . . .). Instantly we are thrown back to the Guinizellian *Al cor gentil ripara sempre amore*, and Dante's use of that doctrine in the *Vita Nuova*, in the *Donne ch'avete*, and more specifically in the companion sonnet, *Amor e 'l cor gentil son una cosa*. Dante is here informing us that he is repudiating a doctrine which he had once embraced. And yet that is the way of the *Inferno*, so dominated by indebtedness or identification and supersession. Francesca's love did not rise to the level of philosophy, just as her "cor gentil" is not that nobility of soul, which, as Dante tells us in the important chapter XXI of the *Convivio*, has the capacity to understand the "universal form" by means of the "intelletto possibile." Yet, it is indicative that in a poem so dominated by the motif of return, Dante will return to this moment of the *dolce stil novo* in cantos XXIV and XXVI of the *Purgatorio*, where these same instincts that are here wayward are the very ones which when properly directed will yield the high reward of Beatrice. Interestingly enough, in between the cantos where Dante defines the "sweet new style" and the meeting with Guinizelli, he describes in canto XXV the development of the possible intellect that he had set forth in the *Convivio* IV.xxi.

Given this measure of former participation there is no wonder that Dante should be troubled at the fates of the young lovers. This is even more important in Francesca's second response (beginning with line 121). The magic moment of the first kiss is recaptured: when the now never-to-be-parted lovers were reading the story of Lancelot and how the beautiful and "desired smile" ("disiato riso") of Guinevere was kissed by so great a lover, with the consequence that "he, who never shall be parted from me, all trembling, kissed my mouth." The book was indeed a Galeotto, a pandar. By means of the aura of romance, the illusion of literature, they were brought to endure a terrible reality. Even linguistically, as Poggioli reminds us, Francesca's use of so heavy and physical a word as "bocca"—where there had been the "disiato riso"—forms an unconscious commentary on the love that she is describing.[5] Indeed, while not quite a *Madame Bovary*, the story Francesca tells is an anti-Romance, where the myth of courtly love is undercut by reality and its consequences. The contrast is even more overwhelming between Lancelot, "cotanto amante" and the present Paolo, who kissed her "tutto tremante," and who we suddenly realize has not spoken a word throughout the entire scene, but weeps silently. When Masaccio or Michelangelo came to depict the expulsion from Paradise, they did not have to go much further than this picture of fallen love in canto V, Dante's own paradise lost.

The important alignment of cantos, all dealing with the Florentine political theme and prophecies of Dante's exile, commences in canto VI. While the story of the *Commedia* is in the visit to the afterlife, the plot is made up of the revelations that announce his exile. In addition to canto VI, these revelations occur in cantos X and XV. If we add canto VII, where the important discussion of Fortuna takes place, we see that in these cantos where Dante learns of the terrible blow he is about to suffer he is at the same time acquiring the means for coping with it. Ciacco, the first Florentine Dante meets in Hell, almost immediately identifies himself in political terms: in the fair life you "citizens" called me Ciacco. By alluding to the envy rampant in Florence Ciacco proceeds in condensed and cryptic manner to summarize the long struggle between the Whites and the Blacks that would result in the exile of the Whites (a history that was told in Chapter 3). The first presentation of a Florentine brings us into contact with the tragic events of 1300–1302. Dante suggests the basis for future developments when, still the naive apprentice on the way, he eagerly inquires about the Florentine heroes of a previous generation, those great names that fired his own youthful imagination and had become part of his civic consciousness. In recoil from the ominous future, Dante reaches back into the section of the Florentine past that seemed to promise security, back to Farinata (X), Aldobrando degli Adimari (il Tegghiao), and Jacopo Rusticucci (each placed with the great Guido Guerra in canto XVI), Arrigo (unknown), and Mosca dei Lamberti (XXVIII). Ciacco, who was known for his biting tongue, wastes no time in disabusing Dante's innocence. They are among the blackest souls in Hell, he informs Dante. Rather than offering any security, those great names from the past are actually part of the disaster Dante is moving toward, and from which he needs to liberate himself. Just as Dante is compelled to reevaluate the totality of his attachment to his city, so he must revise his attitudes toward those great civic exemplars. Dante's own personal growth and preparation for exile are dependent upon his realization that the very heroes and legends that he so revered are themselves part of the mind of Hell.

The next big step in this so-called "municipal theme" is canto X, where Dante meets Farinata and the father of Guido Calvalcanti. But before that scene an important acquisition (as well as recantation) is made by Dante in canto VII. This canto, with its central discussion of Fortuna, is not generally considered to be part of the municipal theme and Dante's exile. Yet, it is the one major theoretical statement in all of the *Inferno* (in addition to canto XI, where the moral theories that explain the structure of the *Inferno* are given) and provides Dante with the necessary lights (as far as those of the *Inferno* go) to respond to Brunetto Latini in canto XV. In *Convivio* IV.xi Dante noted the injustice of the ways riches are acquired. His conception of Fortune there was definitely a pagan conception, against which intelligence is forced to contend. He repeats that notion dramatically when he asks Virgil, "Who is this Fortuna who so has the goods of the world within her claws ["branche"]?" It is upon this last word that Virgil builds his entire discourse (70–96). Fortuna is not a beast but is, rather, a blessed handmaiden of the Lord. Just as the planets have their own directing "intelligences" to their movements so, too, the distribution of worldy goods, of riches, and of power, are directed by a divine agent, and that is Fortuna executing the will of Providence. This medieval conception of Fortuna differs from that of the classical deity as much as it does from the important alteration that Machiavelli will bring to the concept.[6] She is beyond human intelligence: "Your wisdom cannot strive with her." Consequently she is not really subject to human control. It is natural, then, that in the *Convivio*, where Dante has not come to accept his exile, his conception of Fortuna involves inequity; but in the *Commedia*, where his own developing attitudes and acceptance of exile are so central a part of the drama (however much he still knows himself to be a victim of injustice), Dante's conception of Fortuna must change to that of an essentially benign minister of God's will.

Canto X of the *Inferno* has been praised for its dramatic qualities, Farinata's "sudden" address to Dante, the intervention

of Cavalcante Cavalcanti, and then the imperious return of
Farinata to their previous conversation, almost as if there had
been no interruption. This is the ambience, with its sense of
potent energy out of which emerged the brilliant character of
Guido Cavalcanti. While he is not present in the canto, the lines
spoken by Cavalcante and Dante are a monument to his dead
friend. He himself evidently had adhered to the Epicureanism
(technically, the belief that the soul dies with the body) prevailing in Florence, and here uniting Guelph and Ghibelline alike.
This helps us to understand why the perspectives of those suffering its pains do not rise above the present things that Dante will
accuse himself of following in his confession before Beatrice.
Farinata's vision does not rise beyond party and *patria*; consequently what should have been a friendly encounter between
two compatriots meeting on the lonely road of exile turns out to
be a hostile repetition of the Florentine civil wars of 1248–66.
Cavalcante's does not rise above concern for his son, and when
he mistakenly gathers from Dante's words that his son is dead
(as he soon would be in August 1300), he falls back into his tomb
and does not reappear. From within the ruling classes of Florence of the generation before Dante's birth, no higher perspectives emerge than those of party and family. Dante regards this
as the necessary background to the major purpose of the canto,
a dramatic and poignant explanation of what separated Dante
from Guido Cavalcanti.

Guido's surprised father wishes to know why his son is not
accompanying Dante if he is making this exceptional journey
by "altezza d'ingegno." The father's words and Dante's response
lend credence to a kind of rivalry existing between the friends,
and in this canto, where the limitations of Epicureanism are
revealed, the essential difference between them has to do with
Virgil and Beatrice, the sources of faith and larger belief that
came to Dante's rescue in cantos I and II. "I do not come by
myself," is Dante's response to Cavalcante;

he that waits yonder is leading me through here, perhaps [to her]
whom your Guido held in disdain.

He does not mention Virgil by name, indicating that Guido
was also blind to Dante's epic faith. And yet, that same generosity
of faith with which Dante opened himself to the larger vision

of Virgil is that which is leading him to Beatrice. And this larger vision was that which Guido (called "sdegnoso") scorned.

During the short exchange between Dante and Cavalcante, Farinata did not move, but sat there, unbending in his pride. After Cavalcante's relapse, Farinata advises Dante that he will soon learn how hard it is to return from exile. At this point identification catches up with supersession. Literally and figuratively, Dante, the White Guelph, will be allied with his former enemies the Ghibellines, as he himself must come to acknowledge the finality of exile. And just as Farinata was able to wonder why the Florentines were so unrelenting in regard to his family, so Dante in his epistle can ask, "My people, what have I done to you?" Farinata and his limited vision are in the process of being superseded, but in the general similarities that emerge between his fate and that toward which Dante is moving a partial likeness also emerges.

Cantos XV and XVI are next in the aligned series of cantos dealing with exile and Dante's attitudes toward Florence. Yet they are also part of a group of cantos that need to be considered together, XIV to XVII, forming a strong nucleus in the center of the *Inferno* that can be profitably compared with the central cantos in the *Purgatorio* and the *Paradiso*, in all of which important revelations are made of a municipal and historical nature. In these central cantos of the *Inferno* Dante begins to realize the full extent of his separation from the values of his city. As a consequence these cantos are permeated by a sense of weariness brought on by the perspective of historical decline (another element of relationship with the central groups in the other two *cantiche*). The brag of Capaneus, with which canto XIV opens, seems spiritually out of place in this section dominated by the Old Man of Crete, the physical image for Dante's sense of historical decline. The statue of human history is taken from the Book of Daniel and represents the traditional four ages of history (of gold, silver, brass, and iron), though its right leg, upon which most of its weight is placed, is made of clay. This last addition is Dante's version of the present. The statue's back is turned toward Damiatta (or Egypt) but it faces Rome, suggesting what ought to be the true direction of human history. Except for the head of gold, each part has a fissure though which drip the tears that make up the rivers of Hell. Thus the direction of history reinforces the downward-tending topog-

raphy of Hell, and is the necessary prelude to the culminating
encounter with the Florentines in the upper Inferno.

We have already discussed Brunetto Latini's role not only in
the formation of Dante but in that of an entire generation
(Chapter 1). It is no accident, then, that the framing situation of
canto XV should be pedagogic in language, in purpose, and
in structure; however, the drama of the canto comes when this
pedagogic format is reversed by the moral realism of the piece.
For his imaginary journey, as well as for coping with his
coming exile, Dante has another teacher. Here, as in
canto X, the Florentine ambience is transcended by Virgil,
again not named but simply referred to as "this one." It
is Virgil, what he means and what he leads to, who is bringing Dante home ("e reducemi a ca per questo calle"). Not
only does Virgil's larger historical vision, his sense of the providential mission of Rome, prevail over what Dante found
among his local models; so too does his imagination. Just
as when Dante passed beyond Guido Cavalcanti, so
here too, an aesthetic supersession is involved.

Yet Dante must express his great indebtedness to the man
who helped bring Latin culture back to Florence, who thought
philosophy was the "somma cosa" and politics the "plus
haute science." He will always cherish the fatherly image
of the man who taught him thus how man makes himself
eternal. In his fatherly role Latini adds to the series of prophecies concerning Dante's exile. Being a man of letters and
a scholar with some historical perspective, he takes the
causes of exile back even farther than the divisions between
Guelphs and Ghibellines, Whites and Blacks, back to more
fundamental divisions in Florentine life, those between the
Etruscan inhabitants of Fiesole and the victorious Roman
colonial families. Since Dante is of this "holy" Roman seed
it is only natural that he should encounter hostility. The conflict
is ages old: the same battle between the saving remnant and
the destructive forces that was fought out in the heavens is
carried on at the level of history between the heir of Rome and
its enemies. In response, however, Dante, compelled by con-
science, must also express his spiritual separation. Latini had
informed Dante of what fortune held in store for him. Clearly
benefiting from Virgil's interpretation of the nature of Fortuna
in Canto VII, as well as from his advice following the

encounter with Farinata, Dante replies that he is ready for whatever might happen: "che all' Fortuna, come vuol, son presto." He adds that this additional prediction of coming misfortune he will reserve for commentary by a lady, Beatrice, who will provide him with other means for understanding the course of his life. Rather than looking at his life as shaped simply by Roman history and ancient rivalries, he will place these happenings in the pattern provided by the vision of God. Clearly, then, the altered conception of Fortune is a major step in Dante's separation from the Florentine intellectual climate as well as in his readiness to accept his exile.

The remarkable dramatic encounter of canto XV has tended to overshadow the meeting in canto XVI with the political leaders of the generation before 1266. Two of these men he had inquired of from Ciacco. A special fire comes to Dante's poetry as he meets the men who inspired his youthful imagination:

I am of your city, and your deeds and honored names I have always recounted and heard with affection. (58–60)

The temptation here is a kind of emotional self-abandonment, a throwing of oneself down to the level where these great figures suffer their spiritual torment. Here, too, a moral brake is applied as Dante separates himself from their fates. Dante's growing strength and independence were observed in his responses to Farinata and Latini. Here his development is made clearer: Dante does not inquire of his elders as to the ways of the world; rather, it is he who provides the information. In response to their concern whether "valor and courtesy" are still alive in Florence, Dante assumes the function and the stance of the Old Testament prophet as, with uplifted face, he denounces the "gente nova e' subiti guadagni" (73–75). Both Ciacco and Brunetto Latini had condemned the avarice, the pride, and the envy of the Florentines. To this listing of evils Dante now adds two more of a sociological nature: the swelling of the Florentine population by the influx of newcomers from the surrounding countryside and the new possibilties of quick wealth. These thirteenth-century developments,

against which Cacciaguida will complain, served to
weaken the Roman and Christian bases of the Florentine
society. In Dante's mind, the presence of thse new forces only
makes more necessary the restoration of the Imperial
order.

The reeducation of Dante has been completed in regard to his vision of Florence, the object of his most intense
commitment. It is fitting that at this point a major
break should occur in the structure of Hell. The descent on
Geryon is not only prospective in its meaning—looking
ahead to the experiences of fraud—but it is retrospective
as well, representing Dante's separation from a major
illusion, his innocent attachment to Florence. For the first
time we learn that he has been wearing a cord, with
which he had hoped to take the leopard in canto I
(106–108). He now removes this cord, rolls it up, and hands
it to Virgil, who throws it as a signal into the deeper abyss
of lower Hell. This ritual scene has defied interpreters. We
do not really know the meaning of the cord, or of its removal.
Yet obviously there is a connection between the encounter with
deeper fraud and the kind of painful moral schizophrenia
that Dante has just experienced. Also, by removing the
cord Dante seems to be removing the final vestiges of some
sort of tie, and the natural one would be to his city. It
would seem that by this act Dante is finally cutting loose
and ready to face the larger world without his naive
and—as it turned out—ill-founded reliances. The impression
we receive is that of a Dante who, except for the faithful
presence of Virgil, is terribly alone, as he will have to be
throughout his exile.

In an effective passage (XVII.106–14) Dante suggests
again the fates of Phaeton and Icarus. Is his flight
similarly foolhardy, an act of *follia*? Terrified by this
journey out into the void, when Dante looks around him all
he can see is the "beast" (Geryon, upon whose back he and
Virgil are making the descent). One can imagine Dante's
own feelings, the doubts and misgivings he must have been
subject to, when, cut off and alone in exile, he found himself
alienated from both parties, Whites and Blacks. Indeed,
wherever he looked he may have only seen the beast. An
yet, in the centrally located cantos of the *Paradiso*, when

the same question arises (in fact, the same similes) Dante will be reassured by the more appealing Cacciaguida that he is not Phaeton or Icarus, but rather Hippolytus. The use of these similes and their parallel use in *Paradiso* XVII indicate that there is some sense to associating the incidents of the cord and Geryon with Dante's own developing conviction (however much it might be ridden by anxiety) that in his conduct before and after exile, he has been guided by the best standards of reason and faith.

V *Malebolge*

The Malebolge, that eighth circle in whose pockets ten species of simple fraud are punished, shows clearly how in character, tone, and theme the lower Hell differs from the upper. For one thing, fame has lost its efficacy. Benefiting from the pattern of honor established by the noble pagans in canto IV, the magnanimous sinners such as Pier della Vigne (canto XIII) or Brunetto Latini still had some faith in their good words, their good deeds, or in the appeal of their attachments. As a consequence they still want their good names to be kept alive and to have their stories told. In the eighteenth canto, however, we encounter shame, reluctance to have one's name or crime known, since it has to do with pandering—even, in the case of one Venedico Caccianemico, the sale of his sister—and seduction. Under these conditions revelation in the lower Inferno occurs with greater difficulty, in obvious contrast to the eagerness with which most of the noble sinners in the upper Hell wanted to be remember. But it could also be argued that the impressions of nobility and grandeur of the upper Hell conceal a fact that is all the more treacherous: if one's own life is a horror what does it matter if one is remembered in his books, as Brunetto Latini requested? As we descend into the lower Hell unpalatable reality is at least recognized for what it is. Hence the drama of divestment preparatory to the descent on Geryon: rather than the illusions of humanism let the facts stand plain, Dante seems to say, as he strips to meet the raw situation of Hell itself. Better the reality than the appearance.

In the lower Hell Virgil is an anomaly, and his heroic

humanism is out of place. There are few "great" peoole
in the lower levels. The only illusion of grandeur is provided
by Ulysses in canto XXVI and of course his precursor Jason
in canto XVIII—and in each instance, whether by context
or by commentary, their appearance is tarnished. In these
depths more and more of street life is presented, as the art
itself assumes the aspects of medieval popular tastes. In
cantos XXI and XXII, a kind of medicval grotesquerie is
revealed. In canto XXIV an addition to the line of prophecies is made by Vanni Fucci, but this time not as a
means of forewarning and defense but rather as a hostile
act of revenge (133–51). And in the earlier cantos (XXI
and XXII) the theme of irrational challenge is carried on
not by classical figures but by farcical types from medieval demonology.

The numerically central encounter of the lower Hell, the
meeting with Ulysses, is not separated from the "municipal
theme" that had so dominated the episodes of the upper
Inferno. Canto XXVI begins with a diatribe against
Florence, where the city is appropriately satirized for its
expansionism that only seems to yield more subjects for Hell
(five of the thieves in the preceding section were Florentines).
Dante does give his city some credit: he provides a great
humanistic figure, Ulysses, to stand for its restless energies
and agile intelligence. There are personal likenesses with
Dante as well. In several ways Ulysses is Dante's own
prototype, that part of Florence in himself that he must
exorcize if he is ever to enjoy peace and satisfaction. When
Virgil informs Dante that Ulysses, along with Diomed, is
within the horned flame in the eighth bolgia, Dante bends
toward it with desire (68). And yet this arch-adventurer is
precisely that part of himself that he must restrain. Consequently, Dante's way up toward the bridge over the
bolgia is made with difficulty; he climbs on hands and feet,
significantly up the rocks made by the earthquake following Christ's death (13–18). The sight below involves Dante
so intensely that it prompts and authorial intervention
where Dante, moved by the fate of Ulysses, vows to restrain
his genius by means of virtue, so that he may not live
to rue his own special endowments (19–24). If we think
back to that man of "ingegno," Guido Cavalcanti, and

forward to Beatrice's charges against Dante in the *Purgatorio*, it is clear that in some respects the *Commedia*, despite its necessarily universal moral appearances, is not a poem about Everyman, but about men richly endowed with fine intellects and many talents. The most gifted among them, it would appear, are in greatest danger of falling—hence Dante's need to hug the rocks, to make sure his actions and his words are guided by virtue and truth. Yet these same energies which now burn destructively—even self-destructively—are the very energies that return the soul to God when properly directed. Again forging a link with Dante, Ulysses is the only pagan soul in Hell who has, if dimly, gained a view of the mountain of Purgatory. Yet in that sight of that high goal he himself was destroyed, unlike Dante, as not possessing the proper means to reach its heights. The great supports provided by grace, here represented by Virgil and Beatrice, were denied him.

In one sense, then, a kind of heroic greatness invests Ulysses by means of his own historic status and the kinds of energies he represents. But in another, in his association with the fraudulent counselors, with the cunning shifts of the intellect that had such disastrous consequences for Italy, there are distinctly less noble implications, as the cleverly woven texture of commentary reveals. More specifically, Diomed and Ulysses are being punished for three offenses: the deception of the Trojan horse, the rhetorical skills that persuaded Achilles to enter the war, and the theft of the statue of Pallas. Even by pagan standards, then, Ulysses has grave ethical shortcomings. Nor does his stature gain by the fact that, in the roster of sinners in Dante's lower Hell, we encounter instances of all three offenses (including by means of the last-named crime an association with the abhorred Vanni Fucci). And if we remember the events of 1301–1302 whereby, with the connivance of Boniface and Charles of Valois, the forces of Corso Donati secretly reentered Florence, we can see that Dante had no reason to admire the man who conceived the ambush of the Trojan horse.

As a farewell address, Ulysses's advice to old age is fraudulent. He simply urges his men to go down in style. Everything around him has dwindled. Left now with only one boat and a small number of followers, he must deal with another residue, the obvious brevity of his remaining years, or, as he significantly phrases it, "questa tanto picciola vigilia / de' nostri sensi ch'é del rimanente." Literally he is the old man urging one last encounter with the unknown sea, the unpeopled world; no higher object seems to compel his endeavor than to add to his experience. It is natural that Ulysses, who finds nothing in the pagan world commensurate with the fire of his own desires, should perish shortly after catching sight of the mountain of Purgatory, which he cannot comprehend. Ulysses with all of his grandeur cannot serve as Dante's model; his sheer dynamism, his commitment to experience itself, cannot offer the peace and fullness that Dante requires. Yet, he is a noble antagonist, perhaps the greatest in the poem, and Dante will feel compelled to return to Ulysses's flight on two occasions in the *Paradiso*, just as he will continue to do battle with the arguments that Francesca presented.

Cantos XXVI and XXVII should be considered together. They both deal with "fraudulent counselors," the one legendary and the other historical and contemporary. Normally, in the *Commedia*—witness *Inferno* V—these two facets of a sin are presented in the same canto, but here, so important are the size and scope of the characters that two cantos are required. Dante seems concerned to bring the mythic appeal of Ulysses into some contemporary setting, to get a better focus on him by associating him with some palpable reality that Dante knew well. More specific parts of the two stories suggest this association, it being crucial that the "crises" in the lives of Ulysses and Guido should take place when they are both old men. Of the young lovers Paolo and Francesca he needed to know the "prima radice" of their love (its conclusion was all too apparent); now, as we descend deeper into the realities of the larger social world, Dante wants to know how great men came to their end.

While Guido is the ostensible sinner in this canto, he is of course victim of an even greater "false counselor," Pope Boniface. If Ulysses is the *personnage regnant* in the lower Inferno, Boniface is its *éminence grise*. In this sense the true reality standing behind Ulysses are the historical events of 1294 and 1300–1302, from the deception used in forcing Celestine's abdication to that involved in the return of Corso Donati and the Black Guelphs. And if we think back to canto XIX, where Dante uses an error to help locate the place reserved for Boniface (among the simoniacal popes), we see that Dante's treatment of Boniface is in keeping with his subtle character—like Satan, not quite present, he nevertheless seems to have had his hand in everything.

Guido, who as a military strategist was more of a fox than a lion, undergoes his own retributive punishment. He is the epitome of the clever counselor caught in his own devices: from the very first simile, where the inventor of the bronze bull in which the Sicilian tyrant Phalaris roasted his victims was the first to suffer in the device, to the last exchange, where the devil is able to use logic to outwit Guido, the unifying motive of the canto is that of the wily beguiled, the smart being out-smarted. Within the canto, however, the moving center of dramatic appeal does not have to do with such dramatic irony, but rather with the presentation of Boniface in the grips of a desperate and terrible passion. Following his career as a military leader, Guido in old age began lowering his sails and gathering in his ropes (in obvious contrast to Ulysses): he repented and became a Franciscan. This change of heart, he tells Dante, would have saved his soul. But at this time Boniface himself had need of a counselor. The Roman family of the Colonna had not accepted Celestine's resignation or, as a consequence, the legitimacy of Boniface. For a year and a half they maintained themselves in their strongholds, thus making Boniface's power in Rome incomplete. The picture that Dante draws of this ambitious Pope in the grips of a hungry passion is among the most dramatic in the *Inferno*: he is as needy as Constantine coming to be cured of his leprosy. To such an extent does he seem hectic and drunken that Guido on hearing his request is astonished and remains silent. Boniface, however, reassures him that he has the power to "open and close" the ways to heaven (powers, he scornfully adds, for which his predecessor, Celestine, did not have great regard). Incidentally, in the *De Monarchia* III.8, where Dante disputes the papal use of Christ's words to Peter (conferring the powers to bind and loose), he specifically denies the Pope any power to absolve a sinner when the sinner is not penitent. The "dark cherubim" who wrests the soul of Guido from Francis will show that one cannot be

absolved without repentance and that one cannot repent and at
the same time commit the sin (114–20). Guido, however, certain
that he has been cleansed in advance of his sin, succumbs and
breaks his own vow. His words of counsel are now not part of the
subjunctive maneuvering that we associate with his political
background, but are rather the clipped and condensed apothegm
of proverbial political cunning. "Lunga promessa con l'attender
corta" (large promise with scant observance) will bring Boniface
the victory he desires. The real false counselor is Boniface, who
shows his diabolic qualities by corrupting others.

VI Cocytus

At the beginning of canto XXXI, Dante reflects on the fatherly
role of Virgil, who followed his rebuke of Dante at the end of
canto XXX (Dante had been paying too much attention to a
quarrel) with assurances of continuing assistance. Dante will
require such confidence in the realm of Cocytus, where various
forms of treachery are punished, since this area carries to the
last length the discrepancies between appearance and reality
that have been so predominant in the *Inferno*. The sector of
Cocytus begins with an anticlimax and ends with one—thus
fulfilling the antiaesthetic of Hell itself—and in between, in the
stories of Bocca degli Abati and Ugolino, we witness the final
exhaustion in Hell of two of the prime resources of human life,
fame and children.

A thorough reversal of the powers of creation takes place in
the ninth circle, where the treacherous are punished. Dante
addresses "this misbegotten crowd": it would have been better
for them had they been born sheep or goats (XXXII.13–15), and
we recall the passage of *Convivio* IV.xxi, where Dante laments
how terrible it is when the great instinct to return to God becomes
misdirected. No eager self-representation prevails here, no
desire to be known: each keeps his face down in the ice in which
their bodies are submerged. The final direction of the *Inferno* is
toward silence and the perversion of those few rewards of which
the earthly city was thought capable. Whether by accident or
some other hidden purpose ("will or fate or chance") Dante kicks
one of the victims. This victim is Bocca degli Abati, who pre-
cipitated the catastrophe at Montaperti for the Florentine
Guelphs by treacherously cutting off the hand of the standard-
bearer. At this evident signal of collapse, the Guelphs, who were

about to sustain a large assault, panicked and fled. So intense were feelings about the defeat at Montaperti that the family of Farinata, who had led the Ghibelline forces against the Florentine and other Guelphs, continued to be punished because of it (X.85–86). In this pit, however, we are far from any glimmer of nobility or claim to higher motive that might attend the personality of a Farinata. Dante, having some suspicion, asks Virgil to pause so that he might find out the identity of his victim. As he might have done in the upper Inferno he promises fame on earth in exchange for the still-unknown Bocca's story. Dante's eager energy and innocence little reckon with the total blankness, the utter, dread nihilism that inhabits these realms. Bocca does not want his name to be kept alive. What he wants is the opposite of that, the total obliteration of his existence:

What I crave for is the opposite. Take thyself hence and do not vex me further, for thou ill knowest how to flatter in this depth. (94–96)

Beginning at XXXII.124 and extending through much of canto XXXIII, the meeting with Ugolino and his narration transcend the logic of his placement. His terrifying story has little to do with the betrayal of country (hence his location in the Antenora) but it has much to do with Dante's "full experience" of what life has become; it is profoundly continuous with Dante's presentation of the mentality and values of Hell. This key episode of the lower Inferno instils in Dante the feelings of horror and a disgust which he will carry with him when he meets Satan, the very principle of evil. It concerns the second of the two values by which man affirmed his identity and his continuity in history and in time. This explains the collocation of the Bocca degli Abati episode with that of Ugolino; just as in the one, glory or fame had been reduced to its opposite, silence, so in the other procreation, the natural means of extending oneself, is transformed into reversion, and life is forced back on itself. In the overall arrangement of Hell these are the principles that explain the placement of these two scenes.

In the Ugolino episode the awful cunning of the pitiless intelligence—here represented by Archbishop Ruggieri, who had nailed shut the tower in which Ugolino and (in Dante's account) his four sons were imprisoned, thus starving them to death—has taken the source of human affection and made it an instrument of ultimate pain. The unyielding hardness of the motivation responsible for the death of Ugolino and his children is suitably fixed in the icy dimensions of Cocytus, where all of existence has finally congealed. The horror of the story comes from its dramatic and vivid realization of the father's terror, the kind of parental helplessness that is known only in nightmare. That Dante's intention was to exploit this relationship and the theme of progeny is shown by the freedom with which he dealt with historical fact: the people who died by enforced starvation with Ugolino were not all his sons—two were his grandsons; and they were not all children—three were adults.

The canto is dominated by a sense of reversion. Whereas normally (and this is a developing theme throughout the Renaissance, one used most notably by Shakespeare) the resemblance of the child to the parent is a pleasurable recognition of continuity and a modest denial of death, when Ugolino looks into his sons' faces, he sees instead mirrored there his own fears and grief (55–58).[7] And when one of the boys sees his father gnawing his knuckles, thinking that he does it out of hunger, he offers him their flesh to eat (61–63), a second anthropophagal suggestion added to the fundamental detail of Ugolino's chomping on the head of Archbishop Ruggieri.

In this penultimate picture of the decayed human story, man's lot has been brutalized: Ugolino is reduced to "groping"—he is blind from hunger—over the bodies of his children, calling after them. The same brutalization works its way into the father's bereavement and the form his revenge has taken. His eternity in Hell is spent gnawing on the head of the archbishop, the man responsible for the imprisonment, and he is consumed by an insatiable and impotent lust for revenge, which could never be adequate to the loss of his children.

The vision of Hell must end not in anger but in moral and aesthetic disaffection. This explains why the Ugolino episode is not even climactic—it is only the clinching argument in a slowly developing case—and why there is no tragic dimension or any grandeur surrounding his figure. We can also understand why the position of Ulysses is central but not penultimate in the lower Hell. He would be too powerful in his appeal, too humanistic, too inviting of human empathy to rank so close to Satan, for which encounter Dante requires feelings of distance and disgust. These are the emotions conducive to a determined separation from what the world of history had become.

CHAPTER 6

Commedia: Purgatorio

I *The Temporal Realm*

A S the one realm of the *Commedia* which exists in time, the
Purgatorio is marked by a sharp sense of time and change.[1] It
differs from the *Inferno*, so dominated by fixity and obsession, as
it also differs from the other eternal realm, where the saints are
certain and at rest in their total dedication to God's intended role
for them. After the "dead air" of Hell, Dante's delight is re-
awakened when he observes the changing morning color, "dolce
color d'oriental zaffiro. . . ." The very facts of time and change
suggest possibility and hope. Nevertheless, change, while delightful, bears a heavy weight in the course of the *Purgatorio*, as it
shows the destructive tendencies of time. A dominant impression
received from the *Purgatorio* is that of sheer bodily decay, and
the passing of all those things that had been once thought to be
firm and compact. Nature itself, although possessing a bright
changefulness, still controls vast processes that are so ominous for
the fragile human being. Very early, the third and the fifth cantos
of the *Purgatorio* deal with desperate death agonies. Yet the aim
of the poem is to reinforce the strength of the spiritual that begins
to dawn in this *cantica*. Offsetting the strong impressions of disintegration in society and in the individual—down to his very
physical body—are the possibilities of renewal, of spiritual regen-
eration, of communion and continuity. The contest of the two, the
downward decline of the body and the rising strength of the spirit
and regained individual purpose, accounts for the major lyrical
mode of the *Purgatorio*, where isolated spirits are struggling to
find themselves in a rapidly disintegrating world. This lyricism
depends upon memory of the way they had been and sober
recognition of the way they are now; the *Purgatorio* could be
called the lyric of memory.

While the *Inferno* is dramatic, if only apparently so, the *Purgatorio* is recessive, with a sense of "interiority" and reassessment. In Dante's great "trilogy," it seems to be a place of pause, of reconsideration, different in its spiritual activity from the high-energy poems on either side (comparable in this regard to *Paradise Regained*, another "purgatorial poem" in its middle position between *Paradise Lost* and *Samson Agonistes*). In the *Purgatorio* painful rebuilding starts, as the mind of man strives to sort out its priorities. Therefore, despite its lyricism it is also a place of rigorous scrutiny of prior allegiances, where dire exclusions need to be made.

Whereas in the *Inferno*, with its antiaesthetic and its final feelings of disaffection, Dante had been mainly a passive observer, in the second *cantica* he moves toward being an active participant. The only way he can purge himself of evil inclinations is to enter into the positive discipline of penitence. This is to say, of course, that suffused as it is by the lyricism of memory, Purgatory is a place where one sets one's ethical nature in order by obedience to the Law. When Dante insists that both for the race as for the individual the spirit can only be reached through the Law, he is simply recapitulating the Christian view of history: the Law preceded the advent of the spirit. Consequently the guardian of the access to Purgatory is Cato, whose most sacred memory Dante has already invoked in *Convivio* IV. While Cato died in quest of liberty (and in this he is Dante's great model), his first words call into effect stern principle. Who are you, he demands, as he confronts Virgil and Dante, to come to Purgatory directly from Hell? "Are the laws of the abyss broken?" The severity of tone will be used by Beatrice when, in the Earthly Paradise, she compels him to confess his sins. Purgatory is lyrical in its resources and devoted to the spirit, but its means and its methods are exacting.

The greatest victim of this hard system is Virgil. In a book so dominated by interiority, his carefully prepared "rejection" (in effect, he too is superseded) provides the dramatic element. His is the summary case of an entire series of rejections, which produce the tensions in the *Purgatorio*. In fact, the tensions might be more serious and far-reaching than those in the *Inferno*, because Purgatory's stern regime does not reject debased or otherwise marred virtues but rather legitimate and valuable earthly concerns. The relations between man and wife, the values of progeny, the attachment to the polis, art, fame—all those things of humanistic value are subordinated to the struggle for salvation. Purgatory is the place of critical choice, where decision must be made between those things useful for life and those needful for salvation. But if these great values are depreciated, the depreciation is a temporary one; once priorities have been established and the soul is more certain of its faith—as will be the case in the *Paradiso*—then those qualities of life that make for a richer earthly existence are returned in a larger scheme of human values.

This drama of cruel choice begins in the very first canto, when Virgil tries to placate the stern lawgiver Cato by promising to carry report of his kindness to his wife, Marcia, in the Limbo of virtuous pagans. But Cato's response indicates that here in *Purgatorio* the old connections no longer prevail. The blandishment of good report that worked so well in the upper Inferno is again ineffective, since Cato has no thought of his wife "now that she dwells beyond the evil stream." However, if Dante's journey is sponsored by a lady of Heaven, "non c'è mestier lusinghe"— there is no need for flattery. The phrasing is similar to that used by Bocca degli Abati and suggests one of the paradoxes of Purgatory, where many of the values that were violated in the *Inferno* are here voluntarily rejected.

In the second canto, Dante meets his old friend Casella. The *Purgatorio* contains a number of such warm encounters between friends. Dante asks him to sing again one of the songs of love "that used to quiet all my longings." Immediately a warning is raised against the dangers of using art as a substitute gratification for the processes of moral purification. The song that Casella begins to sing is the philosophical *canzone Amor che ne la mente mi ragiona*, which makes his auditors so content "as if nothing else touched the mind of any." This aesthetic ravishment is brusquely interrupted by the morally centered and serious Cato, who rebukes their slackness in climbing the mountain which will make God manifest to them. Temporal urgency with its ethical end takes precedence over the temporary satisfactions of music. In the Purgatory it is not art but themselves that they must make and regain their original likeness to God.

Throughout the *cantica* such important revisions of humanistic ideology are made. And in almost every case the argument is made against external or vicarious reliances that seem to be substitutes for the individual's need to set his own soul in order.

In canto VII, Sordello can summarize in a memorable statement how unreliable are the powers of descent: "Rarely does human worth rise through the branches, and this He wills who gives it that it may be sought from Him" (121–23). In this canto, where the negligent princes engage in a philosophical reflectiveness that they had avoided in life, Dante returns us to *Convivio* IV, where he had argued that true nobility does not reside in *schiatta*, or family line, but rather in the God-given capacity for every one to understand the form of his own being. Insofar as faith in lineal descent prevents this individual philosophical development, where man comes to understand himself in relation to the spiritual forces of his own being, then it needs to be devalued as being too vicarious and unreliable. In *Paradiso* XVI, however, under much different conditions, Dante will glory in his line.

Similarly in canto XI, the human reliance on fame will be scrutinized and found to be too much a part of the irrational processes of nature that promise no stability based upon science and art. Fame is only a cry moving from popular figure to popular figure. Later in the *Purgatorio*, however, in cantos XXI to XXII, XXIV, and XXVI, Dante will defend the stability of certain poetic traditions.

Despite the temporary and relative devaluation of art within its boundaries, the *Purgatorio* is the supreme *cantica* of the arts and artists, of poets and discussions of poetry. There is only one poet in the *Inferno* (Bertran de Born, to whom Dante refers in *De Vulgari Eloquentia* as an example of a poet who wrote illustriously on the subject of war, II.ii), and not many more in the *Paradiso* (two, if in addition to Folco of Marseille we add David of the Psalms). But in the first half of the *Purgatorio* we meet the musicians Casella and Belacqua, the poet Sordello; in the deflating context of canto XI, we hear of the two Guidos, Guinizelli and Cavalcanti, the painters Cimabue and Giotto, and we meet the miniaturists; in the upper reaches of the Purgatory, we learn of Dante's classical connection with Statius, and his contemporary source of inspiration, Guido Guinizelli, and before him the Provençal Arnaut Daniel. Particularly in these latter cantos the subject matter itself is poetry. Dante meant it literally when in the invocation he declared, "But here let poetry rise again from the dead." Not placed among the damned or among the saints, poets seem suited to the particular combination of qualities displayed in the *Purgatorio*: the sense of struggle and yet the hopefulness, the dawning individual spiritual growth in the midst of almost universal signs of decay and dissolution, the role of memory and the lyricism.

And along with the resurgent poetry Dante's own larger philosophical and political speculations emerge, his political thought in cantos VI and XVI, his philosophical thought in cantos XVII to XVIII and XXV. The fitting cap to this *cantica*, where time and the ethical preside, is Dante's full presentation of the *beatitudo huius vitae*, the right workings of Church and Empire, as figured in the allegorical scenes of the Earthly Paradise.

II *The Struggle toward Purgation*

Unlike the *Inferno*, where single imposing characters dominate the scene, the cantos in the *Purgatorio* seem to be given over to several characters whose various stories Dante can alternate and weave together into a total poetic structure. As an aspect of the prevailing code of fellowship (and in contrast to the "atomistic" or individualizing characteristics of the *Inferno*), in the *Purgatorio* there seems to be more of a relationship between cantos and a greater tendency on Dante's part to "group" cantos, where several in a series are linked by a common theme or mood. In the ante-Purgatorio, Dante meets those sinners whose repentance was delayed and as a consequence must undergo a waiting period before they start their actual penitence. Here the central moment seems to be the political diatribe inspired by Sordello and the meeting with the negligent rulers in canto VII. In this sense, then, the emphasis on the violent deaths of the preceding cantos provides the background of individual suffering that is a consequence of the political misrule. Cantos III and V serve the added purpose of impressing the reader with the conditions of mortality from which the aspirant spirit must seek to free itself.

In canto III Dante meets the great Manfred, the illegitimate son of Frederick. Dante, who in *De Vulgari Eloquentia* refers to him as *benegenitus*, relies on contemporary reports as to his appearance, "fair-haired he was and handsome and of noble appearance." Manfred is an example of the surprises inherent in divine mercy. His sins, he tells Dante, were horrible, but still he was pardoned. This is another canto to be joined with *Inferno* XIX and XXVII, suggesting limitations on the power of the papacy. As an excommunicate, Manfred was denied burial in the lands of the Church, and yet the soul of this Ghibelline leader was saved. While granting some efficacy to the papal ban, Dante is always reminding the Church of the greater powers of God: "By their curse none is so lost that the eternal love cannot return while hope keeps any of its green" (133–35). And finally, the episode with Manfred ends, as will so many in the *Purgatorio*, with a request for prayers, "for much is gained here through those yonder."

The contumacious Manfred can be joined with penitents in canto V, not only because of the lateness of his repentance but also because of his violent death. Jacopo del Cassero, Buonconte da Montefeltro, and La Pia all inhabit canto V, and the struggle involved in their deaths and the emphasis on their death-agony (at least in the case of the first two) give an early impression of the tenor of the *Purgatorio*, its emphasis on the fragility of the body, the separation of the soul from the body, and the terrible aloneness of the individual at this moment of struggle. An angel and a devil dispute over Buonconte's soul, thus recalling the debate that occurred at his father's death (*Inferno* XXVII). Here, however, the prior recourse to Mary is sufficient to defeat the devil and save his soul. In disgust, the devil can only work his vengeance on the hapless body.

As was the case with the exhumed body of Manfred, so Buonconte's mortal remains are scattered by the wind and the rain before being buried under the flood's debris. The storm that the devil precipitates in retaliation suggests in fuller detail the great and hostile forces of nature against which the human spirit tries to realize itself. As we reflect on how small is the voice of the human spirit in the wake of such rampaging nature we also realize that we have been prepared for one of the most typical speakers of the *Purgatorio*, La Pia. The turbulence of the natural elements calls to mind the tumult and the violence of the social scene against which she registers her own gentle plea. As in life, so even here in the *Purgatorio* her presence is recessive, overshadowed. In these matters, in her discreet language and in her gentility, she is sister to Francesca in *Inferno* V and to Piccarda (to be encountered in *Paradiso* III). All three were women caught up in a violent world of brutal men, and yet their responses to that world differed. The selflessness of La Pia's gentility comments upon Francesca's self-defense (although not until Piccarda is presented can we, in the expanding system of the poem's cross-references, deliver full judgment on each of them). Yet, even in relation to these sisters, La Pia is passive and without the all-consuming commitment, in the case of the one to eros and in that of the other, to caritas. For the more subdued energies of the purgatorial process, La Pia's might indeed be the representative voice.

The shifts from the fifth to the sixth cantos in both the *Inferno* and the *Purgatorio* involve movement from an aristo-cratic setting of delicate passion to a more robust urban setting. Nevertheless, *Purgatorio* VI, where Dante makes his first major political statement of the poem, is prepared by the experiences of bloodshed that precede it. The poetic drama suggests that connection be made among the personal experiences of Manfred, Buonconte, and even La Pia with the public disruption in the relationships between the Church and the Empire.

In Hell any warmth of embrace is absent; in Purgatory the mere mention of the name Mantua stirs Sordello to move from his leonine reserve toward a fellow townsman, Virgil. This surge of feeling brought on by the love of place forms an ideal connection that serves as a model from which Dante can judge the disorders of the Italy of his day. In canto VI we are given a page from Hell which accounts for the urban dimension of its opening simile of men playing at dice (one not quite in keeping with the mood of Purgatory). Yet, in contrast to Hell, the increased height and illumina-tion of the Purgatory allows causal explanations of Italy's ruin. Here in canto VI, as later in canto XVI (also introduced as a page from Hell), Dante presents us with his theory of collapse. These cantos, along with the allegori-cal visions of the Earthly Paradise, remind us that for all of its spiritual "interiority," its lyric of memory, one of the main and continuing ends of the *Purgatorio* is historical and ethical.

"Ahi, serva Italia," Dante begins the invective that will have other echoes from Petrarch to Machiavelli through-out the Italian Renaissance. A masterpiece of political poetry, its passionate force and argument cover in its different movements the breakup of the three main forces that had prevailed in Dante's age, the commune, the papacy, and the Empire. As always, Dante looks to the evidence. Italy's cities are torn by civil war; within the walls that were intended for protection citizens gnaw at one another. The families that bear authority from the emperor (Dante mentions the Montagues and the Capulets) are feuding with each other. His address points to two causes for this condition. The first is the intrusion of the papacy into political matters (91–96) and the second is the failure of the German emperor, Albert, to appreciate fully the importance of his Roman heritage, the fact that Italy is the "garden of the Empire" (97–117). Whereas in cantos XIX and XXVII we witnessed some of the individual sins of Boniface and his predecessors, here we are shown the ruinous public consequences of their policies. The people who are supposed to be devout should let Caesar sit in the saddle of government. In so doing the papacy would be following Christ's example when he assigned to Caesar the things that are Caesar's. The Church is ill-equipped to control the horse of the body politic which grows headstrong and willful through lack of correction.

Finally, in poetry at its most sarcastic, Dante inveighs against Florence (127–51) not for its neglect but for its hyperactivity, for a changefulness that indicates a lack of true seriousness, especially when contrasted with Sordello's gravity and deliberate movements. Florence, in its feverish need to change laws, offices, coinage, and habits, resembles a feverish woman who thinks she can find relief from pain by constantly altering her position in bed.

Like many other cantos in the *Purgatorio* (in fact it is a model example), canto VIII should be noted for the absence there of any dominating character, and for the variety of the multiple themes that Dante interweaves and brilliantly coordinates so that a stunning unity is achieved. The opening simile of canto VIII ("Era già l'ora che volge il disio / ai navicanti e 'ntenerisce il core . . ."), with its feelings of nostalgia, of yearning, and of separation provides the emotional background to Nino Visconti's indignation over his wife, who has remarried (and hence does not pray for him), as well as to the encounter with the serpent. The souls here sing Saint Ambrose's hymn "Te lucis ante," whose purpose was to guard the soul against the demons of the night and from dreams. This first action of the poem, where prayer and faith are required in the simple combat with emotional longing, prepares us for the central dramatic action of the canto, where the angels of grace repulse the serpent, which, significantly enough, given the emotional sensibility of the opening simile, bears a strong erotic component.

So overjoyed is Dante at the salvation of his friend Nino Visconti, the grandson of Ugolino, that he abandons his authorial distance and intervenes directly: "Noble Judge Nino, what joy it was to me when I saw thee not to be among the damned!" Nino Visconti summons Conrado Malaspina to his encounter. Their stories are joined since each expresses Dante's faith in the "single just man"—with Nino it is his daughter Giovanna, who against all bad example continues to remember her father in prayer, and the Malaspina are honored for persisting in the ancient virtues in the midst of a degraded world. Dante is pleased to inform Conrado of the fame and honor his house receives thoughout Europe (121–32), an encomium occasioned by the reception Dante was given, apparently by Moroello. That house continues to practice the traditional aristocratic virtues, those of the purse and of the sword—that is, generous patronage and military courage. Conrado replies that, within seven years, which would be sometime in 1306, Dante would learn from personal experience of the hospitality and generosity of his house (perhaps, also, in the person of Moroello, of its military prowess as well). The canto that begins with a sense of separation and of isolation ends in reunion and in hope, and thus serves to summarize the nature of Purgatory.

In canto IX a dream announces Dante's readiness to proceed to the higher order of active purgation (in fact in cantos XIX and XXVII dreams also announce Dante's access to new experience). Given the introspective, meditative nature of the *Purgatorio*, it is natural that Purgatory should be the place of dreams. There are none in the *Inferno*, or in the *Paradiso*, where there is no need for dreams, since experience itself is transcendent. Dante's dream has some of the emotional overtones of canto VIII: "Nell'ora che comincia i tristi lai / la rondinella presso alla mattina . . ." (At the hour near morning when the swallow begins her plaintive songs . . .). The language in

the background of the dream is expressive of the conditions
of Purgatory itself: the mythical story of savage violence
in memory of which the swallow sings, the growing division of
the mind from the body, the sense of lonely pilgrimage, and
controlling all the sense of a saddened lyricism. But in
contrast to these elements is the imperial nature of the
royal eagle that carries Dante off to a higher experience.
As Ganymede was ravished up to heaven, so Dante in
his dream is subject to an equally violent experience, where
his whole being seems to be shaken. It is a threshold dream,
announcing a new reality in Dante's life. When he awakens Virgil
informs him that a lady—Lucy—had come to bear Dante aloft.

The remainder of the canto (70 ff.) is devoted to the allegorical account of Dante's entrance as an active participant in Purgatory proper. As he does in *Inferno* IX Dante
here alerts the reader to the fact that the higher matter
at this point has caused him to express it with a higher art
(70–72). As in the *Inferno* cantos IX and X prepare Dante
for his entrance into a new section of the *cantica* (that
of Purgatory proper), and as in the *Inferno* they also take
us back to the proemial foundations of cantos I and II.
It is as if in each *cantica* the content of the introductory
cantos is being expanded and intensified throughout the
remainder of the book. The angelic porter at the top of the
three stairs is so refulgent with the three virtues he represents that he, like Cato, prefigures paradisal transcendence. The porter is a father-confessor who carries the
sword of justice, whose vestments are the color of ash, and
who inscribes seven Ps (representing the Latin word for sin,
peccatum) on Dante's forehead. In this action Dante is
submitting himself to a process of purification, which he will
undergo on each of the seven terraces of Purgatory. After
successfully passing through each terrace, the appropriate "P", representing that sin, will be removed. Once they all
have been removed Dante will be prepared to enter the
Earthly Paradise; he will have been returned to his original sinless nature.

The sins purged on the terraces are the seven cardinal
ones: pride, envy, wrath, sloth, avarice (and its cohort,
prodigality), gluttony, and lust. Procedure on the terraces
is fairly consistent. At first we are given positive *exempla*,

of which the first is always taken from the life of Mary, and the others alternately relative to biblical, pagan, or mythological lore. These are instances that represent the proper exercise of the virtue which counters the sin being purged. Although Purgatory functions under the hard rule of law, its true purpose is to discover the models that permit man to transcend restraint and prohibition. Hence the primary stress on the positive examples. There then follow personal encounters between Dante and the penitents, after which Dante witnesses the great examples from mythology and ancient history of those who succumbed to the sin in question. What we notice is that Dante is on the same level with the penitents whom he meets. Since Dante is himself an active penitent there is a parity in their conditions. Unlike what happens in the *Inferno* and in the *Paradiso*, the souls on the way to purification do not serve as models; instead a common bond of interests exists between them and Dante, a community of endeavor and suffering. Consequently, none of the encounters is "heroic." Purgatory is not a place of avoidance or of transcendence; it is, rather, a place of fellowship, where Dante himself actively undergoes purgation.

The next major step in the *Purgatorio* is in canto XVI, where Dante encounters Marco of Lombardy. This canto actually is part of a group of cantos commencing with XIV, where the problems of Church and State are seen in a larger philosophical context of decline, free will, and Dante's psychology of positive attachment. These cantos should then be compared with the central ones of the *Inferno* and with the same in the *Paradiso*. Just as the infernal group begins with a picture of decline, the statue of the Old Man of Crete, so these begin with Guido del Duca's sense of the fallen families of Romagna, a litany of decline as moving as the great vision of mutability in *Paradiso* XV and XVI. His recitation is preceded by a graphic account of Tuscany's decay along the course of the Arno. The more of the land's flavor that the Arno acquires, the worse it becomes. In fact, its descent is something like the slope in Hell, moving from the hogs (Casentino) and snarling dogs (Arezzo) to the wolves of Florence (insatiable in their needs) and ending with the foxes of Pisa.

Canto XVI stands out from the lyrical, meditative spirit of the *Purgatorio*. The depiction of Romagna's decline is here followed by a larger discussion of Italy's decline. In fact, because of its political nature it acquires some of the properties of the *Inferno*. Evocations are indeed infernal as Dante enters the stormy atmosphere of anger: "Gloom of hell or night bereft of every planet." Marco Lombardo is a perfect type to explain the world's decay; that is to say, he is Dantesque. He has knowledge of the world ("Del mondo seppi") and a love of heroic virtue. This statement, coupled with Guido del Duca's (37–39), causes Dante to wonder what is the cause for decline, the reason why few people strive to attain that ancient excellence. Is the cause in the stars or in ourselves (51–63)? Showing a lingering tendency to irascibility (also Dantesque), Marco considers this to be a stupid question: "The world is blind and indeed thou comest from it," he answers Dante. In fuller response (67–129) Marco defends human freedom, connecting this canto with the two that follow it. The defense of human freedom, of the importance of education and ethics, of good cultivation and practice, we saw was central to the doctrine of nobility in *Convivio* IV. In each case, Dante—and here Marco or later Virgil—shows that despite the basic dispositions and tendencies received at birth, still man has the free will needed to secure salvation. Not only do these cantos attack the notion of a necessary decline, they refute Francesca's message from *Inferno* V. Her sense of tragic necessity in love is one of the continuing arguments of the poem. Here and in the *Paradiso* Dante will reassert what amounts to the cornerstone of the poem, his belief in human freedom.

In accord with Dante's arguments in the *Convivio*, Marco does not deny planetary influences at the time of birth or certain natural dispositions. Yet, in each case, he feels man has superior gifts of reason and free will, which if well nourished can give the proper direction to these innate qualities. This leads into the largest part of the argument (79–120), which could be summarized as crediting a "free necessity," the freedom that man the creature has to return to his creator: "To a greater power and to a better nature, you, free, are subject, and that creates the mind in you which the heavens have not in their charge."

Freedom is a qualified, not an absolute, power. We are free to discover and develop our better natures; that is, we have the power to direct the natural qualities imprinted by the heavens toward their moral and ethical fulfillment. The argument now is no longer one of nature, but rather, as it was in the *Convivio*, one of nurture. The world is declining because the nutritive forces that should be sustaining man's moral nature are lacking.

Here Dante's view of the consequences of the collapse of government are correspondent to his theories of personality, the psychology of positive attachment that is the personal dynamic of his poem. In Dante's conception, the soul is animated by a powerful energy seeking its satisfaction; this, as the *Convivio* tells us, is a basic drive to return to God and is called *horme*. If this desire receives poor models or is otherwise misdirected, it can become an infernal one, desperate in its dissatisfaction. The central poetic passage is a famous one, but also quite reminiscent of *Convivio* IV.xii (with its sense of acceleration in each misstep), "Esce di mano a lui che la vagheggia. . . ."

From his hand who regards it fondly before it is, comes forth, like a child that sports, tearful and smiling, the little simple soul that knows nothing, but, moved by a joyful Maker, turns eagerly to what delights it. At first it tastes the savor of a trifling good; it is beguiled there and runs after it, if guide or curb do not divert its love. (85–93)

In this world-view Dante persistently addresses two major needs of man and human society: permanence and power. So powerful is human appetite (hence the threat posed by the she-wolf at the outset of Dante's journey in *Inferno* I) that it must either be guided by superior ethical models or be restrained by the law. Power is needed to restrain the rampant desire (this is the curb required) and the vision of permanence is needed to satisfy it fully (this is the guide). This was the point at which, for Dante, the system broke down. The overextension of the political interests of the Papacy has worked social and religious harm. Marco complains that the pastor that leads the way ruminates but does not have the cloven hoof, which is to say that a discrepancy exists between the doctrine and the practice

of the Church: while pretending to represent justice it excludes
those who would exercise justice. But this intrusion has disastrous religious consequences as well. When the people see
those who should be guides toward spiritual values themselves hungering for the goods of the world (against which
Virgil in canto XV warned Dante) in their minds this de-
tracts from these values. The rulers, who are supposed to
have "at least" some idea of the heavenly city, give themselves
over to cynicism at the knowledge of papal practices. The world
produced by their defection is precisely the corrupt world that
Dante had come to know, where neither dedication nor devotion
are taken seriously. Given the nature of man and his need for
sound guidance this can only have disastrous consequences.

And it is to the consequences that Dante's argument, persistently historical, looks. Although this positive example is not
fully expanded, Dante finds support for his insistence on the
separation of permanence and power by the older history of
Rome: "Rome, which made the good world, used to have two suns
which made plain the one way and the other, that of the world
and that of God" (106–108). In real historical time the true
cooperation of the secular and the spiritual powers did exist
(Dante is referring to the divided yet cooperative endeavors of
Constantine and Sylvester, Justinian and Agapetus, and Charlemagne and Adrian). These positive examples will be more fully
presented in *Paradiso* VI; for the moment Dante is doing battle,
as he did in *De Monarchia* III, with the papal argument that the
spiritual power was the sun and the secular power the moon, the
one receiving its light from the other and hence subordinate to it.
Dante argues that the secular and the spiritual constitute two
separate and independent orders which, however, are obliged to
cooperate in ways not always easy to determine. But now, with
the confusion of roles, neither power has respect for the domain
of the other. And for confirmation Dante does not only look to
past evidence, he also looks to present conditions and contemporary events. If you do not believe me, look around you, Marco
cries out, as Sordello did, and Guido del Duca, in the manner of
men impatient with lengthy argumentation. "Pon mente a la
spiga." Look at the fruits of this policy, "for every plant is known
by its seed."

The proof is historical: Lombardy was a peaceful land until the
late 1230s, when Frederick began to experience difficulties with

the papacy (118–20). Before that time, along the land watered by the Adige and Po rivers, in Lombardy, valor and courtesy used to prevail (in contrast to the vice that prevails in the cities watered by the Arno). Historical example confirms the philosophical arguments. Decline is not necessary, but the product of a particular policy; that is, it is the result of historical processes. If such is the case, then the problems are also solvable—hence the great ethical and historical mission of Dante's poem. The same moral purpose that moved the *Convivio* and the *De Monarchia* is at work in the *Commedia*.

Just as Dante connects these large public issues with his personal psychology of positive attachment, so, too, these public cantos (including XIV) are joined (in XVII and XVIII) with his fullest reasonings about love and desire—which serves the added function of explaining the rationale of Purgatory. Virgil begins his explanation of the logic of placement by expressing what can be taken to be one of the basic facts of the animated world of Dante's poem: "Neither Creator nor creature . . . was ever without love . . ." (91 ff.). In these cantos Dante confronts again the force of Amor that had become in Francesca's account an omnipresent and overmastering fate. He argues that there are two kinds of love—the instinctive love of animals, which never errs, and the love of rational beings. Dante here uses a distinction which could be called "right focus." [2] As long as the voluntary love is directed toward the primal good, or God, and observes "right measure" when directed toward secondary goods then love cannot be the cause of sin. It is appropriate that these discussions should take place in the *Purgatorio*, where priorities are being weighed, and indeed "right focus" does seem to be the solution brought by a form of Christian humanism to the demands of a primary love of God, on the one hand, and involvement in the world, on the other. The attitude of "right focus" does not hold worldly things in contempt, rather it enjoins their proper use, provided that the use of them does not tend to negate the highest good. When, however, this elective love attaches itself to the wrong objects (and these have to pertain to one's neighbor's harm) or it follows the good with defective or with excessive vigor, then it is in need of correction. The first three terraces of Purgatory proper correct the badly placed love, that which seeks another's ill, hence pride, envy and wrath (106–26). The fourth circle, at which Dante has arrived in canto XVII, purges weak attachment to the good, *accedia* or sloth, while the upper three terraces which Dante is approaching correct the unrestrained pursuit of goods, avarice-prodigality, gluttony, and lust.

This discussion is continued in canto XVIII, where again Francesca's language is transformed, in another context, into the psychology of positive attachment ("L'animo ch'è creato ad amar presto . . ."):

The mind, created quick to love, is readily moved toward everything that pleases, as soon as by the pleasure it is roused to action. (19–21)

Just as it is the nature of fire to rise, so man's nature disposes him to move toward all objects of pleasure. This pursuit is restless and unending until complete satisfaction is achieved, and it is the principal motive of ascent in Purgatory and Paradise. It can also end in Hell, if its direction is toward unworthy objects; Virgil thus can conclude again that not all situations of loving are valid ones (19–39).

While these philosophical cantos can be regarded as pages from the *Convivio*, the later cantos in the *Purgatorio*, XXI and XXII, XXIV, and XXVI, can be seen as related to the *De Vulgari Eloquentia*. In them Dante meets his full poetic culture, and they are the epic sources, Virgil and Statius, and the very earliest source of his inspiration in the modern poetry of love, Guido Guinizelli. Typically enough for the *Commedia*, so dominated by the motif of return, of looking again at an earlier part of one's life that had been abandoned, the ethos of love poetry is placed higher in the cantos immediately preceding the meeting with Beatrice. It is as if Dante were saying that from Virgil and Statius he acquired his broad public vision, the commitment of his epic to the relations of man and the gods, but that the definition of his own purposes and highest powers must grow out of the earliest sources of his inspiration. In Virgil's great poem, as T. S. Eliot has suggested, we find *labor* and *pietas* but we do not find *amor*.[3] Just as the example of Virgil's historical vision permitted Dante to transcend the "municipal" poets, so the vision of love that was rightly defined in cantos XVII and XVIII and became philosophy by means of the *intelletto possibile* transcends the classical vision. To be a philosopher after all is to be a lover of wisdom.

Cantos XXI and XXII complete the link of poetic continuity

presented in *Inferno* I and IV. Statius, like Virgil, introduces himself by his historical identity. At the time when Titus, Emperor Vespasian's son, destroyed Jerusalem (Dante's historical understanding regarded this as an act of vengeance for the death of Christ), Statius lived as a poet ("col nome che più dura e più onora"—82–87). Already we are informed that Statius, unlike Virgil, lived on this side of the spiritual divide. Thought to be the last classical poet crowned with the laurel and, as Dante suggests, the first Christian poet, he is the intermediate between Virgil and Dante; in fact, he might very well be Dante's surrogate, for his indebtedness to Virgil is very like Dante's own.

Statius's debt to Virgil is two-fold: through him he was a poet and a Christian. In each case the testimony is remarkable.

The sparks that kindled the fire in me were from the divine flame from which more than a thousand have been lit—I mean the *Aeneid*, which was in poetry my mother and my nurse; without it I had not weighed a drachm. . . . (94–99)

Dante is of course following historical record in allowing Statius to register this indebtedness; in his epic poem, the *Thebaid*, Statius himself initiated the tradition when he sent off his poem in the steps of the "divinam Aeneida" (XII.816–17).[4]

Yet, despite his being a great source of inspiration, Virgil cannot be saved. We notice the development of the drama of Virgil's "rejection" as we get closer to the point where he will discern no further. The bipartite view of sacred history will cut remorselessly across the tripartite view of cultural history. This is all the more painful since Virgil's poetry is of great ethical and even religious purpose in the development of the Christian spirit. Dante is finally addressing explicitly a point of view that is implicit in the whole *cantica*. The question constantly implied was why should a Christian who had all he needed for salvation in the Old and the New Testaments read the pagan classical writers? In canto XXII, Statius suggests one answer. Just as some lines of the *Aeneid* warned Statius against prodigality, so the famous lines from the Fourth Eclogue prepared him for Christianity. Under the helpful guidance of providential history the development of classical culture led up to and assisted the development of Christianity, both politically and intellectually.

If Virgil is able to lead Dante up through the Purgatory to the very verge of the Christian revelation that was partially because he too had an inspired sense of human history.

The age turns new again; justice comes back and the primal years of man, and a new race descends from heaven. (70–72)

But if these lines were inspired this also means that he wrote better than he knew. His vision did not become his personal property; rather it was a reading that only later ages saw confirmed by events.

Thou didst like him that goes by night and carries the light behind him and does not help himself but makes wise those that follow. . . . (67–69)

His life is what it was, and for all of Dante's "searching" of Virgil's volume he was unable to find in that restrained and austere rational classical genius the transcendent power of Christian love and the supreme dedication that marked the lives of the saints. Dante could not make Virgil other than what he was.

The defining lyrical, meditative voice of the *Purgatorio* is most keenly heard in cantos XXIII and XXIV, where Dante meets his old friend Forese Donati. Their mixture of friendship and yet detachment, of memory and decay, of the sensed dissolution of the society in which they grew up and the clear recognition of the different paths their lives followed makes of these cantos a masterpiece of meditative and subdued intensity, and the fullest and most satisfying episodes in the *Purgatorio*.

These cantos open with a sense of temporal urgency as Virgil, ever the Roman master of time's use, prods Dante: the time they have at their disposal must be put to better use. It closes with a similar expression, when Forese terminates the meeting with Dante by declaring that he dare not stay longer, for time is precious in Purgatory. Nevertheless, despite the pressures of time and individual responsibility that are the cantos' outer bounds, its inner mood is dominated by the intimacy of old friends. "Qual grazia m'è questa?" Forese cries out upon recognizing Dante. The line calls to mind Brunetto Latini's first words in *Inferno* XV, just as the valedictory similes to each encounter bear some resemblance. Intentionally, it would appear,

Dante invokes the pattern of their old mentor to preside as some sort of silent host over this more fortunate meeting.

The lyrical quality of the canto derives from the conjunction of contrary events and emotions, good news and bad news. Forese's face is "unleaving" (from the verb *sfogliarsi*) and Florence is losing its pulp of goodness (from the verb *spolparsi*). Everything from the individual organism, to the family, to society is experiencing break-up and disintegration. Yet, intermixed with change and decay are examples that withstand Florence's moral decadence. The faithful prayers of Forese's wife have served to advance his purgation (a recantation on Dante's part of the poem where she was maligned?); in her virtuous remembrance she offsets the brazen "toplessness" of the Florentine women. Piccarda Donati is in Paradise showing how different can be the moral destinies of individual members of the same family. She balances Corso, the real author of Florence's woes, who in his own desperate, mad flight is seen to be moving toward the valley where no man can be purged of his guilt, and that is Hell, from which Virgil helped Dante escape. And finally, if Dante reminds Forese of that deplorable episode of their poetic lives, the *tenzone*, he is reminded of a happier period of his young life (they were perhaps coincidental), the time of the *Vita Nuova*, when he composed *Donne ch'avete*. We have already discussed these lines and Dante's response in Chapter 1: where Bonagiunta wants to emphasize the "new departure" of the *dolce stil novo*—that is, its philosophical import—Dante underlines its spontaneity and its integral relation to the circumstances of its origin. Dante's poems are descriptive of the conditions in which they were born. This is the honesty that makes them follow so closely behind their "dictator." And this quality is what really set the "sweet new style" off from the then-prevalent "municipal" poets like Guittone d'Arezzo and others.

The stage is now set for the father of this new style, Guido Guinizelli. But, curiously enough, in between this meeting and the discussion of the *dolce stil novo* Dante interposes a discussion which derives from *Convivio* IV.xxi. Ostensibly its point is to resolve Dante's question as to how spirits can feel physical pain. The real point, however, of the theoretical discussion in canto XXV is to follow again the development of the sperm, the impregnation of the female, and the development of the fetus through its vegetative and animal stages until it reaches the point where it is in a position to receive the *intelletto possibile*—that is, the rational potential for the individual soul to understand the universal forms. Although lodged in the context of scientific poetry (of which it is a very good example), this may be the most important theoretical exposition in the poem. Here Dante shows his intellectual orthodoxy by adopting an anti-Averroistic position. The point at which Averroes went wrong (and he was in several instances directly criticized by Aquinas over this) was in the development of the cerebrum. Since he did not find a suitable physical organ that would be responsible for the *intelletto possibile*, Averroes decided that it was not part of each individual but was rather a universal intelligence, from which the rational intelligence (located in the physical brain) made its deductions and applications (61–66).

Dante's own orthodox position is that the *intelletto possibile* is infused by the divine spirit at the moment when the development of the cerebrum is complete (67–75). While independent in coming from God, this capacity still evidences those particular qualities that make up the individual soul, the given characteristics of a person. This means then that salvation lies in the capacity of the individual soul to realize the universal form of its own being. Hence Dante's Paradise is made up of many diverse, individual beings. This greater philosophical possibility of growth is placed between the definition of the "sweet new style" and the economium to Guide Guinizelli, as if to suggest the kind of development that Dante himself enjoyed but which grew out of his early commitment to the poetry of love.

In the words of one Italian commentator canto XXVI is a superb tribute to the first modern literary tradition. Here Dante makes poetry out of literary remembrances ("poesia nata su ricordi letterarii").[5] The poetics of *De Vulgari Eloquentia* is transformed into a "situazione lirica." [6] The meeting with Guido Guinizelli can be compared with the meetings with Sordello and Statius, all establishing lines of poetic continuity. Just as the *Purgatorio* exhorts and celebrates communion with the dead, so it establishes continuity with the past. Where the individualism of the *Inferno* results in discontinuity, in the more communally minded *Purgatorio*, where no individual seems to dominate single cantos, man's achievements are acknowledged to be part of a continuity. The past is alive in the *Purgatorio*, and thus Dante can credit the continuing fatherhood of Guinizelli,

The father of me and of others my betters, whoever have used sweet and graceful rhymes of love. (97–99)

As long as Italian poetry is written, the very ink with which his poems were written will be praised. This is Dante's modulated yet affirmative praise, and all the more affirmative and hence resistant to the disclaimers of *Purgatorio* XI, because it is modulated. And just as Dante indicates that Guinizelli was also the father of "others my betters" (Guido Cavalcanti) so the now chastened Guinizelli points to Arnaut Daniel, "il miglior fabbro del parlar materno," and acknowledges his own indebtedness to the poetry of Provence. In the more polemically assertive *De Vulgari Eloquentia* (as in the *Convivio*), where Dante was driven to defend the legitimacy of Italian verse he had to distinguish it from the Provençal. Here in the Purgatory he can show the continuity between the two, and thus pay the splendid tribute to Daniel of having him speak in his native Provençal, perhaps the most stunning performance in the entire *Commedia*.

Dante completes the process of restoration when in canto XXVII he passes through the fire that purges lust. The significance of this step is underlined when Virgil compares it to that other crucial experience with Geryon. He would regard the passage through the fire as a similar act of faith in his own skill and guidance. But if Dante survived the conditions of exile by entrusting himself to Virgil, such reliances are not sufficient this time when we are dealing with vices that might be *connaturali*. Reason itself, which is largely cautionary, cannot muster the positive energy required to take Dante beyond the ordeal of lust. The energies that were misdirected in the *Inferno* need to find a more positive goal. They need to be redirected, not rooted out. Consequently, however useful and needful is Roman law and reason, what is required for him to achieve fulfillment is the thought of Beatrice. When he hears Virgil mention the name "that ever springs up in my mind," Dante's force and energy return and he is willing to pass through the flames (34–57).

Virgil's valedictory words herald Dante's new commencement. The spiritual peace and intellectual freedom that the three beasts from *Inferno* I had kept him from attaining are what Virgil's schooling has given him. In fact, all the powerful impulses that were so misdirected in the *Inferno*, will find their satisfaction, here. "That sweet fruit which the care of mortals goes to seek on so many boughs shall today give peace to thy cravings" (115–17). Using reason and skill Virgil has led Dante through the steep and the narrow; henceforward Dante will no longer need his guide because spiritually and physically he has attained that freedom which at the beginning of the *Purgatorio* Virgil informed Cato was his quest. "Free, upright and whole is thy will." It would be an error not to follow its promptings. Not at the beginning of the journey but at the end that is a return to the beginning, Dante finds something paradisal in the notion that now his instinctive reactions might be right. This is not a world of transcendence, but rather a spiritual state located in human history where nature operates at the best of her capacities. The fiction that best embodies this mental condition is the Earthly Paradise.

III   *The Earthly Paradise*

In the Earthly Paradise, Dante brings together in a dazzling unity the mythic, the personal, the ritualistic, the historical, and the prophetic elements of his poem. These elements, so diverse in theme and poetic quality—in fact, the cantos are sometimes disparaged as inferior poetry—are connected by their concern with God-given justice, a personal justice that is attained and a collective justice that can only be advocated.

By having the myth of the Golden Age subsumed under the larger myth of Eden, Dante is permitted two additions to the terrestrial paradise. The first is the concept of justice. Secondly, the role of Virgil's Virgin not only allows for Matelda, the guardian of the Earthly Paradise, but also for the more important presence of Beatrice. Beatrice is that quality which had been missing from Dante's life for over ten years. In fact, the point of the poem has gone beyond what it meant to be lost in the dark wood; it has proceeded to an understanding of what is meant by Beatrice's absence. While obviously the *Commedia* is larger than Beatrice, it is nevertheless true that to approach Beatrice is to approach the meaning of Dante's quest.[7]

Appropriately the personal encounter with her occupies the middle two cantos of the Earthly Paradise. It also occurs in the midst of the pageant of Revelation. A sudden light flashing through the divine forest announces, in canto XXIX, the approach of this allegorical spectacle. Dante indicates the heightened significance of his new material by invoking the assistance of the muses, particularly Urania, in his attempt to put in verse things that are hard for thought (37–42). The pageant is preceded by seven candle lights (the seven gifts of the Holy Spirit), and there follow then in order the twenty-four elders, representing the Books of the Old Testament; the four winged creatures, representing the four Evangelists; and within this group moves a triumphal chariot on two wheels and drawn at the neck of a griffin. The griffin, with the eagle's head and wings and the body of a lion, represents Christ in his divine and human natures. There are other details, as well, but all told the pageant stands for the Church with its full historical and theological resources.

At the moment of this revelation, Virgil has obviously nothing more to contribute. In canto XXX, Beatrice appears, and Dante, by way of habit, turns to Virgil with words that echo the *Aeneid* (IV.23): "conosco i segni dell'antica fiamma" (I know the marks of the ancient flame). But in this direct encounter with the spiritual and religious truth of his own life (where for the only time in the poem Dante's own name is spoken), Dante must stand alone and Virgil, his "dolcissimo patre," to whom he gave himself for salvation, can be of no help. Sternly representing the no-nonsense attitude of the *Purgatorio* and its ethical needs, Beatrice advises Dante not to shed any sentimental tears for Virgil, but rather to worry about his own salvation.

Beatrice proceeds to instruct Dante as to the significance of his straying. So blessed was he by nature and by grace that any kind of right training and good practice ("abito destro")—the educational and ethical concerns of the *Convivio*—would have produced admirable results (109–17). But the very strength of the original endowment also means that the results of misdirection are all the more disastrous. This explains why the damned in Hell have some elementary attractiveness, and why, for characters like Ulysses or Corso Donati, the enormity of their sins derives from the power of the original endowment. Hence, the dynamic of parallel extremes that prevails in the poem: from Heaven to Hell, from the very best to the very worst, the antipodal structure of the poem depends upon this basic sense of great human potential. Lucifer was after all the brightest angel.

In his lucid exposition Charles Singleton has shown that at the most basic level what Adam lost by his sin was the sense, or vision of, God.[8] At the same basic level, and perhaps that is the only clear one in this case, some such meaning applies to the

period of "straying" in Dante's life, the period coincidental with
Beatrice's ten-year absence (from her death in 1290 to the fictional
time of the poem in 1300). Her own accusations and Dante's confession support a more general interpretation of Dante's defection. First she reproaches him that when she died and changed
from body to spirit she became less interesting for him (127–32),
meaning that Dante's interests became largely material (witness
his interpretations of Fortuna or of Roman history). In his own
confession (XXXI.34–36) Dante, again adhering to the same level
of generality, confesses his reliance on "present things." These
absorbed his interest after Beatrice's death. And finally, in canto
XXXIII, Beatrice refers to Dante's misplaced commitments as a
"school" whose doctrine was as far from the "divine" as the dis-
cord on earth is from heavenly joy (85–90). Rather than specific
doctrinal errors, the real error in Dante's ways could be called a
more general loss of the sense of divinity and a concentration on
those things that do not last, that are only of "breve uso." In fact
the entire scene of accusation and confession can be restricted to
generalities because we have already been given in the *Inferno*'s
full detail the nature of the false allegiances which Dante had to
sever.

Following this intensely personal confession, the last two cantos
of the Earthly Paradise turn to the role of justice in the public
world, where understandably the results are far different. Like a
splendid army wheeling around, the pageant executes a turn,
and Dante and Statius follow it through a wood, now empty of
people. Like the forest itself the tree around which the procession
now gathers is denuded, all the fault of the first parents. On the
literal level, this is the tree of the knowledge of good and evil, the
injunction against which Adam (XXXII.37) and Eve (XXIV.115–
17) had violated. Consequently, built into the allegorical reading
of the cantos must be the basic story of obedience and disobe-
dience to God's will. Later, in canto XXXIII (56–72), Dante will
be more specific: the height and the shape of the tree (it is an
inverted cone) indicate that it is something set apart and serving
God's particular purposes. Then Dante goes on to state directly
that by the signs and prohibitions it should be known that at the
moral level of interpretation the tree stands for God's justice on
earth.

In the moral-allegorical interpretation of this scene, obedience
to God's plan of justice is enjoined upon the two highest institu-

tions, the Church and the Empire. Just as Christ on the cross brought life back to the first violated tree, so here the Griffin's actions serve as an example to Christ's Church if the stripped tree of justice is to reflourish in human life. But the proper observance of God's plan entails two different kinds of actions, one of abstention and one of cooperation. The prohibition that the Griffin in his exemplary actions directs to the Church is that, unlike Adam, it does not eat of this tree. That strips of this tree were used on the terraces of the gluttonous suggests a proper attitude of renunciation toward the goods of life. (Although technically they are different, it is very difficult, generally speaking, to separate this tree of God's justice, which is his plan for the right functioning of human society, from the tree of life and human history itself.) The Griffin's abstention is an act of obedience: "Blessed art thou, Griffin, that dost not pluck with thy beak from this tree, sweet to the taste, for the belly writhes in pain from it" (XXXII.43–45). By violating God's prohibition, by taking to iself what is God's justice, the Church consumes goods that it can ill digest.

Yet, this is only one-half of the Church's necessary relation to God's will. By some connection, not clearly understood by Dante, the Church does have a positive relation to God's justice. Just as Christ's cross redeemed Adam's tree, so the wooden trunk of the chariot when attached to the tree causes it to spring back to life. God's idea of justice (the moral seems to indicate) is not served when the Church actively takes hand to the tree and its goods; but neither is it served when the Church and the vision of permanence that it has in its custody is divorced from the exercises of justice. Justice is a divine principle to which both Church and State must be subservient. This has been Dante's consistent position throughout the *Commedia*, one that will be more clearly and more forcefully expressed in the *Paradiso*.

Beatrice, having witnessed the ideal workings of Church and State implied in the Griffin's actions, next shows Dante the historical realities that have frustrated that plan (109–59). Beginning with the persecution of the early Christians by the Roman emperors and extending to the slap at Agnani and the removal of the papacy to France in Dante's own time, the many scenes suggest the disasters that have contravened the right working of the ideal order: rather than cooperation first the Empire and then the Church exceed the limits imposed upon their right function-

ing. But things, of course, cannot be left there. In canto XXXIII
Dante shows his essential hopefulness in the providential design.
Beatrice prophesies the coming of a new leader, "the five hundred,
ten and five" (37–45). Commentary is generally agreed that this
new "deliverer" can only be a secular monarch—an heir to the
monarch, presumably Henry VII of Luxembourg. There was of
course much precedent for such numerical prophesying, where
numbers were transposed into letters—the five hundred, ten and
five becoming the DXV, or the DVX (*dux* or *duce*, and hence
leader).[9]

While the result of this and other fervent prophecies would
prove to be unhappy, Dante himself has managed to regain the
right order of his individual being. Dipped into the restorative
waters of Eunoe (just as he had been submerged in Lethe, where
sins are forgotten), Dante completes the process that was begun
in *Purgatorio* I (again with the emphasis on personal renewal):

From the most holy waters I came forth again remade, even as new
plants renewed with new leaves, pure and ready to mount to the stars.

While the purgatorial process restores Dante to the original
intended form, it does not provide him with complete fulfillment;
its aim is to make him ready, or disposed (*disposto*, as we shall
see, is an important word), to climb to the stars. The three-part
heroic structure of Dante's poem insists upon these modulations.
Dante's psychology of positive attachment was misplaced in the
Inferno. At long last, after a painful process of correction in the
Purgatorio, his misdirected motives have been righted. It is now
left for Dante to realize the fullness of his nature assisted by the
great saints and martyrs.

CHAPTER 7

Commedia: Paradiso

I *Principles of divine comedy*

A S the fullest expression of divine comedy, the *Paradiso* represents the height of Dante's poetic achievement. In this last
cantica of his great trilogy, Dante is more than elsewhere the poet
of faith. The *Paradiso* is his Book of Psalms, and he is a David
invaded by the holy spirit, taken over by his material, whose
willing scribe he has become. His poem is a work in praise of
"the glory of Him who moves all things." His *commedia* has
become a *poema sacro*, even, as did David's, a *teodia*. The poem
is literally a song in praise of the mystery, the wonder, the power,
and the love of the divine nature.

With his acute aesthetic self-consciousness Dante was aware
of the experimental nature of his last book, as well as of the difficulties involved in figuring forth or finding the physical equivalents for the most intense moments of spiritual joy. His language
frequently becomes exclamatory; it becomes saltatory, leaping
from one bright moment of illumination to another. And yet
these intensities are lodged in a coherent system, a cosmos of
sights, sounds, and images. Principles of dramatic variety—
present in the other two books—are spread out over a wider
emotional range, as we move from the lyricism of marvelous joy
to dialectical discriminations over vexed theological problems,
to inspired identifications with models of the Christian ascetic
ideal, to moral outrage and bitter invective, all coordinated and
alternated within an imaginative structure of extraordinary poetic
power and consistency.

The *Commedia* is devoted to transcendence. It was not for
Dante, the aspirant poet of high hopefulness and energy, to rest
his case with the restraint and containment of the *Purgatorio*.
In the *Paradiso*, the true heroic paideia of fulfillment is reestab-

lished. Dante's poem gives expression to those figures from the past whose living force and memory, whose continuing historical impact, seem to defy death and in the totality of their commitment and message inspire in those who have absorbed their meaning and message a remarkable feeling of uplift and identification. In the encounters with such figures as Francis, Cacciaguida, or Bernard Dante is carried beyond himself. What the *Paradiso* does is to revive the model theory that was present but misused in Hell. The models that should have inspired him and directed his way did not do so. They were in effect false gods. In the *Paradiso* the true relations of paideia are restored as Dante responds to the likenesses offered by the superior models.

By this revival of the model theory in the *Paradiso*, we observe the parallel extremes that exist between the two outer poems, and learn something about the nature of divine comedy. As a theodicy, it asserts the essential validity of creation. This means that although the energies and the use of heroic models were misdirected and inverted in Hell, such energies and heroic models are not themselves ruled out. Their basic force and idea and their true intent remain intact. They only need to be utilized and directed properly. For this reason an essential ingredient to divine comedy is the "second chance," the fact of repetition. Many paradigmatic situations of the *Inferno* will be repeated in the *Paradiso* with far happier results. Paradise will successfully complete the heroic possibilities that were denied in Hell. The mold itself remains, only to be reinvested with greater validity and more appropriate personages, as we shall see when the meeting with Cacciaguida in many respects duplicates the paradigm of the meeting with Brunetto Latini.

The *Paradiso* is consequently a poem of fulfillment and of completion. It is the fulfillment of that which the earlier *cantiche* are a prefiguration. Aesthetically, it rounds out the network of reference, the elaborate system of anticipation and retrospection— in short, the remarkable poetic performance that the *Commedia* is. The *Paradiso* is the poem not of time but of eternity, the poem where human vision approximates the fullness of the divine. The family lines that have been so separated come together, as we learn the fate of the last of the Donati. The parallels suggested by similar placement are also completed, as Piccarda summarizes and transcends the line of Francesca and La Pia, and Justinian does the same to the political argument initiated by Ciacco and continued by Sordello. The total design becomes clear in *Paradiso*, in a way that cannot but be embarrassing for those who linger over the *Inferno*. By simile and direct address we are asked to look back again on the road we have traveled and reflect on how far we have come from the "mad flight" of Ulysses.

In order to show the height of the occasion to which he must rise, Dante in canto I goes beyond the Nine Muses and invokes the aid of Apollo; Dante would become a vessel of Apollo's power (just as Paul was the "vas d'elezion")—such transcendence is required if Dante is to be worthy of the laurel. In his search for the poetry of self-transcendence Dante requires such inspiration. This invocation has, however, a very specific cultural context. Well before Petrarch's own coronation (an event that came to symbolize for the literate West the beginning of the poetic renascence) Dante himself cherished the reward of the laurel. Later, in canto XXV and in his correspondence, we shall see that this was not an empty projection.

Turning from the inspiration that comes from without, Dante next addresses the human will and its heroic resolve. The pursuit of the laurel has fallen into neglect since the time of Statius, and this lapse Dante attributes to the failure of human aspiration, to a vision of life that is insufficiently heroic (the unstrung bow of which Marco Lombardo complained). But Dante's own pessimism about the present becomes optimism in regard to the future and his role in it. As Virgil helped Statius, so Dante's own work might inspire the poets who follow him:

A great flame follows a little spark. Perhaps after me prayer will be made with better words so that Cyrrha may respond.

This terminates, as Dante's letter to Can Grande informs us, the prologue of the poem.[1] But in the prefatory verse to canto II Dante again addresses the innovative achievement of his poem. "L'acqua ch'io prendo già mai non si corse." The waters that I take were never sailed before. Dante is a poet who knows what he is about: he is the first poet to put the Christian story, told through the history of his times, into an epic form and style derived from the classics.

Dante then shows his own sense of a divided readership. This division in his appeal had been present ever since the philosophical love poems. Those who follow him in a "piccioletta barca" ought to be wary about putting out to the high seas: their meager conception of the philosophical role of poetry will only result in their getting lost. Dante's poem is intended for the other few who early enough in their lives began the study of philosophy (the "pan delli angeli" which Dante in the *Convivio*, a much more popular work, tells us he gathers from the table of the true philosophers).

II *Doctrine and Example*

As he informs Can Grande in the epistle concerning the *Paradiso*, Dante's method is to mix argument ("definitions, division, proof, refutation") with "the setting forth of examples." [2] Of the first five cantos four are largely devoted to doctrinal matters and only the third canto to the kind of personal encounter at which Dante excelled. Despite the warning at the beginning of canto II, the new reader may feel that Dante miscalculated in making the early going of the *Paradiso* so heavy with doctrine. Yet Dante insists on the connection between the two: personal encounter exemplifies the doctrine and in turn leads to further questioning and the need to resolve further problems and doubts. The *Commedia* is an *Argo* of the intellect as well as of human action and inspiration, and it is just this intellectual heroism that fuses the cantos of argument with those where the heroic qualities are exemplified.

In these theoretical passages Dante lays down the basic principles of the *Commedia*. They are unified by Dante's insistence on the primacy of moral purpose and ideal end as being the true causative factors in the universe. Perhaps the best explanation of this faith is in George Santayana's essay on Dante in his *Three Philosophical Poets*, where he provides the background for Dante's spiritual idealism in the intellectual revolution effected by Socrates and Plato more than sixteen hundred years earlier. Socrates in the *Phaedo* showed his disappointment in earlier physical interpretations of the universe. He came to see the world as a "work of reason. It must be interpreted, as we interpret the actions of a man, by its motives." While, as Santayana concedes, this makes for poor physics, it does express a serious morality.[3]

By discussing the physical principle of Dante's ascent in canto I, Beatrice is really affirming a spiritual truth: man's capacity to respond to, and to reach out for, higher objects and truths is a natural fact, part of an instinct that returns man to God. The order of the universe is based upon such motivation: its objects follow physical laws and its creatures follow instinctive behavior. The same is true for "creatures of love and intelligence," or humankind. It is just as "natural" for them to rise to the Empyrean, that is, to respond to truths that lead them to an understanding of the universal forms. It is natural for man to be a thinker and a philosopher.

Nevertheless, unlike the lower orders of the Creation governed by physical law or instinctive behavior, man is free, free to fall as well as to rise. In the *Paradiso* Dante continues in his essential purpose of showing the ways of salvation that are available to man but also of explaining the reasons for his straying. In this third *cantica*, however, causality becomes less and less historical and more and more metaphysical. While never denying the historical failures of Church and State, still from the more philosophical perspective of the *Paradiso* Dante's thought comprehends more basic defects. In canto I, Beatrice uses the analogy of the artist who cannot achieve his design because of some defect in the material, "perch'à risponder la materia è sorda. . . ." This unresponsiveness in the material, a kind of perversity, finds its analogue in a man who will not respond to the promptings of divine grace. In canto VIII Charles Martel will propose another explanation of the all-too-evident human failure, while in canto XIII an even more pessimistic one will be offered. All of these explanations are touched by the air of resignation that shows itself from time to time in the *Paradiso*.

The discussion in canto II, while directed toward the spots on the moon, actually reinforces the message of canto I. The principle of causation in the world is not material or mechanical but spiritual. This was one of the important lessons Dante had to learn before he could accept the rightness of Roman rule. In fact, the image is the same as that of the *Convivio* IV. iv: the smith's hammer is the instrumental cause but guiding the hammer is the smith's rational intent, the efficient cause. Thus the spots on the moon are not caused by any thinness or rarity of substance, but rather derive from the nature of the angelic order controlling the moon's planetary life. A "diverse virtue makes diverse alloy" with the particular body that it influences (139–40). Using the analogy of the Fixed Stars, Dante sees this same principle operating throughout the universe: "Different virtues must needs be fruits of formative principles" (70–71). As Sinclair remarks in his commentary to this canto, it is a "great discourse on a small subject," one that not only allows Dante to develop his cosmology but his principle of diversity as well, a diversity based upon spiritual causes. The next canto will exemplify the unity that can emerge from this diversity.

It is significant that the first speaker for the Paradise is a woman. The meeting with Piccarda Donati in canto III balances the presence of the Virgin at the end of the poem, emphasizing that the new form of *virtù*, not present in the classical models that Dante followed, was feminine. In fact, in both the *Inferno* and the *Paradiso* the first contemporary to be encountered is a woman. Francesca and Piccarda, together with La Pia in the *Purgatorio*, constitute the first triptych of the poem, the first possibility of bringing out of their discrete positioning in the different *cantiche* personages whose qualities reflect on one another. Since La Pia in the *Purgatorio* is a paler version of Piccarda, the great contrast is between Francesca and Piccarda. Each speaks of a love of transcendent force, one which totally overwhelms the individual. But Francesca's love is tragic; it is somehow not ony a victim of violence but implicated in violence as well. This is *l'amore* that involves *la morte*. When she declares that love led them both to one death, she actually blames love. Consequently Dante threads her account with an ironic commentary that inspires distance and finally a lack of compliance on the reader's part. Piccarda's account inspires no such restraint but rather openness to the full force of her exemplary virtue.

One line in Piccarda's response to Dante is among the most celebrated in the poem and is exalted by Matthew Arnold as a touchstone of the grand style in poetry, "E'n la sua volontade è nostra pace." [4] This abandonment of self does not mean an imprisonment in the self (or in another) as it does for Francesca, but rather a vindication of the self through the discovery of God's will. The eros of Francesca does not lead to the freedom and the philosophical growth as does the *caritas* of Piccarda. From Piccarda's story it is evident that every soul can come to understand the controlling principles that redeem its existence from randomness, giving it a coherence, a history and a completeness; and that these principles make not for tragic failure but for human fulfillment. From her account Dante can then see represented the answers to the questions raised in canto II:

It was clear to me then that everywhere in heaven is Paradise, although the grace of the Supreme Good does not rain there in one measure. (88–90)

Beyond that of approximately similar placement that in outline, at least, invites comparison, the other principle of collocation is familial. Here in canto III is completed the first of the family triptychs, the Donati, with Forese in Purgatory, Piccarda in Paradise, and Corso, moving rapidly in the direction of Hell and fully representative of its destructive and dissatisfied energies, just as Piccarda is representative of full contentment. As Cunizza will say of her brother Ezzelino, the firebrand of the north, "from one root came all of these different branches" (*Paradiso* IX.31). This reflection has several consequences. Although the scene is in Paradise, still there must be some melancholy, some edge of sadness touched as once again we experience the break-up and dispersion of a family. The very tripartite structure of the poem suggests this centrifugality. But the conjunction of the different stories also brings out the "full picture," the sense of completion, that is part of Paradise. The other personage in canto III, herself part of a familial triptych, reinforces this view. She is Constance, the female source of those Swabian powers, Frederick II, mentioned in *Inferno* X and Manfred, in *Purgatorio* III, in whose absence the destructive energies of a Corso Donati go unchecked. This further explains why Piccarda and Constance are together in canto III, as Dante shows the connection between the private fates and virtues and the larger public world in which they are inextricably involved.

Canto VI is unique in being the only canto in the *Commedia* that is entirely devoted to the words of a single personage. From the beginning to end, the single speaker is Justinian, almost as if Dante did not want to interpose himself in this unfolding of providential history. As part of his expansive network of connections, Dante aligns this sixth canto of the *Paradiso* with the sixth cantos of the other two *cantiche*, all of them devoted to political issues. In *Inferno* VI, Dante encounters the first Florentine in his poem, Ciacco, and the subject of their talk is strictly municipal. In *Purgatorio* VI, Dante's diatribe against "servile Italy" is the first broad political statement in the poem, one dealing with Italy's deplorable state, the vacant imperial throne and the restless and ineffectual energies of Florence. In his rising vision Dante takes

even more under his purview when in *Paradiso* VI he comprehends not only Florentine and Italian politics but the whole
course of providential history.

Justinian's survey thus completes the single line of political
speculation that was initiated by the events of 1300–1302, discussed in the *Convivio*, more fully in the *De Monarchia*, politically
outlined in *Purgatorio* VI, in the Marco Lombardo episode and
in the allegory of the Earthly Paradise. In each of these works
Dante consistently argues for the independently derived
authority of the Empire, while suggesting that in some way this
secular arm of God is related to the spiritual vision of the Church.
Dante's political thought is neither theocratic nor secular. For
this reason *Paradiso* VI, is crucial: it shows by historical example
the tenuous but proper connections of the Church and the Empire.
While difficult to spell out, nevertheless this connection has been
hinted at in other works: Marco Lombardo tells us that a secular
power is required which has at least some sight of the heavenly
city. In "some way" Dante argues in the last book of the *De
Monarchia* the Empire is dependent upon the Church.

Almost as a prelude to his narrative Justinian shows that he
was able to accomplish his great task of codifying Roman law
only after Pope Agapetus had instructed him on the dual nature
of Christ (he had been a Monophysite, believing only in the divine
nature of Jesus). As soon as his steps moved with those of the
Church (another metaphor suggesting common purpose) he was
able to undertake and complete his divinely inspired task—"and
I gave myself wholly to it" (22–24). Dante is an idealist but not a
utopian: he can point in the past to a place and a time where the
kind of cooperative relationship he has in mind actually existed.

There are three great events in Justinian's account of continuing
Roman history, and each of them shows some interpenetration of
the religious and the secular. While the story of Rome is largely
secular, it shows through its roll call of great heroes a special
kind of divine endorsement, its heroes being the equivalents of
the saints and martyrs of Christian history. As a consequence
Justinian's narration begins with the death of Pallas, the son of
Aeneas's ally Evander. The sacredness of martyrdom, a kind of
personal touchstone for Dante throughout the poem, hallows the
origin of Roman history as it does Christian history. It is clear, as
it was in the *Convivio* and the *De Monarchia,* that the Roman
heroes are illustrious not only because of individual merit but

because they are instruments in the divine plan. The next great turn of the hinge of history occurs at the time of Caesar, when the divine will saw fit to bring the world together in a peace appropriate to the birth of Christ. The greatest triumph of interconnection between the powers of the Empire and Christianity occurred when the divine will made Titus (the son of Vespasian) its instrument for avenging the punishment of Adam's sin, the desruction of Jerusalem seen as revenge for Christ's crucifixion. Thus the third and last great turning-point of providential history, one marking the reestablishment of the Imperial ideal in more modern times, comes during the reign of Charlemagne, when he aided the Church under attack by the Lombards.

The epic narration has an ethical application (97 ff.), which expands upon earlier charges levied against the Ghibelline and the Guelph parties (31–33). The same "viva giustizia," God's living justice in history, transcends exact definition, and also transcends the dualities and oppositions of earthly antagonisms. Just as Dante's aim in the *Paradiso* is to bring concord out of diversity, so his other great purpose is to transcend partisanship. Dante was not happy being either Guelph or Ghibelline. The cause of the former was taken over by Philip of France, while the Ghibellines made the divine principle of justice a property of party. Like Milton, Dante could only become a party of one, one who had a larger sense of disinterested public service and love of justice than fierce political partisanship could tolerate.

Dante's sense of himself as more a friend of justice than of party, and his willingness to pay the price for his choice, accounts for the second presence in canto VI. For the reasons already indicated, the *Commedia* is a poem of likenesses, and a special fervor and intensity (as well as extended space) attaches to those models who bear within themselves a similarity to Dante's own character or fate. Exiles, martyrs, and all who suffered for unpopular (or even erroneous) beliefs send a shock of recognition through Dante, and are models of identification for his own difficult experiences. It is fitting then that after Justinian's pennant-waving account of Roman history Dante should turn to the fate of the single just man, Romeo of Villeneuve, who after remarkable service to Raymond Berenger of Provence became the victim of calumny. As Romeo (whose name means "one who made a pilgrimage to Rome") had come to the court, "humble and a pilgrim," so he chose to leave the count's service rather than continue to suffer under false accusations. And in so doing he becomes the model of the man who refuses to allow his mind to be tainted by the injustices done against him—"if the world knew the heart he had, begging his bread by morsels, much as it praises him it would praise him more" (139–42). In Dante's complex referential system, the role of Romeo contrasts sharply with that of Pier della Vigna, who committed suicide rather than suffer under the accusations of the envious. Although not similarly placed, nevertheless they are coordinated enough in basic story, to show how Dante is manipulating two models: one who represents no way out, and the other who is a guide to Dante's own way of coping with exile and slander.

Justinian's account of providential history must be complemented in canto VII by the story of sacred history. The great moments of sacred history between the "last night" and the "first day" are the cardinal moments out of which Dante builds this canto, just as Milton used them so effectively in his *Ode on the Morning of Christ's Nativity* and *Paradise Lost*. The material is further linked to canto VI by the lingering question: How could Titus have justly punished an act that was inherently just? But the real point of the discourse and its true connection with canto VI lies in the exposition defending the theoretical and logical necessity of the belief in Christ's dual nature, his divinity and his humanity. This belief, which emerged from the Councils of the early centuries of the Church, is associated with the other major conciliar achievement, that of the Trinity, which will become dominant in canto X. The divine solution seems the best of the alternatives offered. Man could not possibly redeem himself, nor could God freely pardon him. Hence, the providential wisdom was just and profound in requiring the humiliation of the second person of the Trinity, who in turn would permit man, by imitation of his life and death, to restore in his soul the divine image that was lost at the Fall (112–20).

As Dante rises to the circle of Venus he must once again confront the important point of astral determinism, especially in matters of love. The world once believed to its peril, he says in the opening lines of canto VIII, that "mad love" ("folle amor") originated in this planet. This is the kind of love for which at the outset of the *Inferno*, Francesca was an apologist. But in his Christian comedy the love that Dante extols is that of freedom, one allowing the possibility of intellectual development, not fatality. Consequently, in this canto where the earlier meeting with Charles Martel is enshrined, Dante is remembered by the *canzone* that announced his own new philosophical development, *Voi che 'ntendendo*. Furthermore, love is placed in a context of good government (lines 73–84 contain political advice for Charles Martel's brother, Robert of Sicily, who seems to have declined from the standards of the Angevin house) and philosophical discussion. In this canto, from recollections of a Charles whom he briefly knew, Dante is drawing his model of the ideal ruler—a gracious and generous patron, a lover of both poetry and music, a ruler concerned with the welfare of his subjects, and, finally, a philosopher. Had he lived longer the' political turmoil between Guelph and Ghibelline might have been resolved by means of his marriage to Clemence, the daughter of Rudolph of Hapsburg. But Charles was another of Dante's defeated hopes, an earlier Henry VII, who was not allowed to realize his potential. It is this experience that forms the necessary background to the metaphysical discussion at the end of the canto. One could almost say that Charles Martel was to Dante what Hamlet was to Shakespeare, and the extended discourse in each case is used as a means to suggest the kind of ruler each would have been.

The question that is finally addressed in the canto is one that was raised in the related canto VII of the *Purgatorio* and that has behind it the full argument of *Convivio* IV. How is it that such differences, and more than simple differences, such decline, can occur between parents and children ("Com'esser può, di dolce seme, amaro?"). Charles Martel begins his discourse (94–112) by reaffirming the spiritual order of the universe—matter similar to that set out in canto II. But this leads to far more interesting speculations (113–38) that begin by showing the reasons for Dante's commitment to the city and lead to his sense of divine comedy. Dante concedes as a self-evident proposition that the best existence available to man is in the city—his life would be far worse were he not a *cive*, a citizen of a political entity. The *Commedia* exists within the dimensions of the city: Hell as a place of disorder is a *città dolente;* Dante can rest only a brief time in the garden of the Earthly Paradise, his true destination being the heavenly city, that city of which Christ is a Roman; and the central cantos of both the *Inferno* and the *Paradiso* are concerned with Dante's definition of himself in relation to Florence.

At the basis of urban life is the principle of diversity, various people with various skills banding together for mutual benefit. Only the city can muster a symphony orchestra. Therefore, since the city itself is necessary to human welfare and diversity is part of the attractiveness of the city, it follows that people must be born with different inclinations and endowments at birth. Thus divine providence sees to it that we are by a kind of natural aptitude lawmakers, soldiers, priests, or artisans (the last example, Daedalus, not mentioned by name but by a periphrasis crucial for this context, "he that flew through the air and lost his son"—122–26).

But this principle of diversity so necessary for the city is also the root of its undoing. As Sordello tells us in *Purgatorio* VII, men do not receive virtue through the loins, but rather from God himself. Were every child to inherit his father's whole worth, one would be what he is because of what his father was. The same kind of historical presumption would set in that Dante had so combated in *Convivio* IV, where he insisted that it was not the *schiatta*, the family line, that was important, but rather the individual's capacity to realize his own form of being, to rise by the capacity of the possible intellect to a secure understanding of himself in relation to divine principles. This larger understanding accounts for the philosophical felicity that converted exile into a fortunate fall. By being uprooted from his city Dante was forced to come to terms with the universal principles of his being. It is for this reason that in divine comedy historical values and generational continuity are disturbed, and that instead of lineal values or linear direction we are subject to sudden shiftings, to tragic risings and fallings, the system of parallel extremes rather than a middling level of social order. In order to show his power, to bring mankind back to to himself, the divine wisdom bestows different aptitudes on different members of a family (127–32). This is God's will and one of the surprises of divine comedy: "the begotten nature would always take a like course with its begetters if Divine Providence did not overrule" (133–35). Dante's examples (Jacob and Romulus) are archetypes of basic divisions in human experience, where from the very outset their differing natures can set brother against brother. Diversity, the positive principle of earthly felicity, is also the basis of division, and ultimately of historical and social unrest. These are Dante's most serious efforts (already reflected in the historical explanation of Brunetto Latini in *Inferno* XV as to the root of hostility in a specific city) to account for failure in the most crucial forms of social organization.

Canto IX, with its suggestions of sexual energy, seems to be far from the metaphysical speculations of the preceding canto, but it is nonetheless just as significant. In the divided stories of Cunizza and her brother Ezzelino, that "firebrand" from the north, another family completes its story. Ezzelino, a tyrant, his sister, a courtesan, were born of the same root. Yet that same passion finally led Cunizza to God. This is the most Dostoevskian canto of Dante's poem, where the sinner becomes the saint. In the single case of Cunizza a repetition prevails that also exists in the *Commedia* as a whole; by this second chance, individuals are allowed to look back on their lives and see under a noxious effect a good principle which when given proper direction can be set right. Divine comedy allows such recovery, that "second sight," where the very force that in its misdirection was the cause of trouble can be seen again as the principle of salvation. This is what is meant when Cunizza confesses that although the light of Venus had overcome her (we think back to the prologue of canto VIII): "I gladly pardon in myself the reason of my lot and it does not grieve me—which may seem strange, perhaps to your crowd ["vostro vulgo"]" (34–36).

That Dante should not only place a known courtesan in Paradise but also justify it according to God's superior plan needs some explaining. Consequently Folco, in his discourse, returns to the problem. Folco was the troubadour poet who later became the bishop of Marseille and combated the Albigensians. Not Dido nor Hercules burned more than he did with the fire of deluded love. Yet, he goes on to declare, he does not repent. Rather he rejoices that one and the same energy led him beyond tragic love, so that he was able to see the divine principles underlying his own life: "here we contemplate the art that makes beautiful the great result, and discern the good for which the world above wheels about the world below" (103–108).

Moreover, even the sexual generosity of a great love has in it a selflessness that transcends the getting and the spending, the trafficking in goods that seems to have consumed the sight of those whose vision was supposed to be higher. Consequently the canto's final section (127–42) is an invective against the careerists in the Church who have been corrupted by the gold florin of Dante's native city. The "decretalists" neglect the Gospels and the fathers of the Church in order to study the more profitable canon law. There is a coherence in Dante's attacks on the canon lawyers and all those other servants of the institution of the thirteenth-century Church that seemed to have cut itself off from the original impulse of the Christian religion: Innocent III and Boniface VIII, the defenders of papal supremacy, were themselves canon lawyers. Their thoughts, Dante complains, are not directed toward the spiritual message of Christ, toward Nazareth, where the angel Gabriel made the great Annunciation.

III   *The Middle Cantos, X to XXII*

In the canto of the sun Dante is no longer under the shadow of the earth, and this new level of being calls for a new proem (1–27) in praise of the Trinity and the superbly functioning physical order of the universe. Just as much as those who look back to the authentic Christian beginnings, so those who regard the heavens show the selflessness and dedication required of the true lover of wisdom. Therefore Dante can urge his readers to raise their sights to the circling heavens (7–12).

Canto X contains the pantheon of medieval thinkers whose brilliance surpasses that of the sun. Their contemplation of the mysteries of the Trinity satisfies all their needs (49–51). The logical interpreter of this philosophical gathering is the great synthesizer Aquinas. Just as Virgil was the mediator between Ulysses and Dante, so Aquinas mediates between Dante and each of the figures, forming as it were the twelve points of the sun's face. It is in the large synoptic tradition of Aquinas that Dante approaches these makers of the medieval mind.

From this gathering three figures stand out, two by inclusion and one by omission. They are Boethius, the eighth named, Siger de Brabant, the last, and Augustine. In the facts of Boethius's life, of his being falsely charged and imprisoned and then put to death, Dante sees a likeness to those of his own (the nine lines devoted to Boethius are more than those devoted to any other single figure in the circle). Boethius was one of the two philosophers to whom Dante turned after the death of Beatrice, and throughout his life, and especially here in the *Paradiso*, the arguments exposing the world's false promises and transiency, which he had first learned from Boethius, are increasingly evident. He came from martyrdom to "this peace": the rhyme words "mondo fallace" to "questa pace" by means of "martiro" will be exactly the words Cacciaguida, another likeness, will use in canto XV.

Siger had been Aquinas's polemical antagonist in life, syllogizing "invidious truths." That is, under the doctrine of the double truth he had discounted many important articles of faith essential to Dante's poem, such as free will and the immortality of the soul. Still he too is saved and in fact stands next to Aquinas. For Dante there was a saving power in the devotion of Siger to his ideas and his suffering because of them, another likeness to Dante himself. While it is remarkable that Augustine is exempted from this list that is only because he is reserved for greater things. In fact Augustine will take his place in the third tier of the Empyrean, just below John the Baptist, in the company of Francis and Benedict, representing at its highest point (even higher than Thomas) the philosophical tradition behind Dante, as Francis does the mendicant, and Benedict the monastic (*Paradiso* XXXII. 34–36).

The vision of spiritual harmony among these figures (that suggests the final concordant image of the clock) leads to the opening invective in canto XI against the careerism that is uninspired by any higher sense of service or dedication. Under the guiding spirit of Aquinas, Dante reasserts the common spiritual purposes of the two great orders founded contemporaneously in the early thirteenth century, the Franciscan and the Dominican. Love and knowledge, the great forces of Dante's world need to be conjoined, and indeed they had been in God's great plan of restoring his Church. Rather than rivals—as they appeared to earthly eyes and earthly ambitions—they were really allies. It is fitting, Dante writes (XII.34–36) that they be introduced together, "so that, as they fought for one end, their glory should shine together."

Cantos XI and XII each have two purposes, then. In the first a Dominican, Thomas, eulogizes the life of Francis, only to follow that praise with a condemnation of the Dominicans; in canto XII, a Franciscan, Bonaventura, praises Dominic, following that great story with an account of the decline of the Franciscans. In each of these accounts, the saint's origin is placed in a specific geographic location. Such placement represents the transcendent nature of his inspiration. Francis comes out of Assisi with the force of the sun rising out of the East. This explains the problem that Erich Auerbach first encountered when he approached canto XI and found that it contained none of the homely anecdotes and intimate details that went into the making of the saint's legend through the course of the thirteenth century. The saint's role was not tied to his character but rather to the role assigned him by Providence; "the personal reality of the saint had to be subordinated to his office, it had to shine forth from the office." [5] Yet while the details that Dante offers from Francis's life represent the transcendent nature of his mission, they can be quite concrete in showing the ascetic nature of his calling. Here in the *Paradiso,* almost for the first time (there were some premonitions in *Purgatorio* XXIII and XXIV) we are shown the ascetic ideal that will be so dominant in Dante's portrayal of the spiritual life. It will also form a standard by which the lapse of the religious orders can be measured. Without slighting the appeal that the contemplative life held for Dante we can understand why, in an important essay, Giorgio Petrocchi could claim that Dante's description of the ascetic life is the spiritual key to the *Paradiso.* [6]

The ascetic ideal that Francis fulfills is the imitation of Christ. While his individuality is consumed in this office (in obvious contrast to Ulysses's fire), nevertheless Francis did make a distinctive contribution to that ideal. If, as Auerbach has pointed out, the imitation advocated by Bernard and his followers led to contemplation and a mystical union, that of Francis is based upon "the imitation of the poor and humble life of Christ." What Francis effected was a "concrete renewal" of the succession that had been discarded for more than 1100 years; "no one else reformed the idea of integral succession from the bottom as he did." [7]

From the account showing Francis's marriage to poverty and the powerful growth of his appeal, two events assume importance. The first is the renunciation of his patrimony and the second the papal acceptance of his order. In the first case, acceptance of a life of poverty amounted to a denial of his earthly father and absolute dedication to his heavenly father. Against the charges of "follia" and the ever-present images of the foolish and overreaching son, Dante's own resolve may have been strengthened by this example of Francis. Artistically the same may have been true. Secondly, Francis consumed by his mission, did not shy away from taking his case before Pope Innocent III in 1210 in order to receive approval for a new religious order. He did not succumb to "viltà" for being a merchant's son, "but royally he opened his stern resolve to Innocent and had from him the first seal upon his order" (88–93). In these lines Dante suggests the cultural and historical significance of the revolution he effected.

Francis's originality is especially shown in the fact that he was a merchant's son, which Dante underlines by mentioning his father's name, Pietro Bernardone. The "viltà" that he had to discard is the same cowardice that Dante had to overcome in *Inferno* II before he could—a wonder to all—embark on a poetic adventure in emulation with the *Aeneid*. In both religious and literary life, and this is clearly Dante's understanding, these two sons of the burgeoning urban culture had an epoch-making impact.

The account of Dominic's life in Canto XII starts by locating him in a significant place. But, as with Francis, this localization does not personalize him, rather it makes of him and his inspiration something of a cosmic force. From the West and from Spain had come this "amoroso drudo," this holy athlete of the Lord. Francis representing the force of love comes from the East (at least metaphorically), Dominic the intellectual, from the West and these two great forces of love and knowledge converge. Together they stand for an ascetic ideal that is centripetal and cohesive in its power; sociologically this was all the more relevant and crucial in the thirteenth and fourteenth centuries, whose centrifugal attractions of money, goods and power, of sheer mobility, Dante had come to fear.

A lingering question provides the material for much of canto XIII. In canto X, Thomas had declared that into Solomon was infused so much wisdom that its equal has never since existed. If this is the case, what about Adam or Christ? But this answer itself, as in other instances, does not seem to justify the endeavor; rather Dante's larger intentions seem to be two-fold: to reaffirm the creative processes of the universe (31–111) and to issue warning against hasty or false conclusions (112–42). With all this, the important lines in the explanation are not those that reveal the fulfillment of the great chain of being, but rather those that show a strange and almost hidden defect in it. Here in canto XIII explanation goes beyond those offered by Marco Lombardo or by Charles Martel; the system itself is described as suffering a breakdown when recalcitrant matter is not fully receptive to the divine intent. Through a basic lack of synchronization, or harmonization of purpose, the wax of the material is not perfectly ready to receive the imprint of divine purpose. This means that ideal intention is realized only part of the time and in varying degrees. The same tree can have better and worse fruit. Diversity here is not generic, but rather qualitative within the same species. This means that perfect creation is almost impossible, and that man must be resigned to the fact that nature works defectively, "like the artist who has the skill of his art and a hand that trembles" (67–78). While this strain of thought was present in the *Convivio* and in the *De Monarchia*, and is in fact well known from Aquinas, it is not allowed to remain only an idea in the *Paradiso*, but rather takes on a new historical validity as Dante reflects on the defeat of all his great hopes.

Cantos XV to XVII, the physical center of the *Paradiso*, also form its personal and moral center, for there Dante learns from his true father the real meaning of Florence and derives from him more accurate information about his approaching exile as well as means for coping with it. There is some significance in the fact that Dante also derives his poetic purpose from this gruff old Crusader, literally addressing Dante from within the cross composed of holy warriors like himself. It is of some importance when one discovers a spiritual father, but joy is even greater when the spiritual father also turns out to be the biological father. For then the spirit is united with the flesh. And it is appropriate that this union should take place under the aegis of the Trinity. In fact one purpose of the *Commedia* is to bring the exiled son back together with the true father. The model-theory operating throughout the poem is based upon this quest for the father, which in turn calls for comparison between the two central encounters, that with Brunetto Latini in *Inferno* XV, and that with Cacciaguida here.

Each of these paradigms is in part like the other: each represents a father-figure, each concerns itself with Florence, and each contains prophecies affecting Dante's personal fate. Yet here the comparison stops. With Brunetto Latini the model-theory is dysfunctional; it is marred by role reversal (the student is on top, the teacher below), hidden agenda and restraint. The indebtedness that Dante faithfully records is matched by a greater sense of poetic and spiritual supersession. With Cacciaguida a proper *paideia* prevails, and Dante feels himself elevated to joyous identification with his progenitor: "You are my father, you give me all boldness to speak, you uplift me so that I am more than myself" (XVI.16–18). In this contrast we observe the working of "repetition" in the structure of the *Commedia*. The father mold is not discarded; rather it is retained and after an arduous process reinvested with its true value. This means of course that while revelation in the *Commedia* is progressive, it is also retrospective. We cannot truly judge Brunetto (or for that matter, Francesca or Pier della Vigna and the others) until we know Cacciaguida, or Piccarda or Romeo. In this further sense, the *Paradiso* communicates a sense of completion, of rounding-out impressions that were earlier left fragmentary. In the *Inferno* our own judgments were equal to the light afforded by the level of experience; now we understand the totality of all meanings.

The meeting with Cacciaguida is marked by convergences. As a Crusader, Cacciaguida represents the ideal cooperation of Church and Empire; he informs Dante of a Florence that while a secular city still existed within the belt of religious purpose (the bells of the Badia were still heard within the first wall); and he himself affirms at once his earthly being and his spiritual nature when he says that in the Baptistery (for Dante the spiritual center of Florentine civic life) he became at once a Christian and Cacciaguida. Later in canto XXV Dante will insist that his own religious-poetic efforts can only be suitably crowned in the same Baptistery.

For these reasons Cacciaguida is a better representative than Brunetto Latini of the true nature of Florence, and it is in regard to this idea of an historical Florence that Dante identifies himself. His own poetic purpose and personal nature are intricately tied up with the real meaning of his city. The myth of his city is a conservative one; back there in the hazy time of its first modern growth, Florentine life was marked by a kind of hard primitivism and restraint. The Florentines were a "sober" people not given to excesses of any kind. The way of life was cohesive and close to the materials provided by the locality itself: one of the prominent men of the community still wore leather and bone. In fact, Florence had not yet known the effects of trade with the East; in neither dress nor habits was its style luxurious. The centrifugal tendencies of the economic revival had not yet dispersed Florentine merchants and bankers throughout the Middle East and Europe, and wives, Cacciaguida tells us, were still assured of their burial place (in contrast to the present). The major culprit in Cacciaguida's account is the population explosion fueled by immigration from the countryside. Not only did population growth itself change the old way of life, but these new people brought in divergent ways, and the mixture was harmful to the health of the city.

Canto XVI thus becomes a litany of decline, of the loss of the names once prominent in the active life of the city. It can be compared to Guido del Duca's lament in *Purgatorio* XIV. And while Cacciaguida can blame the new people and the growth in population for this decline, his lesson in mutability remains incomplete until he rises to a metaphysical level beyond the ethical and historical and sees his city under the sway of Fortune. The Boethian strain heard in *Inferno* VII here is filled with a more specific and poignant meaning:

All your affairs are mortal, even as yourselves, but in some things that last long this is concealed, and lives are short; and as the turning of the moon's heaven covers and lays bare the shores unceasingly, so fortune does with Florence. (XVI.79–84)

Between the poles of caring and noncaring Dante's poem revolves. On one hand Dante's prophetic stance, vitally concerned with a political and religious *renovatio*, virtually forbids him to turn his back totally on events and their causes. But yet another part of his nature must be willing to place the fortunes of his city and himself in the perspective of universal change.

Canto XVII is the most personal of the three, where Dante learns of his own fate, his involvement in this chain of historical events as well as his means for transcending history. Throughout the *Inferno* the fears that Dante had to overcome were those of overreaching. Was he a Phaethon or an Icarus in his poetic ambitions and in his sense that not he but his city was in the wrong? The allusions of *Inferno* XVII are naturally enough repeated in *Paradiso* XVII. Just as Phaeton had turned to his mother in order to be reassured, so Dante turns to Beatrice and to Cacciaguida in order to reassure himself about the predictions he had heard throughout the *Inferno*. We see here the importance of the historically based encounter with Cacciaguida. Unlike Ulysses, to whose flight the word "folle" would be later applied, Dante in his mobility was not centrifugal, but rather centripetal. He has behind him the historical connections and physical and biological roots from which he derives sustenance and for which Cacciaguida is the natural spokesman of fatherly reassurance. Dante is not a rebel against the earlier Florence and its true meaning, but rather against what Florence had become. She is the false stepmother as, continuing the image of the young man, Dante is no longer Phaeton or Icarus but rather Hippolytus, the just son wrongly accused (46–48).

In precise terms, suggesting his comprehension of the human suffering involved, Cacciaguida shows Dante the earlier stages of his exile (31–69): his separation from the mad and ungrateful company of fellow exiles, so that he was right in making himself a party of one, and the hospitality extended to him by Bartolomeo della Scala and later by Can Grande della Scala (70–93). Finally he urges Dante not to envy his enemies, since his own life, or fame, will far outlast their infamy (94–99). But it is precisely this future life and the possibility that his own poem might jeopardize his later fame that is the occasion for Dante's defense of his historical method in the poem. In the letter to Can Grande, Dante shows its nature as a comedy; in the proem to canto XXV, he calls it a *poema sacro;* here in the presence of the voice of Florentine history itself, he defends its historical basis. Cacciaguida's response to Dante's fears becomes something like a second preface (similar to the opening of Book IV of the *Decamerone*), where Dante is reacting to the reactions to his first two *cantiche.* Why should Dante have used specific historical cases? Would it not have been better to use fictionalized and mythic characters? Dante is right in coming to the defense of one of the most distinctive and important features of his poem, its historical nature. Cacciaguida's first reaction shows Dante's own straight-ahead will and moral purpose: Put away falsehood. Express everything that is part of your vision (and here we see as a defense, fidelity to experience). And let them scratch where they itch (127–29). And since the aim of the poem is ethical, that aim can only be enhanced by historical veracity. There will be less of an inclination to doubt or dismiss well-known episodes of contemporary history. For this reason, then, despite the presence of some no-accounts in the *Inferno,* the *Commedia* is a poem of significant people, people whose falls and whose stories are true and representative (136–42). For this reason then in Dante's poetic universe the historical becomes the typical. And in this, in his own contribution of historical types to the mythic repository of modern literature, Dante is more like Shakespeare than Milton.

There is one other important feature of the poem that becomes clear in these cantos. In canto XVIII, still in the planet of Mars, Dante is associated with the Nine Worthies (37–48). The bewildered and uncertain central character who set out with Virgil on a pilgrimage that was terrifying has now become the meritorious hero of his own Christian epic, not without reason later to be called a *Danteid*. Dante is the epic hero of his own poem, and this transformation is completed in the cantos where he receives full and painful confirmation of all the horrid prophecies. This coming together of the "good news" with the "bad news" helps explain the crucial decision Dante made in regard to his poem, that of antedating it, of placing it in the year 1300 so that he can fictionally anticipate as not yet having occurred events that had already happened. What Dante in effect discovered after his exile, that is, the personal resources and means for coping with it, is dramatized as a developing reality prior to that event. What Dante's temporal strategy allows is for this realization of exile to coincide with the full means for coping with it. Terrible recognitions and their remedies coincide; catastrophe and resolution are cotemporal. This formula is essentially antitragic, if not comic, imitating the Christian pattern whereby the Resurrection soon follows the Crucifixion. Only the time-system adopted by Dante would permit this dual purpose, the parallel development of the hero and his agony until both lines reach their height of development at the same time.

Cantos XXI to XXII show the wide range of Dante's sympathies, evidence again of his evolution. In these two related cantos, Dante, the son of a city, who grew up under the tutelage of Brunetto Latini and his brand of civic humanism, shows his own appreciation of the contemplative-ascetic ideal that motivated the spirituality of the Middle Ages. Like that of the other transcendent figures, Damian's account of his life begins with a significant geographic location, that of the monastery in the Apennines, not far distant from Dante's Tuscany. Moreover, in this account, as in those of Francis earlier and of Benedict in the next canto, there is a basic similarity: they are each associated with mountainous places. The danger, the risk, the precariousness of their rugged and heroic calling isolates them from the pleasant valleys. Yet Damian's monastery is not too distant from Tuscany, and the sound of the thunder, of the moral austerity and the terror commanding their existences can be heard in the lowlands, where their life-ideal of absolute dedication held great appeal.

Benedict's account of his work in canto XXII similarly begins at a mountainous setting and the founding of the famous Monte Cassino monastery. As we proceed higher in the *Paradiso*, a kind of historical direction takes hold: the higher up we go the farther back we go. From Francis and Dominic in the early thirteenth century, to Damian in the eleventh, we now are taken back in spirit to Benedict in the early sixth century, and the critical moment when the site of Monte Cassino (and the surrounding towns), crowned by a temple of Apollo and by a grove sacred to Venus, was converted to Christianity. Benedict takes us back to the first victories of Christian monasticism (37–45). But he also serves as an instance of rebuke for the fallen-away monks of Dante's day who find reasons for neglecting the rules he had established.

This attack on the delinquencies of contemporary monasticism is interrupted by a request that will become more dominant as we rise higher toward the Empyrean. Dante's fervent need is to do more than appropriate the living force and meaning of Benedict's life; his desire in fact is to see the saint's actual image. One of the *Commedia*'s great purposes, this need to recover the human image will only increase in dramatic importance in the final cantos. Benedict replies that only in the Empyrean will Dante's prayer be fulfilled; there all things stand where they have always stood because they are not in space nor in time (64–69). This is the vision of eternity required to overcome the bitterly felt experiences of disintegration so prevalent in Dante's world.

Cutting across Benedict's condemnation of the current practices of nepotism and concubinage (73–84) is another perspective, one, as we say, that modifies the ethical-historical import of the poem. This is the larger perspective of simple imperfection, metaphysically shown in canto XIII. Surely the point about Francis, Dominic, Damian, and Benedict as well as the other holy athletes of asceticism is that they as well as their messages were extraordinary. They were not simply individuals but inspired vessels for a tremendous force of renewal and spiritual rejuvenation. In fact they are signals sent by God to reestablish the right way for errant mankind. If, then, to proceed rightly requires superhuman power, to err is to be human. Dante's new vision of eternity and transcendence inclines him toward greater resignation in regard to purely human capabilities. Thus Benedict after uttering his moral outrage can understand why human nature falls away from its great models: "La carne de' mortali è tanto blanda. . . ." Mortal flesh is weak. Later in canto XXVII, Beatrice will utter a similar reflection: the very organic processes of living seem to forbid the continuation of the fervor of saintliness. New beginnings are made, the fire is brought back, but each time it is of brief duration, put out by the sheer weight of mortal existence. There is of course an

ethical reason for this straying: in Benedict's argument the followers have lost sight of the ascetic patterns provided by their
models, Peter and Francis (88–93); and with Beatrice the decline
can be attributed to the lack of a world government (139–41). And
Dante will never lose his hope in a new Redeemer, a great deliverer. Nevertheless along with such messianic fervor and ethical-
historical causality Dante shares a more resigned sense of human
limitations.

The final sections of canto XXII are preparation for the new
poetic material introduced when Dante leaves behind the planetary spheres. As Dante enters the region of the Fixed Stars, the
distributive agency for the individual qualities of life (as described
in canto II), he does so under the sign of the Gemini, that is under
the astral sign of his own birth. We recall that Brunetto Latini
found Dante's signs favorable to learning and philosophy, and now
that early promise is confirmed. As in the meeting with Cacciaguida, so here actual physical origins are confirmed, and
Dante's response is a song of praise (112–20). But this coming-
together of auspicious signs is really a gathering-in of strength
for the purpose of a further leap. To the same signs that have
been so remarkably generous he prays (121–23) for assistance as
he approaches the concluding section of the *Paradiso*, cantos
XXIII–XXXIII.

Within the larger area, however, these closing lines of canto
XXII form a boundary for the next block of cantos ending with
canto XXVII. On the verge of each new experience, Beatrice instructs Dante to look back on the earth and see how far he has
come. This backward vision is an important part of the instructions Dante has left us for reading his *Commedia*: a work built
upon supersession requires retrospection. Borrowing a page from
Cicero's *Somnium Scipionis* Dante now finds the earth contempt-
ible. From his experience of the order of the heavenly planets he
looks down again at our "aiuola," the threshing-floor (the earth)
that makes us so fierce. The word "aiuola" will recur in canto
XXVII when Beatrice again directs Dante's vision down to the
earth. In each case Dante's vision is synoptic, covering the known
world from the Ganges to the Pillars of Hercules. In canto XXVII
the language will be even more suggestive. He has moved six
hours westward so then he will be over Cadiz. Now he is able to
observe the Mediterranean littoral, from its eastern limits out into
the Atlantic; he is able to look back again on the mad outward

journey of Ulysses, "il varco / folle d'Ulisse" and to the eastern shore of the Mediterranean where the abduction of Europa took place (XXVII.82–84). The metaphoric suggestivity of this description shows the remarkable fusing power of Dante's imagination. Toward the West moves Ulysses, the prototype of Occidental man in quest of new experience, and on the dimly-perceived shores of Phoenicia an act of sexual molestation occurs. Intellect and love do not come together. These two misdirected energies of love and intellect (perhaps in the persons of Francesca and Ulysses the most crucial presentations in the *Inferno*) are to be contrasted with the centripetal directions of Francis and Dominic, the one originating in the East (at least by his association with the sun and the play on the name Assisi) and the other coming from the West, each meeting in the transcendent union of opposites. The working combination of these forces of intellect and love was for Dante the contribution of a Roman-centered Europe.

IV   *The Cult of Mary: Cantos XXIII to XXXIII*

Serving as an introduction to the remainder of the *Paradiso* the remarkable twenty-third canto announces a new sensibility and spirit in the poem. Not accidentally it is devoted to Mary, since the purpose of the last cantos will be to make Mary visible. This masterful poem of arranged intermediaries will at last reach the final intermediary, before Dante will witness the Christian Incarnation itself and see the second person of the Trinity, "our likeness." When he asked of Benedict, when he would be able to see the saint's "true semblance," he obviously was preparing us for this dramatic purpose. Here the two tendencies of the poem, metaphysical ascent and historical recession, converge. If to go up is to go back, then at the height of the upward movement we must return to the primordial Christian moment, when, for all time, man's image had been restored to the center of the cosmos. Naturally, then, the culmination of the two movements is a recapitulation of that event when history became ontology.

Unlike any other canto of the *Paradiso*, canto XXIII heralds its new material by opening with an extended, affective simile. "Come l'augello, intra l'amate fronde. . . ." This is the only canto in the whole *Paradiso* that opens with such a simile, reminiscent of the *Purgatorio*, and shows that the new philosophical heights of the poem will be informed by the lyricism of devotion to Mary.

Beatrice's captivation of Dante is such that she must remind him to look to the higher truth of Mary (70–75). She is the fair garden and the rose to which it was granted to bear the "divine word." Through her virtues man has access to divinity, and as was the case historically, so here by means of her man approaches the Incarnation (the process that is begun here and completed in canto XXXIII). Dante shows himself to be a devotee of this cult of Mary: hers is the name that he invokes in morning and evening prayers (88–90).

The next three are the cantos of faith, hope, and charity where Dante is examined by Christ's favorite apostles, Peter, James, and John. Dante is not only asked if he knows the nature of these virtues but also if he possesses them. The lyricism of the introductory canto makes this examination anything but dry. A remarkable and yet steady emotional flow carries the discourse from question to question.

The examination is interrupted in canto XXV by one of those remarkable proems that almost seem to outshine the material of the cantos. A biographical note is useful here. In 1316, letters were delivered to Dante by friends in Florence making it plain that if certain formal conditions were met Dante would be allowed back into Florence. Dante thought the conditions ignominious, the pardon not of the kind to be acceptable to the injured party, particularly a "familiar of philosophy, " a "preacher of justice." [8] In 1319 Giovanni del Virgilio wrote to Dante suggesting that if he were to write a poem in Latin rather than the vernacular, he himself would crown Dante with the poetic laurel in Bologna. Dante's response in the somewhat cryptic language of the Latin pastoral eclogue affirms that the sole place for such a coronation would be Florence.[9] Aided now by his coronation in faith by Peter, Dante finds his own poetic position enhanced. The hand that had trembled under the tremendous assignment now becomes that of the greatest poet of his day. The *Commedia* has become a *poema sacro* (it is called the *sacrato poema* in XXIII.62), inspired by heaven and earth. It, not a Latin poem, is the means by which, if ever, Dante will overcome the cruelty that has kept him outside of Florence. Evidently when Dante stopped working on the *Convivio* he did so because he thought his poem would be a better defense and explanation, a better means of reentrance to Florence. In the eclogue to Giovanni del Virgilio he expresses the confident hope that the *Inferno* and the *Purgatorio*, already completed, and the first ten cantos of the *Paradiso* will help him change his mind. As he affirms in the proem (XXV), the *Commedia* is the work upon which he will base his reputation. Then, if readmitted, he will return with a different fleece (his hair now gray) and as a poet. While Dante had used the phrase "poet" in his earlier prose work, particularly *De Vulgari Eloquentia*, it never had the full resonance it had when attributed to the regular Latin poets. Now a new worth is attached to the Italian phrase as Dante is sure of his own accomplishment, that as a poet of faith he has written an epic that has not only matched anything done by the classical regular poets, but indeed has charted new waters. For Dante the coronation of this accomplishment could only be rightly celebrated in the place where he once received his introduction to faith, the spiritual center of Florentine life (as it was for Cacciaguida), the Baptistery of John.

Having successfully passed the third examination on hope, Dante is stupefied when a fourth and unexpected light has joined the other three. The backward urge of these cantos is taken to its penultimate (cantos XXVII and XXIX will deal with the Fall of the Angels) when this light is identified as that of Adam. Dante's interest in religious origins propels him back to the first father, "l'anima prima / che la prima virtù creasse mai" (83–84). This remarkable re-creation of an ideal conversation with the first father naturally parallels in several respects the earlier one with Cacciaguida. The one is the father in the city, the other the more universal father, the father in the garden. And yet to each Dante has a biological relationship and from each he learns a lesson in mutability. From the first father he learns (103–42) that there were no sacred languages (a conception Dante still held in *De Vulgari Eloquentia*): the diffusion of tongues did not occur because of sin but because of mutability well before the Tower of Babel. Indeed, Adam explains to Dante that no work of mind or hand can last. That man speaks is a necessity, but the form of his speech is constantly changing. Thus the word for God changed in Adam's lifetime, and that is the way it should be, "for the usage of mortals is like a leaf on a branch which goes and another comes." And finally in this meeting dominated by mutability and time—Adam's computations of the time of his creation are laborious but precise—he informs Dante how brief and fleeting was man's stay in that garden existence, to return to which so much energy and time are devoted.

The backward sweep of Dante's genetic imagination reaches its full length in canto XXIX, when Dante, ever prone to mix the bitter with the sweet, brings together the great beginning of the Creation with the prototype of all future falls, the instantaneous making of the angels, the heavens, and the earth, with the abrupt insubordination of Lucifer. In this account Dante shows in what way man can merit salvation. This occurs not at his birth, in the essential given of his talents or nature, nor in the necessary completion of his acts or being, where another kind of grace is required. Somewhere in between, as Erasmus would argue in his famous dispute with Luther, man's merit is involved in his salvation. And this merit depends upon his reaction to his endowments. Should his gifts (like those of Ulysses or Corso, or, perhaps, even Guido) lead him to reject limits, to lose his humility and sense of dependence, his religious reverence, then he himself is damning himself. But should he, like the unfallen angels, remain modest within the limits of his created being, then he participates in, and in a way, merits the further grace and illumination of salvation: "Be assured that there is merit in receiving grace, in the measure that the heart is open to it" (64–66). This conception will help us to understand the exemplary role of Mary in canto XXXIII.

All of the other lights of Paradise grow dim as Dante turns to Beatrice in preparation for the final ascent to the Empyrean. Dante confesses his talents insufficient to describe the effect that Beatrice has on him, and in so doing arrives at a poetry of intense personal lyricism: "Dal primo giorno ch' i' vidi il suo viso . . ." (XXX.28–33). This address is prelude to the more substantial one directed toward Beatrice, when she finally yields her directing role to Bernard in canto XXXI. But before this happens, she shows to Dante the seat reserved for "lofty Harry," Henry VII of Luxembourg, "ch'à drizzare Italia / verrà in prima ch'ella sia disposta" (who shall come to set Italy straight before she is ready for it— again that emphasis on "disposition"). She also shows Dante the Church Triumphant. "Look how great is the assembly of the white robes," where the number of seats allotted for the saved is not far from being filled, suggesting that the world's end is close at hand.

Looking on the great assembly Dante, in a celebrated simile, is like a Barbarian coming from a dismal existence in the North to see the Imperial splendors of Rome. But this comparison gives only some slight indication of Dante's stupefaction when he moves from the human to the divine, from time to the eternal, and from

Florence to a "people just and sane" (XXXI.31–40). As a pilgrim making mental note of all the components in the church that he had vowed to visit, so Dante looks to see all the figures detailed within the ordered petals of the rose. His sight is able to take in the "forma general di paradiso," but when it comes to details upon which to fix his sight he requires new assistance, and this is provided by Bernard, a minister able to lead Dante toward the final vision of Mary.

Like Virgil's departure, so that of Beatrice provides occasion for a magnificent address. In fact, when we think back to Cacciaguida ("Voi siete il padre mio . . ." XVI.16–27), or to Adam ("O pomo che maturo / solo prodotto fosti . . ." XXVI.91–96), we see that Dante has evolved a new kind of poetry, one at which he showed remarkable skill, the poetry of direct address.[10] This form will reach its poetic height in Bernard's final address to the Virgin in canto XXXIII. In a poem marked by such "returns" these lines take us back to the *Vita Nuova*, with the sense of how much new experience has served to fill out Dante's reintegrated vision,

O Lady in whom my hope has its strength and who didst bear for my salvation to leave thy footprints in Hell, of all the things that I have seen I acknowledge the grace and the virtue to be from thy power and thy goodness. It is thou who has drawn me from bondage into liberty by all those ways, by every means for it that was in thy power. Preserve in me thy great bounty, so that spirit, which thou hast made whole, may be loosed from the body well-pleasing to thee. (XXXI.79–90)

This last request will be specifically repeated in the address to Mary.

The remarkable emphasis on physical image that has been so consistent a part of the upper Paradise is added to when Dante in order to express again his surprise at actually seeing Bernard compares it to the wonder of those who have seen the image of Jesus imprinted on the Veronica napkin (103–11). If the sight of Beatrice (Dante spies her "effige") prepares us to see Mary, so the sight of Bernard, by simile, is likened to the vision of Christ.

That Bernard should replace Beatrice and lead to Mary shows the specific historical dimensions of Dante's poem, since it was largely through his efforts that the cult of Mary spread through the twelfth and thirteenth centuries, taking possession of the Church, its cathedrals and its shrines. Thanks to him she became the great object of veneration and joy for Catholic Europe, one to whom, as Dante tells us in canto XXIII, he prayed mornings and evenings. She is the Queen to whom all of the Paradise is subjected and devoted. Amidst the enthroned great assembly of the saints Dante is able to see one light superior to the others, and finally he sees her smile (133–35).

Canto XXXII provides some prosaic relief between the intense lyrical moments of cantos XXXI and XXXIII—it provides the program by which we are to identify the saved arranged like the petals of a rose. Bernard then terminates this central discussion by having Dante look to Mary: "Look now in the face that most resembles Christ, for only its brightness can fit thee to see Christ" (85–87). As with the case of Bernard, so history itself determines Mary's penultimate position. Historically and physically she was the person closest to Christ. In her spiritual relations she also represents the closest that the human can come to the principle of divinity. She must then be the ultimate intermediary, the greatest human example, the principle closest to divinity whom we can still imitate. This is why the last canto opens with Bernard's address to the Virgin.

As was the case with Adam, Mary's comprehensiveness and divine origins are confirmed by her paradoxical relations, relations that transcend nature: "Vergine madre, figlia del tuo figlio." She is the Virgin Mother and the daughter of her son. So, too, on the spiritual plane her qualities are paradoxical: "umile e alta più che creatura." Mary's humility is the cause of her elevation. Although faith, hope, and charity are the cardinal Christian virtues, Dante's poem dramatizes how humility is the ground of these gifts, the basis of one's modest acceptance of whatever grace he may have received. Hence at the second start of the old road, at the foot of the mountain of Purgatory, Dante must descend to the humble reed that renews itself. This virtue and Mary's choice to embody it were not random—she was the fixed goal of the eternal counsel. From all eternity she was known to be the woman most deserving to bear the incarnate Christ. Mary is the chief exemplar because her humility makes her the fittest of women to be exalted by grace. She so "ennobled" human nature, "that its Maker did not disdain to be made its making."

This inspired saltatory address then moves to its main object, which is supplication of aid for Dante. Bernard prays that by her intervention Dante might be able to elevate his vision so as to see the ultimate salvation ("l'ultima salute"), the Trinity, including the Incarnate second person. The second request touches on the later history of Dante as character and poet, and reminds us that just as the pilgrim must return to the world of contingency so Dante the poet-visionary must go on leading his life, with all the weaknesses of the flesh, the fragmentation of purpose, that the battering of daily existence can produce.

This too I pray of thee, Queen, who canst what thou wilt, that thou keep his affections pure after so great a vision. Let thy guardianship control his human impulses. . . .

The last line repeats the kind of universal and simple language that Dante employs in the *Paradiso* to suggest the normality of human defection: "la carne de' mortali è tanto blanda" (Benedict, XXII); "la pioggia continua" (Beatrice, XXVII). So here the enemy is not some great evil, but simple "movimenti umani."

From this accessible human image Dante must move to the harder task of describing his vision of the great principles of the universe in their concrete form. Eight times in the remaining one hundred lines Dante expresses the inadequacy of his memory, his skill or his words to the experience he has had. Yet, the difficulties of approaching transcendence never reduce Dante to silence. After each such admission somehow his courage revives and he finally does leave us with vivid image of what he has seen. The alternation of these two means, the expression of difficulties and then their resolution, causes Mario Casella to call *Paradiso* XXXIII, "the most fragmentary and anxious of the whole poem."[11]

Dante's own endurance is rewarded when he is granted his first superior vision (82–90). He enjoys the abundant grace of being able to look into eternal light.

In its depth I saw that it contained, bound by love in one volume, that which is scattered in leaves through the universe, substances and accidents and their relations as it were fused together in such a way that what I tell of is a simple light.

Finally Dante has come to realize the philosophical capacity of the *intelletto possibile* that was suggested in the *Convivio*. The next lines tell us that Dante believed that he saw "the universal form of this complex." He has come to understand events, history and human conduct in the light of essential principles. From the point of view of eternity things acquire a coherence that they could not have had: they are redeemed from randomness. Outside of this eternal light everything is defective which is there perfected.

In the *Inferno* and especially in the *Purgatorio* we saw how powerful was Dante's sense of sheer dispersion and of mutability, how vast were the universal processes in which fragile human desires and wants were located; we also saw how much he valued centripetality as against centrifugality, the small enclosed nest that Florence had been as against the expanding city that developed. His great need was to see things as coming together, as part of great patterns, all of them having their origin in the great source of light. It is appealing then and quite autobiographical that the binding power of this divine principle should be likened to a book. Dante's own life, split by exile, was almost literally reconstructed and held together by the continuity of his book. The book is a rational cosmos where all things stand together as part of a system of relationships and patterns and where they are understood by wisdom.

Even after the surge of these visions Dante again lapses into poetic inadequacy (106–108). But this check is overcome when Dante's vision into unity becomes a vision into the Trinity (115–20). This complex figure had occupied a predominant position in the *Paradiso* since canto X. One of the poem's great realities, it was perverted in the person of Satan in the *Inferno*, and expressed in the joyful meetings with the great fathers, Cacciaguida and Adam, in Paradise. As a male line it balances the eminence of Mary. Given this personal meaning of the Trinity for Dante it is natural that the union with the Trinity should come at the climax of the poem. In it he finds completed his ultimate purposes: the restoration of man to his divine likeness and capacity. Focusing on the second circle of the Trinity, the reflected light of the Son, Dante sees there "nostra effige," our likeness in Christ. As in a flash Dante then comes to understand the mystery of the union of human and divine nature. He now has reached the summit of the hill he could not reach in *Inferno* I. This act of vision is followed by an act of love, as Dante senses his own will moved by the love that moves the sun and the other stars. Individually he has been granted what the larger collectivity has been denied— that is, Boethius's wish (quoted by Dante in *De Monarchia*) that mankind and its desires be ruled by the same love that rules the heavens.

CHAPTER 8

Conclusion

THE last years of Dante's life were spent at Ravenna, where he enjoyed great recognition and the patronage of Guido Novello da Polenta, the nephew of Francesca. There he died in 1321, not long after completing the last ten cantos of the *Paradiso*.[1] He was given an honorable burial, attended by the leading men of letters at the time, and the funeral oration was delivered by Guido Novello himself. Dante's *Commedia* soon became the *Finnegans Wake* of the fourteenth century: some twelve commentaries of various scope and size appeared before the year 1400. And in time Dante became celebrated in the city that had ejected him. Giovanni Villani included his life and praises in his *Croniche fiorentine* (1321). Boccaccio became the main curator of Dante's reputation, writing a life and then in the academic year 1373–74 delivering the first public lectures about the *Commedia* in Florence (which means of course that Dante was the first of the moderns to find his place with the ancient classics in a university course). Full restoration of Dante to Florence occurred in 1481 when the Signoria financed a splendid edition of the *Commedia*, with commentary by Cristoforo Landino and a prefatory epistle by Ficino himself. In this edition Dante was called the "divino poeta," and in the Venetian edition of 1555 the adjective was applied to the poem's title, which tradition has continued to honor: *La Divina Commedia*.

Some of the critical problems attending the reception of the *Commedia* revealed themselves very early in the poetic exchange with Giovanni del Virgilio. Later, in 1351–53, Boccaccio, having visited Petrarch, was disturbed that Petrarch's reaction to his fellow townsman was not as praiseful as it might have been. In 1359 Petrarch's response to another letter of Boccaccio, now lost, is curious.[2] He considers Dante's poem to be "noble in substance although popular in style." It is the "best of its kind," and he

189

quickly adds what he thinks of the kind. Some twinge of envy is felt in the statement that Dante enjoys great popular favor, but that he (Petrarch) does not need the "windy applauses of the masses." In the manner of Giovanni del Virgilio he concludes that Dante, while a great writer in the vernacular, did not sufficiently use the vehicle that would have insured highest praise, Latin.

This criticism set up a dualism that was to last into the period of full Romanticism, a kind of competition between the reputations of Dante and Petrarch. In the course of the classicizing tendencies of the Renaissance and with the prevalence of the standards of refinement and elegance (we can think of Cardinal Bembo in Italy and Malherbe in France), the "popular" style of Dante was doomed to suffer. In fact, this relative eclipse continued until the nationalistic and historical criticism of the nineteenth century replaced the grammatical and rhetorical standards of the seventeenth and eighteenth centuries. To these readers, whose rhetorical principles favored harmonious musicality of verse, Dante's style in the *Commedia* was rough (it is ironic that the style of the author of the *De Vulgari Eloquentia* was so regarded), and there was no evidence that his major poem abided within the classical unities as expounded in the commentaries on Aristotle's *Poetics* in the sixteenth century. Voltaire could be regarded as an outspoken representative of these views.[3] For him the *Commedia* was a "salmagundi," a potpourri of various styles, and its mixture of the heroic and the comic meant that the *Commedia* was neither comic nor heroic, but bizarre. As a matter of fact, Dante never achieved a great influence in France. His reception there was nothing like the continuing influence he exerted on English poetry (and eventually on Anglo-American letters) from Chaucer to T. S. Eliot.[4]

In the midst of full classicism and enlightenment, where Dante's poem was considered not only popular in style but even as lacking nobility of substance, Giambattista Vico initiated the modern reevaluation of Dante. In his *New Science* and in his introduction to the publication of an ancient commentary on the *Commedia* Vico was struck by one fact: Homer, the greatest poet of the classical world, wrote before the rules either of Aristotle or of Longinus were known.[5] In this sense a historical parallel existed between Dante and Homer, since Dante's powerful performance also predated the reintroduction of classical standards and rules. This poetic fact helped Vico derive a conclusion of great cultural importance: poetic wisdom and the creation of poetry may require a faculty to which philosophical wisdom and the creation of philosophy are antithetical.

By the very nature of poetry it is impossible for anyone to be at the same time a sublime poet and a sublime metaphysician, for metaphysics abstracts the mind from the senses, and the poetic faculty must submerge the whole mind in the senses: metaphysics soars up to the universals, and the poetic faculty must plunge deep into particulars.

Vico's approach bore two important implications for the nineteenth century, the great age of Dante. One was historical: Dante had to be understood in relation to his times (for Vico, this meant a Dante who possessed some of the concrete historical powers of the precedent age of barbarism; consequently Dante himself was a historical poet). The other was the legacy of the divided Dante; a Dante who would have been an even greater poet had he not been so interested in philosophy. The problems raised by the first and the dilemma of the second would preoccupy the Dante criticism of Francesco DeSanctis and Benedetto Croce.

Given the somewhat smug, certainly blithe, dogmatism of the eighteenth century, the historical purpose of the nineteenth can be attributed to motives of generosity. Its critical practitioners wished to understand and judge a work in regard to the particular events and ideas of its own time. This faith in historical criticism soon determined the situation in which DeSanctis found the state of Dante studies. On one side were the grammatical and rhetorical critics judging Dante by standards alien to his poem; on the other side were historical scholars of facts and currents of ideas, perhaps not judging the poem at all.[6] For DeSanctis neither approach by itself succeeded in elucidating the spirit and the poetic principles, the organic form and the procedures of Dante's poem. His aim was to apply history to literature, to show how the tensions of Italy's historical situation (divided between its classical heritage and its Christian past) helped create in the *Commedia* a poem about heaven and earth.[7] In fact, the virtue of the poem, its poetic greatness, derives from the special transformation the earthly figures undergo when perceived in the light of the eternal.

In one sense this tension helped produce the great vision of the *Commedia*, but in another it encouraged the critical problem of the two Dantes. The one is the poet of real-life passionate figures and the other the poet of pale, allegorical ideas. The end result of this division is that DeSanctis rarely extends his critical interests beyond the *Inferno*. He almost literally ignores two-thirds of Dante's poem. Two critical terms from the canon of Romanticism control DeSanctis's evaluations: one is compassion, a fellow feeling for the sufferings of Dante's characters, and the other is dramatic interest (lost are the ethical and religious judgments of classical reason and Christian faith). In his great essay on Francesca, DeSanctis does not protest that divine justice is wrong in punishing the pair of lovers, but that the value of her story derives from the dramatic pleasure we receive when we are witness to a brave woman, acknowledging her sin and error, yet still bidding for the gentle feelings of love.[8] It is this Romantic element (he will call it Byronic) that Croce in his turn will attack.

Croce, writing in the early twentieth century, was strongly anti-Romantic. His Dante is a man of faith, judgment, and will. In criticizing the Romantics Croce clearly has DeSanctis in mind: "They believed . . . that they could not find true passion outside certain confused, agitated, or violent forms or tones of passion, shot through with flashes of illumination serving only to deepen gloom and add exasperation to fury. . . ."[9] One virtue of Croce is that he restored to the twentieth century sections of the *Purgatorio* and of the *Paradiso*.

Nevertheless, like DeSanctis, he persisted in the division that Vico had made (in even more Viconian language): "Dante the poet is not the same thing as Dante the critic, and . . . the acts of poetic creation and of philosophical reflection upon it are two distinct and different acts. . . ."[10] DeSanctis, making the same distinction, separated the *Inferno* from the rest of the poem. Croce, however, applies his distinction to all three *cantiche*, setting aside what he calls structure from what he deems to be poetry. At one extreme this is a valid distinction: certainly we are all distressed by the hyper-literalists who do not discern that the *Commedia* is a rhetorical fiction and that debate over certain elements of the literal ultramundane journey are not too fruitful; moreover at certain times it is clear that the appeal of the story we are hearing (Ugolino's and Ulysses's) transcends the particular logic of its teller's placement in the moral structure of Dante's poem. Croce rightly points to some of the discrepancies between the needs of Dante the poet and the structure of his theological romance. But in most cases, as should be obvious, a sharp demarcation between structure and poetry is arbitrary and philosophically invalid. Either such an approach succeeds by its own rigorous application in impoverishing the poem, and immensely reducing its dramatic value, or its practical application (fortunately) contradicts its own theoretical principles (as Croce's does several times).

Croce has had a large following, but his radical position has also provoked resounding protests. While Michele Barbi was an early leader in refuting Croce, perhaps for our purposes we can point to the very significant anti-Crocean position taken by Natalino Sapegno in the *avvertenza* to his 1955 edition of the *Commedia*. The characteristic feature of this edition, he writes, is its firm resolve to renounce entirely that form of commentary that is called "aesthetic" and is totally given over to underlining particular poetic parts and separating the poetry from the non-poetry. Such an approach he calls a travesty of a poem like the *Commedia*, so unitary in its conception and imagination. His aim is to make apparent the fullness of the "poetic moment" of each canto in relation to its surrounding environment and the total structure in which it is placed.[11]

Far from being the naive remnant of an age of expiring barbarism (Vico), Dante was one of the bright lights of a remarkable culture, whose own historical dimensions he had himself traced in several of his works. He was supremely conscious of himself in relation to that culture, and in what ways he had superseded it. And his aesthetic self-consciousness went hand-in-hand with aesthetic confidence. He was aware that what he had attempted in the *Commedia* had never been attempted before ("L'acqua ch'io prendo già mai non si corse"), and that following his example many would come who would try to place the experiences of their time, controlled by a Christian pattern, in the frame of the large poem modeled after the classical epic.

What strikes us about Dante's achievement is the coherent power of his imagination, the way he was able to bring together a plausible ethic and metaphysic, a reasoned way of understanding human conduct, with the great historical events of his day. In his poem the personal and the public converge and even reinforce each other. He had the supreme power of understanding what was happening to him and the men of his time in the light of the great patterns of the Christian and classical past. This coherent imagination made him a poet of history as no one in the preceding age of "barbarism" had been. And the fusing power of his imagination makes of his work one of the most pleasurable to read that has ever been written.

Dante combines qualities in a remarkable way. His aesthetic

refinement was part of a powerful philosophical vision and ethical commitment. The evident clarity of his philosophical position and the crisis of his times made him a man with an urgent mission, a poet-prophet. Rarely has there been a poet who combined such religious passion with philosophical clarity and rational procedure. Obviously Dante has his Western side of rationalism along with his Dostoevskian side of passionate adventure. In Dante there is no separation among devout religious dedication and political involvement and ethical commitment, just as there is no sharp separation between his religious experience and common-sense reasonableness. Far from being the product of the historical division in Italian culture (as DeSanctis claimed), perhaps Dante, as he himself tells us, had behind him the beneficent influence of an integrated culture, which was of great help to him in his years of exile.

Despite the informing Christian pattern (or perhaps because of it, and the thirteenth-century reformulations of Christian theology) Dante's poem is enriched by great variety. How wide and diverse in its individual parts is the tableau of the saved in the *Paradiso*! Here again Dante's remarkable philosophical thought (and particularly the role of the Thomistic "possible intellect") permits this preservation of diversity in the midst of paradisal unity. In his poem adherence to the Christian pattern is filled out with the events and people of his time. Like Shakespeare—and this is a genuine contribution of DeSanctis's criticism—Dante's great value can be gauged by the types he discovered and created that have entered into the world of reference and association of modern thought. From real historical figures he created universal types. And in so doing he significantly added to the repertoire of modern myth.

Notes and References

Chapter One

1. For a very recent usage of this concept so active in the twentieth century, see I. A. Richards, *Complementarities*, ed. John Paul Russo (Cambridge, 1976), p. 108. Richards, relying on Niels Bohr, uses the phrase in more of an epistemological sense.

2. *A History of Europe*, trans. Bernard Miall from the French of the 8th edition (1936; New York, 1939), p. 89.

3. All quotations from Dante's *Commedia* come from *The Divine Comedy of Dante Alighieri*, trans. John D. Sinclair (New York, 1948), to which canto and line numbers given in the text refer.

4. "Rhetoric and the Classics in Italian Education," *Politics and Culture in Medieval Spain and Italy* (Rome, 1971), p. 621.

5. Quoted by Marvin B. Becker, *The Decline of the Commune*, Vol. I of *Florence in Transition* (Baltimore, 1967), p. 38.

6. See the Chronicle of Giovanni Villani for a description of the habits of the Florentine people shortly before Dante's birth (1259). *Selections from the "Croniche Fiorentine," of Giovanni Villani*, trans. Rose E. Selfe, ed. Phillip Wicksteed (Westminster, 1897), VI, 69. Excellent passages by Dean Church are reproduced in *Aids to the Study of Dante*, ed. C. A. Dinsmore (Boston, 1903), pp. 29 ff.

7. *Il Convivio*, new edition, ed. G. Busnelli and G. Vandelli, with appendixes added to 2nd ed., by A. E. Quaglio, Vol. V, *Opere di Dante* (Florence, 1964); English version, *The Banquet*, trans. Katharine Hillard (London, 1889). Here and throughout the text my references are to these volumes; because Dante's chapters are so brief I avoid page numbers.

8. I.vi, in *The Latin Works of Dante*, Temple Classics (London, 1919), to which all further quotations in the text from the *De Vulgari Eloquentia* are taken. For the critical Latin text see *De Vulgari Eloquentia*, ed. Pio Rajna, *Le Opere di Dante*, Edizione Nazionale, Vol. IV (1896; Milan, 1965).

9. *A History of Europe*, p. 375.

10. Nicola Zingarelli, *Dante*, Storia Letteraria d'Italia (Milan, 1914), p. 22.

11. *Selections from the "Croniche Fiorentine"* VIII. 10, pp. 312–13.

12. "Rhetoric and the Classics in Italian Education," *Politics and Culture in Medieval Spain and Italy*, p. 622.

13. *Li Livres dou Tresor de Brunetto Latini*, ed. Francis J. Carmody (Berkeley and Los Angeles, 1948), to which all citations in the text refer.

14. "Cicero and the Roman Civic Spirit in the Middle Ages and the Early Renaissance," in *Lordship and Community in Medieval Europe*, ed. Frederick L. Cheyette (New York, 1968), p. 300.

15. *Li Livres dou Tresor* II, 5. 2 and *Convivio* IV.iv.

16. "Cicero and the Roman Civic Spirit. . . ," p. 300.

17. Ibid., 292.

18. The critical text of the *Vita Nuova*, ed. Michele Barbi in *Le Opere di Dante*, ed. M. Barbi and others (Florence, 2nd ed., 1960); for the English version, I have used *Dante's Vita Nuova*, trans. with an essay by Mark Musa, new edition (Bloomington, Ind., and London, 1973), to which all citations (chapter numbers only) refer.

19. See the important discussion of this passage in Charles S. Singleton, *An Essay on the "Vita Nuova"* (Cambridge, 1958), pp. 15–17, and in Mark Musa, "An Essay on the *Vita Nuova*," in *Dante's "Vita Nuova,"* pp. 115–17 and n. 7, p. 186. The quotation seems to suggest the scholastic definition of God; see, in relation to Dante, Georges Poulet, *The Metamorphosis of the Circle*, trans. from the French by Carley Dawson and Elliott Coleman (Baltimore, 1966), pp. xi–xii. The young man's words do seem to suggest some moral or spiritual perfection in relation to which Dante is defective. Singleton sensitively reads a prophetic quality into the episode, one looking forward to Beatrice's death. See also M. de Bonfils Templer, *Itinerario di Amore: dialettica di Amore e Morte nella "Vita Nuova,"* Univ. of North Carolina Studies in Romance Languages and Literature (Chapel Hill, 1973), and "Amore e le visioni nella *Vita Nuova*," *Dante Studies*, XCII, 1974, p. 19. This issue of *Dante Studies* contains three other essays on the *Vita Nuova*.

20. See A. Schiaffini, *Tradizione e poesia nella prosa d'arte italiana dalla latinità medievale a Giovanni Boccaccio* (Rome, 1943), pp. 91–94.

21. See *Poeti del Duecento*, ed. Gianfranco Contini, 2 vols. (Milan and Naples, 1960), I.189–225 for a very full selection of Guittone's verse.

22. For Dante's verse that he did not collect himself see Gianfranco Contini, *Rime* (Turin, 1965), p. 32, and for English versions of all of Dante's Italian lyrics, see *Dante's Lyric Poetry*, trans. Kenelm Foster and Patrick Boyde, 2 vols. (Oxford, 1967), to which I hereafter refer in the text.

23. *Poeti del Duecento*, II.460 (all volume and page numbers in the text refer to this edition).

24. *Dante*, p. 55.

25. See the excellent comments of Fredi Chiappelli in his edition, *Vita Nuova e Rime* (Milan, 1965), pp. 6–7, and 41, n.2. These remarks, though brief, are nonetheless valuable.

26. *The Chronicle of Dino Compagni*, trans. Else C. M. Benecke

and A. G. Ferrers-Howell, Temple Classics (London, 1906), to which all book and chapter citations in the text refer. For the Italian see *La Cronica Fiorentina di Dino Compagni*, ed. Isidoro del Lungo (Milan, n.d.). There are no chapter divisions in Book III of this edition.

27. *The Decameron*, trans. Frances Winwar, The Modern Library (New York, 1955), p. 374.

28. *Poeti del Duecento*, II.544, to which all further citations in the text refer.

29. Contini, *Rime*, p. 35.

Chapter Two

1. *The Earliest Lives of Dante*, trans. James Robinson Smith (New York, 1901), p. 83.

2. See Chapter 1, n. 7 above.

3. See the excellent notes, here and throughout the Busnelli-Vandelli edition of the *Convivio*.

4. The changed circumstances of Dante's later position seem to be the simplest explanation of the differences between the *Vita Nuova* and the *Commedia*. The other far more controversial thesis holds that the *Vita Nuova* had another ending in an earlier version; it ended with the consolation being offered by the "donna gentile" rather than with the triumphant return of Beatrice. By this interpretation no contradiction exists between the original *Vita Nuova* and the *Convivio*, but that as Dante conceived the *Commedia* he then felt obliged to retouch the *Vita Nuova* in the light of Beatrice's regained preeminence. This argument suffers by virtue of the fact that no manuscript evidence exists in its support; moreover, the *Convivio* already refers to the *Vita Nuova* as being known and in public view—thus making any major change unlikely. For a discussion of the problem see Chimenz (bibliography), p. 410, and Cosmo, *Guida a Dante*, 3rd ed. rev., p. 42.

5. See Chapter 1, n. 22.

6. See the *Voi che savete ragionar d'amore*, where the "donna gentile" has become "disdainful." The envoy to the *canzone Amor che ne la mente mi ragiona* specifically refutes this charge. The *Parole mie che per lo mondo siete* agrees with the *Voi che savete* and threatens to seek out other more pleasurable mistresses than the haughty one of philosophy. But the *O dolci rime che parlando andate* in turn refutes the *Parole mie*.

7. See the note to *Le dolci rime d'amor* in Foster and Boyde, II. 210 for a clear exposition of the change brought about by these didactic love poems from the Guinizellian love poem addressed to a knowing elite. Here Dante becomes more of the philosopher-mediator, writing in a more popular vein, perhaps even showing some of the virtues of moral directness that had marked the school of Guittone.

8. See the note in Busnelli-Vandelli edition of the *Convivio*, II. 11–12, showing that this was a real *quaestio* in the schools at the time.

9. See the commentary, II. 228, where Foster and Boyde explain the difficulty of finding a suitable English equivalent for *leggiadria*. The word suggests "elegance," "grace," and was used only in courtly literature. In this case, perhaps my expedient of *courtliness* would be an acceptable substitute.

10. In this brief sketch of Dante's poetic interests prior to the *Commedia*, three other sectors of his activity need to be mentioned: his *tenzone* with Forese Donati, his poems addressed to the *pargoletta*, and his *rime petrose*. Sometime before Forese's death in July 1296 and perhaps even as late as 1293—that is, in the midst of the idealized style of the *Vita Nuova*—Dante and Forese engaged in a poetic correspondence that was marked by a bantering exchange of insults (Foster and Boyde, I.148–55; see also the commentary in Contini's *Rime*, pp. 81–93). Although these sonnets are lively and humorous, and even show a mastery of the rough language of popular poetry, years later Dante will have occasion, in the context of the purgatorial struggle (XXIV, 115–17), to be chagrined by their memory. Dante also wrote a group of poems—two *ballate*, a sonnet, and several *canzoni* (the *Amor che movi* and *Io sento si d'Amor*)—addressing a young woman, the so-called *pargoletta* poems (Foster and Boyde, I.114–129). Interpretation has been needlessly complicated by Beatrice's reference (*Purgatorio* XXXI.58–60) to a *pargoletta* as a cause of Dante's straying. The *rime petrose* (named after the "stony heart" of the woman they describe, the so-called donna Pietra) are entirely different; in them we can discern the vivid linguistic energies of the *Inferno*. To such an extent is this so, that Gianfranco Contini, the outstanding student of Dante's *rime*, regards the lady of the poem as a simple device by which to understand Dante's new poetic needs (Contini, *Rime*, p. 149). Bergin demurs from this interpretation (*Dante*, see bibliography, pp. 93–94). Because of the first and most important *canzone* of this group we are able to date their composition as after late December 1296. For a remarkably detailed and suggestive interpretation of this *canzone*, *Io son venuto al punto de la rota*, see Robert M. Durling, " 'Io son venuto': Seneca, Plato and the Microcosm," *Dante Studies*, 93, 1975, p. 95. For a recent, general overview of the criticial attitudes toward these poems see Enrico Fenzi, "Le rime per la donna Pietra," *Miscellanea di studi danteschi* (Genoa, 1966), p. 229.

Chapter Three

1. See Chapter 1, n. 26.

2. Renato Piattoli, *Codice diplomatico dantesco*, new rev. ed.

(Florence, 1950); this "documentary life" of Dante is an extremely useful tool. All citations in the text refer to the item numbers of this edition and can be easily found in this edition either by the date given or by item number.

3. Boccaccio in *The Earliest Lives of Dante*, p. 58.

4. Ibid., p. 88.

5. Early in 1302 (to indicate his active role on behalf of the Whites), Dante was one of eighteen who signed a pledge promising compensation to Ugolino degli Ubaldini for any damages members of his family or their vassals might suffer in supporting the exiles in their war against Florence (Piattoli, 92). When, according to Leonardo Bruni, the Florentines elected as their captain Alessandro da Romena, one of the twelve councilors chosen to aid the captain was Dante. After the defeat at Serravalle (this event, occurring in September 1302, seems to be the reference of Vanni Fucci's prophecy in *Inferno* XXIV), the Florentines turned to the lord of Forlì, Scarpetta Ordelaffi. Dante was apparently the emissary to Forlì to procure his services. This new force invaded the Mugello in March 1303 but was defeated by the Florentine podestà Fulcieri da Càlboli, whose brutalities Dante recorded in *Purgatorio* XIV. Following this defeat Dante may have been dispatched for help to the Scaligers in Verona. By this time the break within the camp of the White forces may have already occurred. For Dante his companions in exile began to be the most burdensome part of his lot. He includes these experiences in the prophecies of both Brunetto Latini and Cacciaguida, *Paradiso* XVII. 61–66. In the meantime another force of exiles was massing to attack Florence. But this army of 1,500 horsemen and 9,000 infantry, some small portion of which actually reached the gates of Florence, was defeated at Lastra. This defeat, taking place in July 1304, may have been the one alluded to by Farinata in *Inferno* X, when he tells Dante that not fifty months will pass before Dante himself will learn how difficult is the art of returning from exile. How long Dante remained at Verona is not known. His stay could not have lasted much after the death of Bartolomeo della Scala in March 1304, because his successor, Alboino, is belittled in the *Convivio* IV.xvi. These must have been the most trying years of exile for Dante, and the beginning of his restless peregrinations, which, as he himself tells us, took him to almost every region of Italy. Important among the northern families who helped support Dante in these years were the Malaspina, whose representative, Currado, revealing himself to Dante in the Valley of the Negligent Princes, is assured that his house "does not despoil itself of the glory of the purse and of the sword" (*Purgatorio* VIII.124–29). In his response Currado informs Dante that not seven years will pass—that is, some time in 1306, before he will know of the beneficence of the house of the Malaspina by personal experience. Indeed, documentary evi-

dence shows that in October 1306 Dante was used in a diplomatic mission on behalf of the Malaspina. Moroello Malaspina, the powerful leader who crushed the Whites at Serravelle and who figures so threateningly in Vanni Fucci's prophecy, was to become Dante's patron, to whom he addressed the epistle covering the *canzone Amor da che convien pur ch' io mi doglia.*

6. *The Earliest Lives of Dante*, p. 89.

7. See Contini, *Rime*, p. 172.

8. See Chapter 1, n. 7.

9. See Chapter 1, n. 6; IX.36 (year 1321), pp.448–50.

10. See *Francesco Petrarca, Prose*, ed. G. Martellotti and others (Milan, 1955), p. 844.

11. *The City of God*, trans. Marcus Dods (New York, 1950), XVI.iv; *Paradise Lost*, XII.33–62.

12. For these Provençal poets see the valuable old edition of H. J. Chaytor, *The Troubadours of Dante* (1902; reprinted New York, 1974). Incidentally, Bertran de Born (*Inferno* XXVIII. 118–42) is alone named as a poet of war because Dante cannot find "that any Italian has yet written poetry on the subject of arms" (II.ii).

13. See Boccaccio's account in *The Earliest Lives of Dante*, p. 65. For a remarkable presentation of the poetic situation surrounding this epistle as well as Dante's Latin exchange with Giovanni del Virgilio in regard to the laurel, see *Dante and Giovanni del Virgilio*, ed. Philip H. Wicksteed and Edmund G. Gardner (Westminster, 1902); the letter to Can Grande is Epistle X in the Temple Classics *Latin Works of Dante*, p. 343.

14. For a few varying approaches to allegory in Dante see Charles S. Singleton, Dante Studies I, *Commedia: Elements of Structure* (Cambridge, 1957); David Thompson, *Dante's Epic Journey* (Baltimore and London, 1974); and, for an excellent description of the cultural context of Dante's use of allegory, Maria Picchio Simonelli, "Vernacular Poetic Sources for Dante's Use of Allegory," *Dante Studies*, XXIII, 1975, p. 131.

15. As expounded by Erich Auerbach, "Figura," *Scenes from the Drama of European Literature* (New York, 1959), p. 11.

16. For another presentation of the importance of this concept see Kenelm Foster, "The Mind in Love; Dante's Philosophy," in *Twentieth-Century Views, Dante*, ed. John Freccero (Englewood Cliffs, N.J., 1965), pp. 54–55.

17. For background to these points see the Busnelli-Vandelli commentary on Book IV, II. 265 as well as the very full appendixes by A. E. Quaglio, IX–XII.

18. One has only to look at the lengthy appendix X, by A. E. Quaglio, to realize how complicated this key notion of the possible intellect is (pp. 393, 401, 403). See also the *Enciclopedia Dantesca.*

19. Quaglio, appendix XI, pp. 404, 405.
20. Temple Classics, *Latin Works of Dante*, p. 351.

Chapter Four

1. Epistle V, in Temple Classics, *Latin Works of Dante*, to which the page numbers refer.
2. "Ut adversentur Domino suo et Uncto suo, romano principi," in the Edizione Nazionale *Opere di Dante*, ed. P. G. Ricci (Milan, 1965). Throughout my translations are taken from the version of Herbert W. Schneider, *On World-Government or De Monarchia* (New York, 2nd rev. ed., 1957). Unfortunately the phrase "et Uncto suo" is left untranslated by Schneider.
3. Here, too, Schneider's version does not indicate the full value of the Latin. Dante declares the goal to be "apprehensivum per intellectum possibilem. . . . ," which Schneider renders, "to be sensitive to intellectual growth," thus slighting the carry-over of the key concept from the *Convivio*.
4. See *Translations and Reprints from the Original Sources of European History*, vol. III, no. 6 (Philadelphia, 1897), p. 20.

Chapter Five

1. Outstanding pages on the lack of formal unity in the *Convivio* are in Auerbach's *Dante: Poet of the Secular World*, pp. 76–80.
2. *European Literature and the Latin Middle Ages*, trans. from the German by W. Trask (New York, 1953), p. 366.
3. *The Earliest Lives of Dante*, p. 94.
4. *Studies in Dante*, First Series (1896; reprinted New York, 1968), pp. 166–97.
5. See "Paolo and Francesca" in *Dante*, Twentieth-Century Views, ed. John Freccero, p. 61.
6. See the classic comparison of Dante's and Machiavelli's treatments of Fortuna in Ernst Cassirer's *The Myth of the State* (New Haven, 1946), pp. 156–62.
7. My own *Renaissance Discovery of Time* (Cambridge, 1972), passim, consult index.

Chapter Six

1. For discussions in English of the *Purgatorio*, see Francis Fergusson, *Dante's Drama of the Mind: A Modern Reading of the "Purgatorio"* (Princeton, 1953), and Bernard Stambler, *Dante's Other World* (New York, 1957).
2. See my *Renaissance Discovery of Time*, pp. 29–30; and *The City of God*, trans. Marcus Dods (XV. 4), from which the concept derives.

3. "Virgil and the Christian World," in *On Poetry and Poets* (*New York*, 1957), p. 147.

4. Trans. J. H. Mozley, Loeb Classical Library, 2 vols. (Cambridge, 1928).

5. From Aurelio Roncaglia, "Guido Guinizelli e !a poesia dei ricordi letterari" in *Antologia della critica dantesca*, ed. Carlo Salinari (Bari, 1968), p. 212.

6. See Sapegno's introduction to this canto in his edition of the *Commedia* (bibliography).

7. See the immensely useful section "Return to Eden," in Charles S. Singleton, *Journey to Beatrice*, Dante Studies 2 (Cambridge, 1958), p. 141.

8. *Journey to Beatrice*, p. 236.

9. See R. E. Kaske, "Dante's DXV," in Freccero, *Dante: A Collection of Critical Essays*, p. 122.

Chapter Seven

1. Epistle X, Temple Classics, *The Latin Works of Dante*, pp. 352–61.

2. Ibid., p. 349.

3. (1910; Garden City, New York, 1958), pp. 71–73.

4. "The Study of Poetry," *Essays in Criticism*, Second Series (London, 1906), p. 48.

5. "St. Francis of Assisi in Dante's *Commedia*," in *Scenes from the Drama of European Literature* (New York, 1959), p. 93.

6. "Dante and Thirteenth-Century Asceticism," in *From Time to Eternity*, ed. Thomas G. Bergin (New Haven and London, 1967), p. 39.

7. "St. Francis of Assisi in Dante's *Commedia*," p. 96.

8. Epistle IX, Temple Classics, *The Latin Works of Dante*, p. 340.

9. See Chapter 3, n. 13.

10. On this point see Erich Auerbach, *Dante: Poet of the Secular World*, pp. 36–37.

11. *Letture Dantesche*, ed. Giovanni Getto (Florence, 1962), p. 2021.

Chapter Eight

1. Why or when Dante moved to Ravenna from the court of the Scaligers in Verona is not clear. Whatever the reason, in Ravenna he was warmly received, even "exalted," if we are to believe Boccaccio. In August 1321 Dante was part of a diplomatic mission to Venice, but evidently returned to Ravenna because of illness, where he died September 13–14, 1321.

2. *Fam.*, XXI. 15; in *Letters from Petrarch*, trans. Morris Bishop (Bloomington, Ind., and London, 1966), p. 176.

3. *Dictionnaire philosophique*, s.v. "Le Dante," *Oeuvres completes*, vol. XVIII (Paris, 1878); trans. Irma Brandeis, in *Discussions of the "Divine Comedy"* (Boston, 1961), pp. 13–15.

4. See Werner P. Friederich, *Dante's Fame Abroad*, Studies in Comparative Literature 2 (Chapel Hill, 1950); and *Dante nel mondo*, ed. Vittore Branca and Ettore Caccia (Florence, 1965); see also Paget Toynbee, *Dante in English Literature from Chaucer to Cary*, 2 vols. (New York, 1909); William J. De Sua, *Dante into English* (Chapel Hill, 1964); Gilbert F. Cunningham, *The "Divine Comedy" into English: A Critical Bibliography 1782–1900* (New York, 1965).

5. *The New Science of Giambattista Vico*, rev. and abridged Thomas G. Bergin and Max H. Fisch (Ithaca and London, 1970), p. 261.

6. See his exposition of the critical situation in two essays, "The Subject of the *Divine Comedy*" and "*The Divine Comedy*: Translation by F. Lammennais with an Introduction to Dante's Life, Ideas, and Works," in *DeSanctis on Dante*, ed. and trans. Joseph Rossi and Alfred Galpin, pp. 3–5, 137.

7. "The Subject of the *Divine Comedy*," pp. 11–14.

8. "Francesca da Rimini," *DeSanctis on Dante*, p. 37.

9. *The Poetry of Dante*, trans. Douglas Ainslie (New York, 1922), p. 253.

10. Ibid., pp. 34–35.

11. *Avvertenza*, pp. viii–ix; see bibliography.

Selected Bibliography

PRIMARY SOURCES

Le Opere di Dante Alighieri, ed. E. Moore and Paget Toynbee. 1894; 4th ed. rev. Oxford: Oxford University Press, 1924.

Le Opere di Dante, ed. M. Barbi and others, 1921; 2nd ed. Florence: Società Dantesca Italiana, 1960.

The *Commedia*: *La Commedia secundo l'antica vulgata*, ed. Giorgio Petrocchi, Edizione Nazionale, vol. VII, Parts I–IV. Milan: Mondadori, 1966–67; *La Divina Commedia*, ed. Natalino Sapegno, 3 vols. 2nd ed. rev. Florence: La Nuova Italia, 1968 (excellent commentary); *The Divine Comedy of Dante Alighieri*, trans. John D. Sinclair. New York: Oxford University Press, rev. 1958 (superb small essays for each canto); *The Divine Comedy*, Bollingen Series LXXX, 3 vols. (2 parts each), trans. and commentary, Charles S. Singleton. Princeton: Princeton University Press, 1970 (the most useful work in English).

Vita Nuova, ed. M. Barbi, Florence: Bemporad, 1932; *Dante's Vita Nuova*, trans. with an essay by Mark Musa, new edition. Bloomington, Ind., and London: Indiana University Press, 1973.

Rime: *Rime della "Vita Nuova" e della Giovinezza*, ed. M. Barbi and F. Maggini. Florence: Le Monnier, 1956; *Rime della maturità e dell' essilio*, ed. M. Barbi and V. Pernicone, Florence: Le Monnier, 1969; *Dante Rime*, ed. G. Contini. Turin: Einaudi, 1965; *Dante's Lyric Poetry*, ed. Kenelm Foster and Patrick Boyde, 2 vols. Oxford: Clarendon Press, 1967.

Convivo: *Il Convivio*, new edition, ed. G. Busnelli and G. Vandelli, with appendixes added to 2nd ed. by A.E. Quaglio. Florence: Le Monnier, 1964. Very dependable.

De Vulgari Eloquentia: *De Vulgari Eloquentia*, ed. A. Marigo, 3rd ed. rev. with appendix by P. G. Ricci. Florence: Le Monnier, 1957; in Temple Classics *Latin Works of Dante*, trans. A. G. Ferrers Howell. London: Dent, 1919; in *Literary Criticism of Dante Alighieri*, trans. and ed. Robert S. Haller. Lincoln: University of Nebraska Press, 1973.

De Monarchia: *Monarchia*, ed. P. G. Ricci, Edizione Nazionale, vol. V. Milan: Mondadori, 1965; *On World Government, or De*

Monarchia, trans. Herbert Schneider. New York: Liberal Arts Press, 2nd ed. rev. 1957.

Epistolae: see complete works above and in Temple Classics *Latin Works of Dante*.

Eclogae Latinae: *Dante and Giovanni del Virgilio*, ed. Philip H. Wicksteed and Edmund G. Gardner. Westminster: Constable, 1902.

SECONDARY SOURCES

AUERBACH, ERICH. "Farinata and Cavalcante" in *Mimesis; The Representation of Reality in Western Literauture*. Trans. Willard Trask. Princeton: Princeton University Press, 1953.

_____. "Figura" in *Scenes from the Drama of European Literature*. New York: Meridian, 1959. A German critic whose influence has been enormous in Italy and in America. His "figural" and "mimetic" approaches suggest the crossroads at which the *Commedia* is situated.

BARBI, MICHELE. *Life of Dante*. Trans. and ed. by Paul G. Ruggiers. Berkeley and Los Angeles: University of California Press, 1954.

_____. *Problemi fondamentali per un nuovo commento della "Divina Commedia."* Florence: Sansoni, 1955. Superb knowledge of Dante and excellent judgment distinguish the work of Barbi who should be consulted by all students.

BERGIN, THOMAS G. *Dante*. Riverside Studies in Literature. Boston: Houghton Mifflin, 1965.

_____, ed. *From Time to Eternity: Essays on Dante's "Divine Comedy."* New Haven and London: Yale University Press. 1967. Some major essays.

CHIMENZ, SIRO. *Dizionario biografico degli italiani*. s. v. Alighieri, Dante. Rome: Instituto dell'Enciclopedia Italiana, 1961.

CLEMENTS, ROBERT J., ed. *American Critical Essays on "The Divine Comedy."* New York: New York University Press, 1967.

COSMO, UMBERTO. *A Handbook to Dante Studies*. Trans. David Moore. Oxford: Blackwell, 1960. But see 3rd Italian edition, *Guida a Dante*, ed. and brought up to date by Bruno Maier. Florence: La Nuova Italia, 1967.

_____, ed. *Dante nella Critica d'Oggi*. Florence: Le Monnier, 1965. Excellent, with full bibliography.

D'ENTREVES, ALESSANDRO PASSERIN. *Dante as a Political Thinker*. Oxford: Clarendon Press, 1955. Attractive thesis now subject to some question (see Limentani, pp. 128–134).

DINSMORE, C.A. *Aids to the Study of Dante*. Boston: Houghton Mifflin, 1903. Excellent summary of Dante criticism in English, 1850–1900.

————. *Enciclopedia Dantesca.* Rome: Istitutio dell 'Enciclopedia Italiana, 1970. Essential work.

FRECCERO, JOHN, ed. Twentieth Century Views. *Dante.* Englewood Cliffs, N.J.: Prentice-Hall, 1967. Excellent choice of some of the more interesting contemporary criticism of Dante's works.

GETTO, GIOVANNI, ed. *Letture Dantesche.* Florence: Sansoni, 1962. Summary of more than a half-century of criticism, canto by canto, of the *Commedia.*

GILSON, ETIENNE. *Dante and Philosophy.* Trans. David Moore. Harper Torchbooks. New York: Harper and Row, 1973.

LIMENTANI, U., ed. *The Mind of Dante.* Cambridge: Cambridge University Press. 1965. A collection of prominent English Dantists.

NARDI, BRUNO. *Dal "Convivio" alla "Commedia."* Rome: Istituto Storico Italiano per il Medio Evo, 1960. Excellent knowledge of the philosophy of Dante's time; some of his conclusions should be approached with caution.

PADOAN, GIORGIO. *Introduzione a Dante.* Florence: Sansoni, 1975.

PIATTOLI, RENATO. *Codice diplomatico dantesco.* 2nd. ed. Florence: Gonnelli, 1950. Very useful.

SINGLETON, CHARLES S. *"Commedia:" Elements of Structure.* Dante Studies I. Cambridge: Harvard University Press. 1954.

————. *Journey to Beatrice.* Dante Studies II. Cambridge: Harvard University Press, 1957. This master of the major school of American Dante criticism should be known to all Dante students.

————. *An Essay on the "Vita Nuova."* Cambridge: Harvard University Press. 1958.

VALLONE, ALDO. *Dante.* Storia letteraria d'Italia. Milan: Vallardi, 1971.

ZINGARELLI, NICOLA *Dante.* Storia letteraria d'Italia. Milan: Villardi, 1914.

Index

Alighieri, Dante

and aesthetic confidence, 159, 193; and aesthetic self-consciousness, 59, 114, 157, 193; and allegory, 47, 70-73, (*Letter to Can Grande della Scala*), 70-71, (*De Monarchia* III), 70-71, 109, 140, 153, 154, 155, 200 nl4; and argument by historical consequences, 137-38, 144-45; and Beatrice, (see also Works: *Vita Nuova*, *Commedia*) 107; and Boethius, 44, 170; embassy to Boniface VIII, 54; speaks out against Boniface VIII, 54; and *Book of Proverbs*, 77; and Cacciaguida, 19; at battle of Campaldino, 42; and the *canzone*, 24, 69; at Caprona, 42; and Guido Cavalcanti, (see also Cavalcanti, Guido), 40, 118; on Church and State, (see also Church—State), 13, 143; and Cicero (*De Amicitia*), 44; and coherent powers of imagination, 193; combination of qualities, 193-94; and Arnaut Daniel (*Purgatorio*), 151; and disposition, 156; and divided readership, 47, 159-60; and *dolce stil novo*, 115, (defined in *Purgatorio*) 149; and the *donna gentile*, 72-73, 74-77, 197 n4; and dreams (*Purgatorio*), 139-40; embassy to San Gimignano, 54; ethics and education, 58; exile (early years), 53, 199 n5; and fame, 128-29, 134; and family, 19-20; and Florence, (see also Florence), 16; need to return to Florence, 55-57; Florentine political leaders, 121-22; and Fortuna, 117, 201 n6; and free will, 142-43; and gentilezza, (see also *gentilezza*), 134; graduated universe, 58; and Guido Guinizelli, 40, 51, 84, 115, 149-51; the patronage of Guido Novello da Polenta, 189;

enters Guild, 52; and Guittone d'Arezzo, 31; and historical decline, 119, 141; *horme*, 58, 86-87, 101, 143; homage paid to Henry VII (see also Henry VII), 90; and inexpressibility, 47; *intelletto possibile*, 58, 61, 85-86, 93, 115, 146, 149-50, 187, 194; and James Joyce, 31, 100; and Brunetto Latini, 23, 40, 58; and *leggiadria*, 49-51; and Niccolo Machiavelli, 137; and the Malaspina (encomium in *Purgatorio*), 139, 199 n5; and Charles Martel, 43; and John Milton, 100, (use of sacred history) 166; and the moral *canzoni*, 48-51; and the "municipal" poets, 23, 31; and Petrarch, 137, 159, 190; philosopher-mediator, 58; and philosophy, 43-47, (conversion to philosophy), 44, development of philosophical thought, 100; commitment to poetry, 24; and poetic circumstances, 27; and his poetic culture, 146-52; and poetic development, 24, 26, 37, 43-48, 49, 52, 100; and poetic followers, 159 - 93; as the poet of history, 193; as poet-prophet, 194; and a poetic renaissance, 61, 114; and poetic subject matter, 24, 40, 68-69; political development, 99, 100, 137-38, 163-64; and progeny (Ugolino), 129-30, (Sordello) 134; and psychology of positive attachment, 108-109, 143, 146; last years at Ravenna, 189, 202 n1; and "right focus," 145; and ideal mission of Rome, 79-80, 100, 103, Roman origins, 22, veneration of Rome, 81; and "single just man," 139; and sonnet, 24; and Statius (*Purgatorio*), 146-48; and supersession, 40, 120, (of Francesca) 145, (of Brunetto Latini)

23, (of Virgil) 146-48, 153; and *"viltà,"* 173; and Virgil, 23, 40, 69, 80, 103, 107, 146-48, 153; and Virgilio, Giovanni del, 189.

WORKS:

Commedia, 14, 87-88; and the *Aeneid,* 103-104; and allegory, 109; and Beatrice as transcendent hope, 109; comparison of central cantos (XIV-XVII), 119, 141-46, 174-78; compared with Milton, 177; compared with Shakespeare, 177; and the device of antedating poem, 177-78; and divided readership, 159-60; as *La Divina Commedia,* 189; and divine comedy, 157-60; Empire, 108; *Inferno* and Florentine division, 120; *follia,* 107, 111-112, 122-23, 166, 176, 181; Francesca, 114-16; and future followers, 193; and historical decline, 149; and historical location, 102; and historical presentation (Virgil), 102-103; and the creation of historical types, 177, 194; historical types (compared with Shakespeare) 194; and the image of the book, 188; and innovation, 193; and integretation of experience and theory, 101-102; *intelletto possibile,* 115, 146, 149-50, 187, 194; and Papacy, 108; as a *poema sacro,* 157; and progeny, 118; and reality of places and things, 103; and structure, 104, 110; structure as a "permitting device," 104; structural similarities of *cantiche,* 140; and supersession, 115; and supersession of Francesca's eros (*Purgatorio*), 146; and variety, 194; and *viltà,* 107; Virgil, 103, 107, 108, 109.

Inferno, and the anti-climax of Dis, 106-107; and anti-papal argument, 127-28; and its atomism, 109-110; and Beatrice, 121; and Bocca degli Abati, 128-29; and Capaneus, 119; and Cavalcanti, 118-19; and Christian patterns, 105-106, 110-111; and Ciacco, 116-17; and Cocytus (perversions of humanistic values) 128-30; contrasted with the *Odyssey* and *Aeneid,* 104-107; and courtly love (Francesca) 114-16; and disaffection, 130; and Farina-

ta, 117-19, (identification with exile) 119; and rejection of Florentine values, 105-06; and *follia,* 122-23; and Fortuna (as part of municipal theme), 117-121, (as different from Convivio), 117; and the separation from Florence (Geryon), 122; and Guido da Montefeltro, 126-28; theologically and aesthetically incomplete, 106-107; and irrational forces of opposition, 111-12; and Brunetto Latini, 120-21; and the loss of "the good of intellect," 110; and Malebolge, 123-28, (and the loss of heroism) 123; and break-down of model system, 106; and the "municipal theme," 116 - 23; new sponsorship for Dante (Virgil and Beatrice) 107; and new directions, 104-105; and Old Man of Crete, 119; and a poetic renaissance, 114; and supersession, 105-106; and trimmers, 112 - 13; and Ugolino, 129-30; and Ulysses, 123-26, (as a fraudulent counselor), 125-26, (personal identification), 124-25, (as part of municipal theme), 124; and virtuous pagans, 113 - 14.

Purgatorio, and active participation, 132; and the arts and artists, 134-35; and meaning of Beatrice's absense, 153-54; and Beatrice's reprimand of Dante, 153-54; and transcendent spirit of Beatrice, 151-52; and bodily decay, 131; and Bonagiunta da Lucca (*dolce still novo* defined), 149; and Buonconte da Montefeltro, 136; and Casella, 133; and Cato, 132-33; and hilosophy of *Convivio,* 149-50; and Forese Donati, 148; and divine justice, 155; and the earthly paradise, 152-56; and Florence (satire) 138; and Guido Guinizelli, 149, 150-52; and Guittone d'Arezzo, 149; and "interiority," 132; and Brunetto Latini, 148-49; and the Law, 132; and lyric·of memory, 131; and Manfred, 135-36; and Marco Lombardo, 141-43; and method of presentation, 138-39, 140-41; its method compared with the *Inferno,* 135; compared with Milton's *Paradise Regained,* 132; and limitations of Papacy, 136; advice to Papacy, 154-55; and representative voice of La Pia, 136-37; and political development, 137-38; and purgatorical consciousness, 132, 156; and rejection of humanistic values, 132-34; and spiritual renewal, 131; and time, 131; and Virgil, 132-33, (his valediction), 151-52; and Nino Visconti, 139.

Paradiso, and Adam, 183; and Augustine, 170-71; and Beatrice, 160-61; and Benedict, 178-79; and Bernard, 185-87; and Boethius, 170; and Cacciaguida, 174-78; and arguments against careerists in the Church, 169-70, 171; and dual nature of Christ, 166; and the ideal relations of Church and State, 164; and the importance of the city, 167; and Damian, 178; and arguments of decline, 167; and the change in opinion on the diffusion of tongues, 183; and principles of diversity, 167-68; and divided readership, 159-60; and divine comedy, 180, (disruption of historical continuity), 168, (Folco), 169, (repetition and the "second chance"), 158; (second chance, Cunizza), 169, (repetition of paradigm, Caccaiaguida and Brunetto Latini), 158, 174-78; and Dominic, 171; and Piccarda Donati (contrasted with Francesca), 162-63; and the examination on faith, hope and charity, 182; and exile, 177; and view of Florentine history, 175-76; and *follia*, 166, 176, 181; and transcendence of Francesca, 166-67; and St. Francis, 171-73; and the freedom of the will (compared with Erasmus), 184; as a poem of history, 177; and human image, 179, 181, 185, 186, 188; and ideal purpose, 160-62; and sense of innovation, 159; and Justinian, 163-65; and the poet's laurel, 159, 182-83; and lyrical quality, 181-82; and Mary, 181-88, (her paradox), 186, (as model of humility), 186; and metaphysical reasons for world's straying, 161, 173-74, 176; and method (doctrine and example), 160; and the revival of the

model theory, 158, 174-75; and monasticism, 178-79; as a *poema sacro*, 182; and the poetry of direct address, 185; and proem to canto XXV, 182; and retrospection, 158, 175, 180-81; and Romeo of Villeneuve, 165-66, (identification with Dante), 165, (contrasted with Pier Della Vigna), 166; and sacred history, 166; and Siger de Brabant, 171; and Thomas of Aquinas, 170-74; and tragedy, 168, 184; and transcendence of dualities, 165, 171-72, 175; and the Trinity, 170, 187-88; and the triptych (Piccarda, La Pia and Francesca), 162, (Forese—Corso—Piccarda Donati), 163.

Convivio, 17, 24, 56-63; and allegory, 70-73; *Amor che ne la mente mi ragiona*, 73; and Aristotle, 82; and avarice, 82; no conflict between *Convivio* and Christianity, 76-77; coincidence of secular and sacred history, 80-81; and intellectual system of the *Commedia*, 58, 74-75; critical problem, 72, 101; defense of Italian vernacular, 53, 58; and its design, 57; *donna gentile* and philosophy (philosophical demonstrations, philosophical persuasions), 76; Frederick II, 82; and *gentilezza*, 78-79, 83-84; and *horme*, 86-87; and the *intelletto possibile*, 85-86; magnify the Italian language, 61; personal defense, 60; and a poetic renaissance, 62-63; and Dante's political thought, 79-82; and psychology of positive attachment, 82; and similitude, (Christ, our likeness), 75, 76, 77; and the *Vita Nuova*, 45, 59; *Voi che 'ntendendo*, 43, 71-73; and wisdom (and Christ), 77.

Epistles, to Can Grande Della Scala, 159; to the leaders of Italy, 89, 91, 92; to the Florentines, 91; to Henry VII, 91-92; bridge between the *Convivio* and the *Monarchia*, 92; "Popule mee," 56.

Latin verse epistle (eclogue to Giovanni del Virgilio), 182-83, 199-200 n5.

Monarchia, and allegory (arguments of

the Papacy), 95-97; argument by historical consequences, 93; Church and State, (ideal relations), 97-99; the *Commedia*, 99; the decretalists, 94-95; the Donation of Constantine, 97; and the figure of paradise, 98; the ideal purpose of Rome, 93; and *intelletto possibile*, 93; and its political circumstances, 92-93; and unity of rule, 93.

Rime, Doglia me reca ne lo core ardire, 48; *Due donne*, 47; *Guido, i' vorrei che tu e Lapo ed io*, 38; *O dolci rime che parlando andate*, 197 n6; *Parole mie che per lo mondo siete*, 197 n6; *rime petrose*, 198 n10; *tenzone* with Forese Donati, 198 n10; *Tre donne intorno*, 48, 56-57; *Voi che savete ragionar d'amore*, 197 n6.

Vita Nuova, 23-41; and *A ciascun'alma presa e gentil core*, 27; and Beatrice's death, 24; and Guido Cavalcanti, 25, 31, 36-39; as a collection of poetry, 24; and prose commentary, 25; and *donna gentile*, 25, 30; *Donna pietosa e di novella etate*, 29; and *Donne ch'avete*, 34-36, 45; and Guido Guinizelli, 32-34; and *Gentil pensero che parla ti vui*, 30; and historical research, 25; and impersonality, 25; and the Italian vernacular, 39; and Dante da Maiano, 31; and *Oltre la spera che più larga gira!*, 30; and *Piangete, amanti, poi che piange Amore*, 29; and Cino da Pistoia, 31; and poetic circumstances, 31-41; and screenwoman, 27; and thresholds of experience, 26, 29.

De Vulgari Eloquentia, 17, 24; and the theory of the *canzone*, 69; and the *Convivio*, 63; and its design, 65; and the diffusion of tongues, 65; and the need for a *grammatica*, 64; and Guido Guinizelli, 67; and Guittone d Arezzo, 31; and Dante's historical sense, 65; and imitation, 64; and defense of the Italian vernacular, 53; a survey of the Italian dialects, 66-67; and the dialect of Bologna, 66-67; and the illustrious literary vernacular, 67-68; and the muncipial poets, 31; and the use of periphrasis, 69; as a poetic, 64, 67;

and the subject matter of poetry, 68-69.

Arnold, Matthew, 162

Aristotle, 16, 21, 82

Auerbach, Erich, 171-72, 200 n15, 201 n1, 202 n10

Barbi, Michele, 193

Baron, Hans, 22

Becker, Marvin B., 195 n5

Bergin, Thomas G., 198 n10

Boccaccio, Giovanni, description of Guido Cavalcanti, 37, 189, 202 n1

Boethius (*De consolatione philosophiae*), 44, 170

Boniface VIII, 13, 19, 54-55

Boyde, Patrick, 196 n22, 197 n7, 198 n9

Brunelleschi, Betto, 37, 90-91

Bruni, Leonardo, (*Life of Dante*), 42, 56, 104, 199 n5

Calboli, Fulcieri da, 199 n5

Capet, Hugh, 18

Carolingian, 13, 14

Casella, Mario, 187

Cassirer, Ernst, 201 n6

Cavalcanti, Guido, 24, 25, 31, 40; exile, 53; *Inferno*, 118-19; and Guido Guinizelli, 32; and the Italian vernacular, 39; and the *Vita Nuova*, 36-39;

WORKS:

"*I' vegno 'l giorno a te 'nfinite volte*," 38; *Vedeste, al mio parere, onne valore*, 31, 37.

Cerchi, Veri de', 53

Charlemagne (see also Carolingian), 13

Charles of Anjou, 19

Charles of Valois, 18, 54-55

Chaucer, Geoffrey, 190

Chiappelli, Fredi, 196 n25

Chimenz, Siro, 197 n4

Church, Dean, 195 n6

Church—State, (see also Papacy, Empire), 13, 143-44; confusion of roles, 101, 143-44; ideal relations, 14, 17, 97-99, 144; new threatening forces (France), 13, 18-19

Cicero, 16; (*de Amicitia*), 44

Clement V, 89, 92

Compagni, Dino (*Chronicle*), History of blacks and whites, 53, 54, 90-91; and description of Guido Cavalcanti, 37

Complementarities, 13, 17-18

Contini, Gianfranco, 196 n21, 196 n22, 198 n10

Cosmo, Umberto, 197 n4

Croce, Benedetto, 192-93; structure and poetry, 192-93

Cunningham, Gilbert F. 203 n4

Curtius, E. R., 102

De Sua, William J., 203 n4

Donati, Corso, 53-55; exile, 53; reign of terror, 55

DuBellay, Joachim (*Defense et illustration de la langue française*), 61; use of periphrasis, 69

Durling, Robert M. 198 n10

Empire, (see also Church-State), 13; 95-99; Frederick II, 14; and neglect of Italy, 138; political role, 101-102; and power, 143-44

Eliot, T. S., on Virgil, 146, 190

Fenzi, Enrico, 198 n10

Fergusson, Francis, 201 n1

Ficino, Marsilio, 189

Florence and Aristotle, 16; Blacks and Whites, 52-55; Buondelmonte's murder, 15; Cacciaguida, 15, 16; and Cicero, 16; civic humanism, 16; civil war, 15; in the *Convivio*, 17; and conservative myth, 175-76; the divided city, 52; and Epicureanism (*Inferno*), 118-19; Farinata, 15; "fast money," (*subiti guadagni*), 18, 121-22; Guelph and Ghibelline, 15; opposition to Henry VII, 91; "new people," (*nouva gente*), 18, 121-22; Ordinances of Justice, 53; comparison with Rome, 16; satire of (in *Purgatorio*), 138; sociological change, 18, in the *De Vulgari Eloquentia*, 17

Foster, Kenelm, 196 n22, 197 n7, 198 n9, 200 n16

Frederick II, 13, 17, 82

Friederich, Werner P., 203 n4

Gianni, Lapo, 24

Guinizelli, Guido, 32-34, 40, 51, 67, 84, 149, 150-52; and Cavalcanti, 32; and *gentilezza*, 32, 33-34; and philosophy, 33; and poetic development, 34, 115; WORKS: *Al cor gentil ripara [reimpara] sempre amore*, 32, 33, 51, 84; *Io voglio del ver la mia donna laudare*, 32, 34

Guittone d'Arezzo, 31, 149

Henry VII, 89-92; coronation, 92; dead, 92-93; deceived by Clement V, 92; defeat, 91; delay, 90; entrance into Italy, 89

Horace, 23

Joyce, James, 31, 100

Kaske, R. E., 202 n9

Landino, Cristoforo, 189

Latini, Brunetto, 20-23, 31, 40, 58, 120-21, 148-49; and Aristotle, 21; and Book of Proverbs, 22; and Cicero, 21, 22; *dittator* (ars dictandi) 22-23; exile, 21; glory, 23; identification with Dante, 21; philosopher-mediator, 56; praise of Rome, 22, Seneca, 21; WORKS: *The Tresor (Li Livres dou Tresor)*, 21; *Tesoretto*, 21; *Rhettorica*, 21

Lucca, Bonagiunta da, 31, 149; and opposition to Guinizelli, 32, 33; in *Purgatorio*, 149; WORKS: *Voi ch'avete mutata la maniera*, 32-33

Machiavelli, Niccolo, 137, 201 n6

Maiano, Danta da, 31

Malaspina, Moreollo, 139, 199 n5

Manfred, 13, 17

Martel, Charles, 43, 167-68

Milton, John, 100, 132, 166

Musa, Mark, 196 n19

Ordelaffi, Scarpetta, 199 n5

Papacy, (see also Church-State) 13, 95-99, 108; advice to, 154-55; Geogory

VII, 14; intrusion into political affairs, 138; limitations described (Purgatorio), 136; spiritual role, 101-102

Petrarch, Francis, 137; and the coronation, 159; and a poetic renaissance (the *Coronation Oration*), 114; response to Dante's poem, 189-90; veneration of Rome, 81

WORKS:

Letter to King Robert of Sicily, 62

Petrocchi, Giorgio, 172

Pirenne, Henri, 14

Pistoia, Cino da, 24, 31, 38

Poggioli, Renato, 115-16

Polenta, Guido Novella da, 189

Poulet, Georges, 196 n19

Quaglio, A. E., 200 n17, 200 n18, 201 n19

Quinones, Ricardo J., 201 n7, 201 n2

Robert of Sicily, 92, 167,

Romena, Alessandro da, 199 n5

Roncaglia, Aurelio, 202 n5

Sanctis, Francesco de, 191-92, 194

Santayana, George, 160

Sapegno, Natalino, 193, 202 n6

Scala, Bartolomeo della, 199 n5

Schiaffini, A., 196 n20

Shakespeare, William, 194

Simonelli, Maria Picchio, 200 n14

Singleton, Charles S., 153-54, 196 n19, 200 n14, 202 n7,

Spenser, Edmund, (*English Poet*), 61

Stambler, Bernard, 201 n1

Templer, M. de Bonfils, 196 n19

Thompson, David, 200 n14

Toynbee, Paget, 203 n4

Vico, Giambattista, 190-91; and the two Dantes, 191

Villani, Giovanni, 20, 189

Virgil, as cautionary reason, 109; and the classical poets, 40-41, 69-70; and genesis of *Commedia*, 103; and historical presentation in *Commedia*, 102-103; and the ideal mission of Rome, 80; and rejection (*Purgatorio*), 132-33; and similarity of theme with *Commedia*, 103-104; valediction to Dante (*Purgatorio*), 151-52

Virgilio, Giovanni del, 182-83, 189, 200 n13

Voltaire, attitude towards the *Commedia*, 190

Wieruszowski, Helene, 16, 20-21

Zingarelli, Nicola, 32